THE GREAT TRAGEDIES
OF
AESCHYLUS,
SOPHOCLES,
AND
EURIPIDES

THE GREAT TRAGEDIES OF AESCHYLUS, SOPHOCLES, AND EURIPIDES

Illustrated by Quentin Fiore

THE FRANKLIN LIBRARY
Franklin Center, Pennsylvania

Printed in the United States of America.

✧ ✧ ✧ ✧ ✧ ✧ ✧ ✧ ✧ ✧ ✧ ✧

CONTENTS

AESCHYLUS

Agamemnon 3

Prometheus Bound 67

SOPHOCLES

Oedipus the King 113

Antigone 183

EURIPIDES

Medea 235

The Bacchae 293

AESCHYLUS

AGAMEMNON

Translated by Richmond Lattimore

CHARACTERS

AGAMEMNON, *king of Argos*

CLYTAEMESTRA, *his wife*

WATCHMAN

HERALD

CASSANDRA, *daughter of Priam and slave of Agamemnon*

AEGISTHUS, *son of Thyestes, cousin of Agamemnon*

CHORUS OF ARGIVE ELDERS

Non-speaking: attendants of Agamemnon; attendants of Clytaemestra; bodyguard of Aegisthus

Time, directly after the fall of Troy

AGAMEMNON

SCENE *Argos, before the palace of King Agamemnon. The Watchman, who speaks the opening lines, is posted on the roof of the palace. Clytaemestra's entrances are made from a door in the center of the stage; all others, from the wings.*

The Watchman, alone.

I ask the gods some respite from the weariness
of this watchtime measured by years I lie awake
elbowed upon the Atreidae's roof dogwise to mark
the grand processionals of all the stars of night
burdened with winter and again with heat for men,
dynasties in their shining blazoned on the air,
these stars, upon their wane and when the rest arise.

I wait; to read the meaning in that beacon light,
a blaze of fire to carry out of Troy the rumor
and outcry of its capture; to such end a lady's
male strength of heart in its high confidence ordains.
Now as this bed stricken with night and drenched with
dew
I keep, nor ever with kind dreams for company:
since fear in sleep's place stands forever at my head
against strong closure of my eyes, or any rest:
I mince such medicine against sleep failed: I sing,
only to weep again the pity of this house
no longer, as once, administered in the grand way.
Now let there be again redemption from distress,
the flare burning from the blackness in good augury.

A light shows in the distance.

Oh, hail, blaze of the darkness, harbinger of day's
shining, and of processionals and dance and choirs
of multitudes in Argos for this day of grace.
Ahoy!
I cry the news aloud to Agamemnon's queen,
that she may rise up from her bed of state with speed
to raise the rumor of gladness welcoming this beacon,
and singing rise, if truly the citadel of Ilium
has fallen, as the shining of this flare proclaims.
I also, I, will make my choral prelude, since
my lord's dice cast aright are counted as my own,
and mine the tripled sixes of this torchlit throw.

May it only happen. May my king come home, and I
take up within this hand the hand I love. The rest
I leave to silence; for an ox stands huge upon
my tongue. The house itself, could it take voice, might
speak
aloud and plain. I speak to those who understand,
but if they fail, I have forgotten everything.

Exit. The Chorus enters, speaking.

Ten years since the great contestants
of Priam's right,
Menelaus and Agamemnon, my lord,
twin throned, twin sceptered, in twofold power
of kings from God, the Atreidae,
put forth from this shore
the thousand ships of the Argives,
the strength and the armies.
Their cry of war went shrill from the heart,
as eagles stricken in agony

for young perished, high from the nest
eddy and circle
to bend and sweep of the wings' stroke,
lost far below
the fledgelings, the nest, and the tendance.
Yet someone hears in the air, a god,
Apollo, Pan, or Zeus, the high
thin wail of these sky-guests, and drives
late to its mark
the Fury upon the transgressors.

So drives Zeus the great guest god
the Atreidae against Alexander:
for one woman's promiscuous sake
the struggling masses, legs tired,
knees grinding in dust,
spears broken in the onset.
Danaans and Trojans
they have it alike. It goes as it goes
now. The end will be destiny.
You cannot burn flesh or pour unguents,
not innocent cool tears,
that will soften the gods' stiff anger.

But we; dishonored, old in our bones,
cast off even then from the gathering horde,
stay here, to prop up
on staves the strength of a baby.
Since the young vigor that urges
inward to the heart
is frail as age, no warcraft yet perfect,
while beyond age, leaf
withered, man goes three footed
no stronger than a child is,
a dream that falters in daylight.

Clytaemestra enters quietly. The Chorus continues to speak.

But you, lady,
daughter of Tyndareus, Clytaemestra, our queen:
What is there to be done? What new thing have you
heard?
In persuasion of what
report do you order such sacrifice?
To all the gods of the city,
the high and the deep spirits,
to them of the sky and the market places,
the altars blaze with oblations.
The staggered flame goes sky high
one place, then another,
drugged by the simple soft
persuasion of sacred unguents,
the deep stored oil of the kings.
Of these things what can be told
openly, speak.
Be healer to this perplexity
that grows now into darkness of thought,
while again sweet hope shining from the flames
beats back the pitiless pondering
of sorrow that eats my heart.

I have mastery yet to chant the wonder at the wayside
given to kings. Still by God's grace there surges within
me
singing magic
grown to my life and power,
how the wild bird portent
hurled forth the Achaeans'
twin-stemmed power singlehearted,
lords of the youth of Hellas,
with spear and hand of strength

to the land of Teucrus.
Kings of birds to the kings of the ships,
one black, one blazed with silver,
clear seen by the royal house
on the right, the spear hand,
they lighted, watched by all
tore a hare, ripe, bursting with young unborn yet,
stayed from her last fleet running.
Sing sorrow, sorrow: but good win out in the end.

Then the grave seer of the host saw through to the hearts divided,
knew the fighting sons of Atreus feeding on the hare
with the host, their people.
Seeing beyond, he spoke:
"With time, this foray
shall stalk the castle of Priam.
Before then, under
the walls, Fate shall spoil
in violence the rich herds of the people.
Only let no doom of the gods darken
upon this huge iron forged to curb Troy—
from inward. Artemis the undefiled
is angered with pity
at the flying hounds of her father
eating the unborn young in the hare and the shivering mother.
She is sick at the eagles' feasting.
Sing sorrow, sorrow: but good win out in the end.

Lovely you are and kind
to the tender young of ravening lions.
For sucklings of all the savage
beasts that lurk in the lonely places you have sympathy.
Grant meaning to these appearances

good, yet not without evil.
Healer Apollo, I pray you
let her not with crosswinds
bind the ships of the Danaans
to time-long anchorage
forcing a second sacrifice unholy, untasted,
working bitterness in the blood
and faith lost. For the terror returns like sickness to lurk in the house;
the secret anger remembers the child that shall be avenged."
Such, with great good things beside, rang out in the voice of Calchas,
these fatal signs from the birds by the way to the house of the princes,
wherewith in sympathy
sing sorrow, sorrow: but good win out in the end.

Zeus: whatever he may be, if this name
pleases him in invocation,
thus I call upon him.
I have pondered everything
yet I cannot find a way,
only Zeus, to cast this dead weight of ignorance
finally from out my brain.

He who in time long ago was great,
throbbing with gigantic strength,
shall be as if he never were, unspoken.
He who followed him has found
his master, and is gone.
Cry aloud without fear the victory of Zeus,
you will not have failed the truth:

Zeus, who guided men to think,

who has laid it down that wisdom
comes alone through suffering.
Still there drips in sleep against the heart
grief of memory; against
our pleasure we are temperate.
From the gods who sit in grandeur
grace comes somehow violent.

On that day the elder king
of the Achaean ships, no more
strict against the prophet's word,
turned with the crosswinds of fortune,
when no ship sailed, no pail was full,
and the Achaean people sulked
fast against the shore at Aulis
facing Chalcis, where the tides ebb and surge:

and winds blew from the Strymon, bearing
sick idleness, ships tied fast, and hunger,
distraction of the mind, carelessness
for hull and cable;
with time's length bent to double measure
by delay crumbled the flower and pride
of Argos. Then against the bitter wind
the seer's voice clashed out
another medicine
more hateful yet, and spoke of Artemis, so that the kings
dashed their staves to the ground and could not hold
their tears.

The elder lord spoke aloud before them:
"My fate is angry if I disobey these,
but angry if I slaughter
this child, the beauty of my house,
with maiden blood shed staining

these father's hands beside the altar.
What of these things goes now without disaster?
How shall I fail my ships
and lose my faith of battle?
For them to urge such sacrifice of innocent blood
angrily, for their wrath is great—it is right. May all be
well yet."

But when necessity's yoke was put upon him
he changed, and from the heart the breath came bitter
and sacrilegious, utterly infidel,
to warp a will now to be stopped at nothing.
The sickening in men's minds, tough,
reckless in fresh cruelty brings daring. He endured then
to sacrifice his daughter
to stay the strength of war waged for a woman,
first offering for the ships' sake.

Her supplications and her cries of father
were nothing, nor the child's lamentation
to kings passioned for battle.
The father prayed, called to his men to lift her
with strength of hand swept in her robes aloft
and prone above the altar, as you might lift
a goat for sacrifice, with guards
against the lips' sweet edge, to check
the curse cried on the house of Atreus
by force of bit and speech drowned in strength.

Pouring then to the ground her saffron mantle
she struck the sacrificers with
the eyes' arrows of pity,
lovely as in a painted scene, and striving
to speak—as many times
at the kind festive table of her father

she had sung, and in the clear voice of a stainless maiden
with love had graced the song
of worship when the third cup was poured.

What happened next I saw not, neither speak it.
The crafts of Calchas fail not of outcome.
Justice so moves that those only learn
who suffer; and the future
you shall know when it has come; before then, forget it.
It is grief too soon given.
All will come clear in the next dawn's sunlight.
Let good fortune follow these things as
she who is here desires,
our Apian land's singlehearted protectress.

The Chorus now turns toward Clytaemestra, and the leader speaks to her.

I have come in reverence, Clytaemestra, of your power.
For when the man is gone and the throne void, his right
falls to the prince's lady, and honor must be given.
Is it some grace—or otherwise—that you have heard
to make you sacrifice at messages of good hope?
I should be glad to hear, but must not blame your
silence.

CLYTAEMESTRA As it was said of old, may the dawn child
be born
to be an angel of blessing from the kindly night.
You shall know joy beyond all you ever hoped to hear.
The men of Argos have taken Priam's citadel.

CHORUS What have you said? Your words escaped my
unbelief.

CLYTAEMESTRA The Achaeans are in Troy. Is that not clear enough?

CHORUS This slow delight steals over me to bring forth tears.

CLYTAEMESTRA Yes, for your eyes betray the loyal heart within.

CHORUS Yet how can I be certain? Is there some evidence?

CLYTAEMESTRA There is, there must be; unless a god has lied to me.

CHORUS Is it dream visions, easy to believe, you credit?

CLYTAEMESTRA I accept nothing from a brain that is dull with sleep.

CHORUS The charm, then, of some rumor, that made rich your hope?

CLYTAEMESTRA Am I some young girl, that you find my thoughts so silly?

CHORUS How long, then, is it since the citadel was stormed?

CLYTAEMESTRA It is the night, the mother of this dawn I hailed.

CHORUS What kind of messenger could come in speed like this?

CLYTAEMESTRA Hephaestus, who cast forth the shining blaze from Ida.

And beacon after beacon picking up the flare
carried it here; Ida to the Hermaean horn
of Lemnos, where it shone above the isle, and next
the sheer rock face of Zeus on Athos caught it up;
and plunging skyward to arch the shoulders of the sea
the strength of the running flare in exultation,
pine timbers flaming into gold, like the sunrise,
brought the bright message to Macistus' sentinel cliffs,
who, never slow nor in the carelessness of sleep
caught up, sent on his relay in the courier chain,
and far across Euripus' streams the beacon flare
carried to signal watchmen on Messapion.
These took it again in turn, and heaping high a pile
of silvery brush flamed it to throw the message on.
And the flare sickened never, but grown stronger yet
outleapt the river valley of Asopus like
the very moon for shining, to Cithaeron's scaur
to waken the next station of the flaming post.
These watchers, not contemptuous of the far-thrown
blaze,
kindled another beacon vaster than commanded.
The light leaned high above Gorgopis' staring marsh,
and striking Aegyplanctus' mountain top, drove on
yet one more relay, lest the flare die down in speed.
Kindled once more with stintless heaping force, they
send
the beard of flame to hugeness, passing far beyond
the promontory that gazes on the Saronic strait
and flaming far, until it plunged at last to strike
the steep rock of Arachnus near at hand, our
watchtower.
And thence there fell upon this house of Atreus' sons
the flare whose fathers mount to the Idaean beacon.
These are the changes on my torchlight messengers,
one from another running out the laps assigned.
The first and the last sprinters have the victory.

By such proof and such symbol I announce to you
my lord at Troy has sent his messengers to me.

CHORUS The gods, lady, shall have my prayers and thanks straightway.
And yet to hear your story till all wonder fades
would be my wish, could you but tell it once again.

CLYTAEMESTRA The Achaeans have got Troy, upon this very day.
I think the city echoes with a clash of cries.
Pour vinegar and oil into the selfsame bowl,
you could not say they mix in friendship, but fight on.
Thus variant sound the voices of the conquerors
and conquered, from the opposition of their fates.
Trojans are stooping now to gather in their arms
their dead, husbands and brothers; children lean to clasp
the aged who begot them, crying upon the death
of those most dear, from lips that never will be free.
The Achaeans have their midnight work after the fighting
that sets them down to feed on all the city has,
ravenous, headlong, by no rank and file assigned,
but as each man has drawn his shaken lot by chance.
And in the Trojan houses that their spears have taken
they settle now, free of the open sky, the frosts
and dampness of the evening; without sentinels set
they sleep the sleep of happiness the whole night through.
And if they reverence the gods who hold the city
and all the holy temples of the captured land,
they, the despoilers, might not be despoiled in turn.
Let not their passion overwhelm them; let no lust
seize on these men to violate what they must not.
The run to safety and home is yet to make; they must turn

the pole, and run the backstretch of the double course.
Yet though the host come home without offence to high
gods, even so the anger of these slaughtered men
may never sleep. Oh, let there be no fresh wrong done!

Such are the thoughts you hear from me, a woman
merely.
Yet may the best win through, that none may fail to see.
Of all good things to wish this is my dearest choice.

CHORUS My lady, no grave man could speak with better
grace.
I have listened to the proofs of your tale, and I believe,
and go to make my glad thanksgivings to the gods.
This pleasure is not unworthy of the grief that gave it.
O Zeus our lord and Night beloved,
bestower of power and beauty,
you slung above the bastions of Troy
the binding net, that none, neither great
nor young, might outleap
the gigantic toils
of enslavement and final disaster.
I gaze in awe on Zeus of the guests
who wrung from Alexander such payment.
He bent the bow with slow care, that neither
the shaft might hurdle the stars, nor fall
spent to the earth, short driven.

They have the stroke of Zeus to tell of.
This thing is clear and you may trace it.
He acted as he had decreed. A man thought
the gods deigned not to punish mortals
who trampled down the delicacy of things
inviolable. That man was wicked.
The curse on great daring
shines clear; it wrings atonement

from those high hearts that drive to evil,
from houses blossoming to pride
and peril. Let there be
wealth without tears; enough for
the wise man who will ask no further.
There is not any armor
in gold against perdition
for him who spurns the high altar
of Justice down to the darkness.

Persuasion the persistent overwhelms him,
she, strong daughter of designing Ruin.
And every medicine is vain; the sin
smolders not, but burns to evil beauty.
As cheap bronze tortured
at the touchstone relapses
to blackness and grime, so this man
tested shows vain
as a child that strives to catch the bird flying
and wins shame that shall bring down his city.
No god will hear such a man's entreaty,
but whoso turns to these ways
they strike him down in his wickedness.
This was Paris: he came
to the house of the sons of Atreus,
stole the woman away, and shamed
the guest's right of the board shared.

She left among her people the stir and clamor
of shields and of spearheads,
the ships to sail and the armor.
She took to Ilium her dowry, death.
She stepped forth lightly between the gates
daring beyond all daring. And the prophets
about the great house wept aloud and spoke:

"Alas, alas for the house and for the champions,
alas for the bed signed with their love together.
Here now is silence, scorned, unreproachful.
The agony of his loss is clear before us.
Longing for her who lies beyond the sea
he shall see a phantom queen in his household.
Her images in their beauty
are bitterness to her lord now
where in the emptiness of eyes
all passion has faded."

Shining in dreams the sorrowful
memories pass; they bring him
vain delight only.
It is vain, to dream and to see splendors,
and the image slipping from the arms' embrace
escapes, not to return again,
on wings drifting down the ways of sleep.
Such have the sorrows been in the house by the
  hearthside;
such have there been, and yet there are worse than these.
In all Hellas, for those who swarmed to the host
the heartbreaking misery
shows in the house of each.
Many are they who are touched at the heart by these
  things.
Those they sent forth they knew;
now, in place of the young men
urns and ashes are carried home
to the houses of the fighters.

The god of war, money changer of dead bodies,
held the balance of his spear in the fighting,
and from the corpse-fires at Ilium
sent to their dearest the dust

heavy and bitter with tears shed
packing smooth the urns with
ashes that once were men.
They praise them through their tears, how this man
knew well the craft of battle, how another
went down splendid in the slaughter:
and all for some strange woman.
Thus they mutter in secrecy,
and the slow anger creeps below their grief
at Atreus' sons and their quarrels.
There by the walls of Ilium
the young men in their beauty keep
graves deep in the alien soil
they hated and they conquered.

The citizens speak: their voice is dull with hatred.
The curse of the people must be paid for.
There lurks for me in the hooded night
terror of what may be told me.
The gods fail not to mark
those who have killed many.
The black Furies stalking the man
fortunate beyond all right
wrench back again the set of his life
and drop him to darkness. There among
the ciphers there is no more comfort
in power. And the vaunt of high glory
is bitterness; for God's thunderbolts
crash on the towering mountains.
Let me attain no envied wealth,
let me not plunder cities,
neither be taken in turn, and face
life in the power of another.

Various members of the Chorus, speaking severally.

From the beacon's bright message
the fleet rumor runs
through the city. If this be real
who knows? Perhaps the gods have sent some lie to us.

Who of us is so childish or so reft of wit
that by the beacon's messages
his heart flamed must despond again
when the tale changes in the end?

It is like a woman indeed
to take the rapture before the fact has shown for true.

They believe too easily, are too quick to shift
from ground to ground; and swift indeed
the rumor voiced by a woman dies again.

Now we shall understand these torches and their
shining,
the beacons, and the interchange of flame and flame.
They may be real; yet bright and dreamwise ecstasy
in light's appearance might have charmed our hearts
awry.
I see a herald coming from the beach, his brows
shaded with sprigs of olive; and upon his feet
the dust, dry sister of the mire, makes plain to me
that he will find a voice, not merely kindle flame
from mountain timber, and make signals from the
smoke,
but tell us outright, whether to be happy, or—
but I shrink back from naming the alternative.
That which appeared was good; may yet more good be
given.

And any man who prays that different things befall
the city, may he reap the crime of his own heart.

The Herald enters, and speaks.

Soil of my fathers, Argive earth I tread upon,
in daylight of the tenth year I have come back to you.
All my hopes broke but one, and this I have at last.
I never could have dared to dream that I might die
in Argos, and be buried in this beloved soil.
Hail to the Argive land and to its sunlight, hail
to its high sovereign, Zeus, and to the Pythian king.
May you no longer shower your arrows on our heads.
Beside Scamandrus you were grim; be satisfied
and turn to savior now and healer of our hurts,
my lord Apollo. Gods of the market place assembled,
I greet you all, and my own patron deity
Hermes, beloved herald, in whose right all heralds
are sacred; and you heroes that sent forth the host,
propitiously take back all that the spear has left.
O great hall of the kings and house beloved; seats
of sanctity; divinities that face the sun:
if ever before, look now with kind and glowing eyes
to greet our king in state after so long a time.
He comes, lord Agamemnon, bearing light in gloom
to you, and to all that are assembled here.
Salute him with good favor, as he well deserves,
the man who has wrecked Ilium with the spade of Zeus
vindictive, whereby all their plain has been laid waste.
Gone are their altars, the sacred places of the gods
are gone, and scattered all the seed within the ground.
With such a yoke as this gripped to the neck of Troy
he comes, the king, Atreus' elder son, a man
fortunate to be honored far above all men
alive; not Paris nor the city tied to him

can boast he did more than was done him in return.
Guilty of rape and theft, condemned, he lost the prize
captured, and broke to sheer destruction all the house
of his fathers, with the very ground whereon it stood.
Twice over the sons of Priam have atoned their sins.

CHORUS Hail and be glad, herald of the Achaean host.

HERALD I am happy; I no longer ask the gods for death.

CHORUS Did passion for your country so strip bare your heart?

HERALD So that the tears broke in my eyes, for happiness.

CHORUS You were taken with that sickness, then, that brings delight.

HERALD How? I cannot deal with such words until I understand.

CHORUS Struck with desire of those who loved as much again.

HERALD You mean our country longed for us, as we for home?

CHORUS So that I sighed, out of the darkness of my heart.

HERALD Whence came this black thought to afflict the mind with fear?

CHORUS Long since it was my silence kept disaster off.

HERALD But how? There were some you feared when the kings went away?

CHORUS So much that as you said now, even death were grace.

HERALD Well: the end has been good. And in the length of time
part of our fortune you could say held favorable,
but part we cursed again. And who, except the gods,
can live time through forever without any pain?
Were I to tell you of the hard work done, the nights
exposed, the cramped sea-quarters, the foul beds—what part
of day's disposal did we not cry out loud?
Ashore, the horror stayed with us and grew. We lay
against the ramparts of our enemies, and from
the sky, and from the ground, the meadow dews came out
to soak our clothes and fill our hair with lice. And if
I were to tell of winter time, when all birds died,
the snows of Ida past endurance she sent down,
or summer heat, when in the lazy noon the sea
fell level and asleep under a windless sky—
but why live such grief over again? That time is gone
for us, and gone for those who died. Never again
need they rise up, nor care again for anything.
Why must a live man count the numbers of the slain,
why grieve at fortune's wrath that fades to break once more?
I call a long farewell to all our unhappiness.
For us, survivors of the Argive armament,
the pleasure wins, pain casts no weight in the opposite scale.
And here, in this sun's shining, we can boast aloud,

whose fame has gone with wings across the land and sea:
"Upon a time the Argive host took Troy, and on
the houses of the gods who live in Hellas nailed
the spoils, to be the glory of days long ago."
And they who hear such things shall call this city blest
and the leaders of the host; and high the grace of God
shall be exalted, that did this. You have the story.

CHORUS I must give way; your story shows that I was wrong.
Old men are always young enough to learn, with profit.
But Clytaemestra and her house must hear, above
others, this news that makes luxurious my life.

Clytaemestra comes forward and speaks.

I raised my cry of joy, and it was long ago
when the first beacon flare of message came by night
to speak of capture and of Ilium's overthrow.
But there was one who laughed at me, who said: "You trust
in beacons so, and you believe that Troy has fallen?
How like a woman, for the heart to lift so light."
Men spoke like that; they thought I wandered in my wits;
yet I made sacrifice, and in the womanish strain
voice after voice caught up the cry along the city
to echo in the temples of the gods and bless
and still the fragrant flame that melts the sacrifice.

Why should you tell me then the whole long tale at large
when from my lord himself I shall hear all the story?
But now, how best to speed my preparation to
receive my honored lord come home again—what else
is light more sweet for woman to behold than this,

to spread the gates before her husband home from war
and saved by God's hand?—take this message to the
king:
Come, and with speed, back to the city that longs for
him,
and may he find a wife within his house as true
as on the day he left her, watchdog of the house
gentle to him alone, fierce to his enemies,
and such a woman in all her ways as this, who has
not broken the seal upon her in the length of days.
With no man else have I known delight, nor any shame
of evil speech, more than I know how to temper bronze.

Clytaemestra goes to the back of the stage.

HERALD A vaunt like this, so loaded as it is with truth,
it well becomes a highborn lady to proclaim.

CHORUS Thus has she spoken to you, and well you
understand,
words that impress interpreters whose thought is clear.
But tell me, herald; I would learn of Menelaus,
that power beloved in this land. Has he survived
also, and come with you back to his home again?

HERALD I know no way to lie and make my tale so fair
that friends could reap joy of it for any length of time.

CHORUS Is there no means to speak us fair, and yet tell the
truth?
It will not hide, when truth and good are torn asunder.

HERALD He is gone out of the sight of the Achaean host,
vessel and man alike. I speak no falsehood there.

CHORUS Was it when he had put out from Ilium in your sight,
or did a storm that struck you both whirl him away?

HERALD How like a master bowman you have hit the mark
and in your speech cut a long sorrow to brief stature.

CHORUS But then the rumor in the host that sailed beside,
was it that he had perished, or might yet be living?

HERALD No man knows. There is none could tell us that for sure
except the Sun, from whom this earth has life and increase.

CHORUS How did this storm, by wrath of the divinities,
strike on our multitude at sea? How did it end?

HERALD It is not well to stain the blessing of this day
with speech of evil weight. Such gods are honored apart.
And when the messenger of a shaken host, sad faced,
brings to his city news it prayed never to hear,
this scores one wound upon the body of the people;
and that from many houses many men are slain
by the two-lashed whip dear to the War God's hand, this turns
disaster double-bladed, bloodily made two.
The messenger so freighted with a charge of tears
should make his song of triumph at the Furies' door.
But, carrying the fair message of our hopes' salvation,
come home to a glad city's hospitality,
how shall I mix my gracious news with foul, and tell
of the storm on the Achaeans by God's anger sent?
For they, of old the deepest enemies, sea and fire,

made a conspiracy and gave the oath of hand
to blast in ruin our unhappy Argive army.
At night the sea began to rise in waves of death.
Ship against ship the Thracian stormwind shattered us,
and gored and split, our vessels, swept in violence
of storm and whirlwind, beaten by the breaking rain,
drove on in darkness, spun by the wicked shepherd's
hand.
But when the sun came up again to light the dawn,
we saw the Aegaean Sea blossoming with dead men,
the men of Achaea, and the wreckage of their ships.
For us, and for our ship, some god, no man, by guile
or by entreaty's force prevailing, laid his hand
upon the helm and brought us through with hull
unscarred.
Life-giving fortune deigned to take our ship in charge
that neither riding in deep water she took the surf
nor drove to shoal and break upon some rocky shore.
But then, delivered from death at sea, in the pale day,
incredulous of our own luck, we shepherded
in our sad thoughts the fresh disaster of the fleet
so pitifully torn and shaken by the storm.
Now of these others, if there are any left alive
they speak of us as men who perished, must they not?
Even as we, who fear that they are gone. But may
it all come well in the end. For Menelaus: be sure
if any of them come back that he will be the first.
If he is still where some sun's gleam can track him down,
alive and open-eyed, by blessed hand of God
who willed that not yet should his seed be utterly gone,
there is some hope that he will still come home again.
You have heard all; and be sure, you have heard the
truth.

The Herald goes out.

CHORUS Who is he that named you so
fatally in every way?
Could it be some mind unseen
in divination of your destiny
shaping to the lips that name
for the bride of spears and blood,
Helen, which is death? Appropriately
death of ships, death of men and cities
from the bower's soft curtained
and secluded luxury she sailed then,
driven on the giant west wind,
and armored men in their thousands came,
huntsmen down the oar blade's fading footprint
to struggle in blood with those
who by the banks of Simoeis
beached their hulls where the leaves break.

And on Ilium in truth
in the likeness of the name
the sure purpose of the Wrath drove
marriage with death: for the guest board
shamed, and Zeus kindly to strangers,
the vengeance wrought on those men
who graced in too loud voice the bride-song
fallen to their lot to sing,
the kinsmen and the brothers.
And changing its song's measure
the ancient city of Priam
chants in high strain of lamentation,
calling Paris him of the fatal marriage;
for it endured its life's end
in desolation and tears
and the piteous blood of its people.

Once a man fostered in his house

a lion cub, from the mother's milk
torn, craving the breast given.
In the first steps of its young life
mild, it played with children
and delighted the old.
Caught in the arm's cradle
they pampered it like a newborn child,
shining eyed and broken to the hand
to stay the stress of its hunger.

But it grew with time, and the lion
in the blood strain came out; it paid
grace to those who had fostered it
in blood and death for the sheep flocks,
a grim feast forbidden.
The house reeked with blood run
nor could its people beat down the bane,
the giant murderer's onslaught.
This thing they raised in their house was blessed
by God to be priest of destruction.

And that which first came to the city of Ilium,
call it a dream of calm
and the wind dying,
the loveliness and luxury of much gold,
the melting shafts of the eyes' glances,
the blossom that breaks the heart with longing.
But she turned in mid-step of her course to make
bitter the consummation,
whirling on Priam's people
to blight with her touch and nearness.
Zeus hospitable sent her,
a vengeance to make brides weep.

It has been made long since and grown old among men,
this saying: human wealth

grown to fulness of stature
breeds again nor dies without issue.
From high good fortune in the blood
blossoms the quenchless agony.
Far from others I hold my own
mind; only the act of evil
breeds others to follow,
young sins in its own likeness.
Houses clear in their right are given
children in all loveliness.

But Pride aging is made
in men's dark actions
ripe with the young pride
late or soon when the dawn of destiny
comes and birth is given
to the spirit none may fight nor beat down,
sinful Daring; and in those halls
the black visaged Disasters stamped
in the likeness of their fathers.

And Righteousness is a shining in
the smoke of mean houses.
Her blessing is on the just man.
From high halls starred with gold by reeking hands
she turns back
with eyes that glance away to the simple in heart,
spurning the strength of gold
stamped false with flattery.
And all things she steers to fulfilment.

Agamemnon enters in a chariot, with Cassandra beside him. The Chorus speaks to him.

Behold, my king: sacker of Troy's citadel,
own issue of Atreus.

How shall I hail you? How give honor
not crossing too high nor yet bending short
of this time's graces?
For many among men are they who set high
the show of honor, yet break justice.
If one be unhappy, all else are fain
to grieve with him: yet the teeth of sorrow
come nowise near to the heart's edge.
And in joy likewise they show joy's semblance,
and torture the face to the false smile.
Yet the good shepherd, who knows his flock,
the eyes of men cannot lie to him,
that with water of feigned
love seem to smile from the true heart.
But I: when you marshalled this armament
for Helen's sake, I will not hide it,
in ugly style you were written in my heart
for steering aslant the mind's course
to bring home by blood
sacrifice and dead men that wild spirit.
But now, in love drawn up from the deep heart,
not skimmed at the edge, we hail you.
You have won, your labor is made gladness.
Ask all men: you will learn in time
which of your citizens have been just
in the city's sway, which were reckless.

AGAMEMNON To Argos first, and to the gods within the land,
I must give due greeting; they have worked with me to bring
me home; they helped me in the vengeance I have wrought
on Priam's city. Not from the lips of men the gods
heard justice, but in one firm cast they laid their votes

within the urn of blood that Ilium must die
and all her people; while above the opposite vase
the hand hovered and there was hope, but no vote fell.
The stormclouds of their ruin live; the ash that dies
upon them gushes still in smoke their pride of wealth.
For all this we must thank the gods with grace of much
high praise and memory, we who fenced within our toils
of wrath the city; and, because one woman strayed,
the beast of Argos broke them, the fierce young within
the horse, the armored people who marked out their
   leap
against the setting of the Pleiades. A wild
and bloody lion swarmed above the towers of Troy
to glut its hunger lapping at the blood of kings.

This to the gods, a prelude strung to length of words.
But, for the thought you spoke, I heard and I remember
and stand behind you. For I say that it is true.
In few men is it part of nature to respect
a friend's prosperity without begrudging him,
as envy's wicked poison settling to the heart
piles up the pain in one sick with unhappiness,
who, staggered under sufferings that are all his own,
winces again to the vision of a neighbor's bliss.
And I can speak, for I have seen, I know it well,
this mirror of companionship, this shadow's ghost,
these men who seemed my friends in all sincerity.
One man of them all, Odysseus, he who sailed
   unwilling,
once yoked to me carried his harness, nor went slack.
Dead though he be or living, I can say it still.

Now in the business of the city and the gods
we must ordain full conclave of all citizens
and take our counsel. We shall see what element

is strong, and plan that it shall keep its virtue still.
But that which must be healed—we must use medicine,
or burn, or amputate, with kind intention, take
all means at hand that might beat down corruption's
pain.
So to the King's house and the home about the hearth
I take my way, with greeting to the gods within
who sent me forth, and who have brought me home
once more.
My prize was conquest; may it never fail again.

Clytaemestra comes forward and speaks.

Grave gentlemen of Argolis assembled here,
I take no shame to speak aloud before you all
the love I bear my husband. In the lapse of time
modesty fades; it is human.
What I tell you now
I learned not from another; this is my own sad life
all the long years this man was gone at Ilium.
It is evil and a thing of terror when a wife
sits in the house forlorn with no man by, and hears
rumors that like a fever die to break again,
and men come in with news of fear, and on their heels
another messenger, with worse news to cry aloud
here in this house. Had Agamemnon taken all
the wounds the tale whereof was carried home to me,
he had been cut full of gashes like a fishing net.
If he had died each time that rumor told his death,
he must have been some triple-bodied Geryon
back from the dead with threefold cloak of earth upon
his body, and killed once for every shape assumed.
Because such tales broke out forever on my rest,
many a time they cut me down and freed my throat
from the noose overslung where I had caught it fast.
And therefore is your son, in whom my love and yours

are sealed and pledged, not here to stand with us today,
Orestes. It were right; yet do not be amazed.
Strophius of Phocis, comrade in arms and faithful friend
to you, is keeping him. He spoke to me of peril
on two counts; of your danger under Ilium,
and here, of revolution and the clamorous people
who might cast down the council—since it lies in men's
nature to trample on the fighter already down.
Such my excuse to you, and without subterfuge.

For me: the rippling springs that were my tears have
dried
utterly up, nor left one drop within. I keep
the pain upon my eyes where late at night I wept
over the beacons long ago set for your sake,
untended left forever. In the midst of dreams
the whisper that a gnat's thin wings could winnow
broke
my sleep apart. I thought I saw you suffer wounds
more than the time that slept with me could ever hold.

Now all my suffering is past, with griefless heart
I hail this man, the watchdog of the fold and hall;
the stay that keeps the ship alive; the post to grip
groundward the towering roof; a father's single child;
land seen by sailors after all their hope was gone;
splendor of daybreak shining from the night of storm;
the running spring a parched wayfarer strays upon.
Oh, it is sweet to escape from all necessity!

Such is my greeting to him, that he well deserves.
Let none bear malice; for the harm that went before
I took, and it was great.
Now, my beloved one,
step from your chariot; yet let not your foot, my lord,
sacker of Ilium, touch the earth. My maidens there!

Why this delay? Your task has been appointed you,
to strew the ground before his feet with tapestries.
Let there spring up into the house he never hoped
to see, where Justice leads him in, a crimson path.

In all things else, my heart's unsleeping care shall act
with the gods' aid to set aright what fate ordained.

Clytaemestra's handmaidens spread a bright carpet between the chariot and the door.

AGAMEMNON Daughter of Leda, you who kept my house for me,
there is one way your welcome matched my absence well.
You strained it to great length. Yet properly to praise
me thus belongs by right to other lips, not yours.
And all this—do not try in woman's ways to make
me delicate, nor, as if I were some Asiatic
bow down to earth and with wide mouth cry out to me,
nor cross my path with jealousy by strewing the ground
with robes. Such state becomes the gods, and none beside.
I am a mortal, a man; I cannot trample upon
these tinted splendors without fear thrown in my path.
I tell you, as a man, not god, to reverence me.
Discordant is the murmur at such treading down
of lovely things; while God's most lordly gift to man
is decency of mind. Call that man only blest
who has in sweet tranquillity brought his life to close.
If I could only act as such, my hope is good.

CLYTAEMESTRA Yet tell me this one thing, and do not cross my will.

AGAMEMNON My will is mine. I shall not make it soft for you.

CLYTAEMESTRA It was in fear surely that you vowed this course to God.

AGAMEMNON No man has spoken knowing better what he said.

CLYTAEMESTRA If Priam had won as you have, what would he have done?

AGAMEMNON I well believe he might have walked on tapestries.

CLYTAEMESTRA Be not ashamed before the bitterness of men.

AGAMEMNON The people murmur, and their voice is great in strength.

CLYTAEMESTRA Yet he who goes unenvied shall not be admired.

AGAMEMNON Surely this lust for conflict is not womanlike?

CLYTAEMESTRA Yet for the mighty even to give way is grace.

AGAMEMNON Does such a victory as this mean so much to you?

CLYTAEMESTRA Oh, yield! The power is yours. Give way of your free will.

AGAMEMNON Since you must have it—here, let someone with all speed
take off these sandals, slaves for my feet to tread upon.
And as I crush these garments stained from the rich sea
let no god's eyes of hatred strike me from afar.
Great the extravagance, and great the shame I feel
to spoil such treasure and such silver's worth of webs.

So much for all this. Take this stranger girl within
now, and be kind. The conqueror who uses softly
his power, is watched from far in the kind eyes of God,
and this slave's yoke is one no man will wear from choice.
Gift of the host to me, and flower exquisite
from all my many treasures, she attends me here.

Now since my will was bent to listen to you in this
my feet crush purple as I pass within the hall.

CLYTAEMESTRA The sea is there, and who shall drain its yield? It breeds
precious as silver, ever of itself renewed,
the purple ooze wherein our garments shall be dipped.
And by God's grace this house keeps full sufficiency
of all. Poverty is a thing beyond its thought.
I could have vowed to trample many splendors down
had such decree been ordained from the oracles
those days when all my study was to bring home your life.
For when the root lives yet the leaves will come again
to fence the house with shade against the Dog Star's heat,
and now you have come home to keep your hearth and house
you bring with you the symbol of our winter's warmth;

but when Zeus ripens the green clusters into wine
there shall be coolness in the house upon those days
because the master ranges his own halls once more.

Zeus, Zeus accomplisher, accomplish these my prayers.
Let your mind bring these things to pass. It is your will.

Agamemnon and Clytaemestra enter the house. Cassandra remains in the chariot. The Chorus speaks.

Why must this persistent fear
beat its wings so ceaselessly
and so close against my mantic heart?
Why this strain unwanted, unrepaid, thus prophetic?
Nor can valor of good hope
seated near the chambered depth
of the spirit cast it out
as dreams of dark fancy; and yet time
has buried in the mounding sand
the sea cables since that day
when against Ilium
the army and the ships put to sea.

Yet I have seen with these eyes
Agamemnon home again.
Still the spirit sings, drawing deep
from within this unlyric threnody of the Fury.
Hope is gone utterly,
the sweet strength is far away.
Surely this is not fantasy.
Surely it is real, this whirl of drifts
that spin the stricken heart.
Still I pray; may all this
expectation fade as vanity
into unfulfilment, and not be.

Yet it is true: the high strength of men
knows no content with limitation. Sickness
chambered beside it beats at the wall between.
Man's fate that sets a true
course yet may strike upon
the blind and sudden reefs of disaster.
But if before such time, fear
throw overboard some precious thing
of the cargo, with deliberate cast,
not all the house, laboring
with weight of ruin, shall go down,
nor sink the hull deep within the sea.
And great and affluent the gift of Zeus
in yield of ploughed acres year on year
makes void again sick starvation.

But when the black and mortal blood of man
has fallen to the ground before his feet, who then
can sing spells to call it back again?
Did Zeus not warn us once
when he struck to impotence
that one who could in truth charm back the dead men?
Had the gods not so ordained
that fate should stand against fate
to check any man's excess,
my heart now would have outrun speech
to break forth the water of its grief.
But this is so; I murmur deep in darkness
sore at heart; my hope is gone now
ever again to unwind some crucial good
from the flames about my heart.

Clytaemestra comes out from the house again and speaks to Cassandra.

Cassandra, you may go within the house as well,
since Zeus in no unkindness has ordained that you
must share our lustral water, stand with the great throng
of slaves that flock to the altar of our household god.
Step from this chariot, then, and do not be so proud.
And think—they say that long ago Alcmena's son
was sold in bondage and endured the bread of slaves.
But if constraint of fact forces you to such fate,
be glad indeed for masters ancient in their wealth.
They who have reaped success beyond their dreams of hope
are savage above need and standard toward their slaves.
From us you shall have all you have the right to ask.

CHORUS What she has spoken is for you, and clear enough.
Fenced in these fatal nets wherein you find yourself
you should obey her if you can; perhaps you can not.

CLYTAEMESTRA Unless she uses speech incomprehensible,
barbarian, wild as the swallow's song, I speak
within her understanding, and she must obey.

CHORUS Go with her. What she bids is best in circumstance
that rings you now. Obey, and leave this carriage seat.

CLYTAEMESTRA I have no leisure to stand outside the house and waste
time on this woman. At the central altarstone
the flocks are standing, ready for the sacrifice
we make to this glad day we never hoped to see.
You: if you are obeying my commands at all, be quick.
But if in ignorance you fail to comprehend,

speak not, but make with your barbarian hand some sign.

CHORUS I think this stranger girl needs some interpreter
who understands. She is like some captive animal.

CLYTAEMESTRA No, she is in the passion of her own wild thoughts.
Leaving her captured city she has come to us
untrained to take the curb, and will not understand
until her rage and strength have foamed away in blood.
I shall throw down no more commands for her contempt.

Clytaemestra goes back into the house.

CHORUS I, though, shall not be angry, for I pity her.
Come down, poor creature, leave the empty car. Give way
to compulsion and take up the yoke that shall be yours.

Cassandra descends from the chariot and cries out loud.

Oh, shame upon the earth!
Apollo, Apollo!

CHORUS You cry on Loxias in agony? He is not
of those immortals the unhappy supplicate.

CASSANDRA Oh, shame upon the earth!
Apollo, Apollo!

CHORUS Now once again in bitter voice she calls upon
this god, who has not part in any lamentation.

CASSANDRA Apollo, Apollo!
Lord of the ways, my ruin.
You have undone me once again, and utterly.

CHORUS I think she will be prophetic of her own disaster.
Even in the slave's heart the gift divine lives on.

CASSANDRA Apollo, Apollo!
Lord of the ways, my ruin.
Where have you led me now at last? What house is this?

CHORUS The house of the Atreidae. If you understand
not that, I can tell you; and so much at least is true.

CASSANDRA No, but a house that God hates, guilty within
of kindred blood shed, torture of its own,
the shambles for men's butchery, the dripping floor.

CHORUS The stranger is keen scented like some hound upon
the trail of blood that leads her to discovered death.

CASSANDRA Behold there the witnesses to my faith.
The small children wail for their own death
and the flesh roasted that their father fed upon.

CHORUS We had been told before of this prophetic fame
of yours: we want no prophets in this place at all.

CASSANDRA Ah, for shame, what can she purpose now?
What is this new and huge
stroke of atrocity she plans within the house
to beat down the beloved beyond hope of healing?
Rescue is far away.

CHORUS I can make nothing of these prophecies. The rest
I understood; the city is full of the sound of them.

CASSANDRA So cruel then, that you can do this thing?
The husband of your own bed
to bathe bright with water—how shall I speak the end?
This thing shall be done with speed. The hand gropes now, and the other
hand follows in turn.

CHORUS No, I am lost. After the darkness of her speech
I go bewildered in a mist of prophecies.

CASSANDRA No, no, see there! What is that thing that shows?
Is it some net of death?
Or is the trap the woman there, the murderess?
Let now the slakeless fury in the race
rear up to howl aloud over this monstrous death.

CHORUS Upon what demon in the house do you call, to raise
the cry of triumph? All your speech makes dark my hope.
And to the heart below trickles the pale drop
as in the hour of death
timed to our sunset and the mortal radiance.
Ruin is near, and swift.

CASSANDRA See there, see there! Keep from his mate the bull.
Caught in the folded web's
entanglement she pinions him and with the black horn
strikes. And he crumples in the watered bath.
Guile, I tell you, and death there in the caldron wrought.

CHORUS I am not proud in skill to guess at prophecies,
yet even I can see the evil in this thing.
From divination what good ever has come to men?
Art, and multiplication of words
drifting through tangled evil bring
terror to them that hear.

CASSANDRA Alas, alas for the wretchedness of my ill-starred life.
This pain flooding the song of sorrow is mine alone.
Why have you brought me here in all unhappiness?
Why, why? Except to die with him? What else could be?

CHORUS You are possessed of God, mazed at heart
to sing your own death
song, the wild lyric as
in clamor for Itys, Itys over and over again
her long life of tears weeping forever grieves
the brown nightingale.

CASSANDRA Oh, for the nightingale's pure song and a fate like hers.
With fashion of beating wings the gods clothed her about
and a sweet life gave her and without lamentation.
But mine is the sheer edge of the tearing iron.

CHORUS Whence come, beat upon beat, driven of God,
vain passions of tears?
Whence your cries, terrified, clashing in horror,
in wrought melody and the singing speech?
Whence take you the marks to this path of prophecy
and speech of terror?

CASSANDRA O marriage of Paris, death to the men beloved!
Alas, Scamandrus, water my fathers drank.
There was a time I too at your springs
drank and grew strong. Ah me,
for now beside the deadly rivers, Cocytus
and Acheron, I must cry out my prophecies.

CHORUS What is this word, too clear, you have uttered now?
A child could understand.
And deep within goes the stroke of the dripping fang
as mortal pain at the trebled song of your agony
shivers the heart to hear.

CASSANDRA O sorrow, sorrow of my city dragged to uttermost death.
O sacrifices my father made at the wall.
Flocks of the pastured sheep slaughtered there.
And no use at all
to save our city from its pain inflicted now.
And I too, with brain ablaze in fever, shall go down.

CHORUS This follows the run of your song.
Is it, in cruel force of weight,
some divinity kneeling upon you brings
the death song of your passionate suffering?
I can not see the end.

CASSANDRA No longer shall my prophecies like some young girl
new-married glance from under veils, but bright and strong
as winds blow into morning and the sun's uprise
shall wax along the swell like some great wave, to burst

at last upon the shining of this agony.
Now I will tell you plainly and from no cryptic speech;
bear me then witness, running at my heels upon
the scent of these old brutal things done long ago.
There is a choir that sings as one, that shall not again
leave this house ever; the song thereof breaks harsh with
menace.
And drugged to double fury on the wine of men's
blood shed, there lurks forever here a drunken rout
of ingrown vengeful spirits never to be cast forth.
Hanging above the hall they chant their song of hate
and the old sin; and taking up the strain in turn
spit curses on that man who spoiled his brother's bed.
Did I go wide, or hit, like a real archer? Am I
some swindling seer who hawks his lies from door to
door?
Upon your oath, bear witness that I know by heart
the legend of ancient wickedness within this house.

CHORUS And how could an oath, though cast in rigid
honesty,
do any good? And still we stand amazed at you,
reared in an alien city far beyond the sea,
how can you strike, as if you had been there, the truth.

CASSANDRA Apollo was the seer who set me to this work.

CHORUS Struck with some passion for you, and himself a
god?

CASSANDRA There was a time I blushed to speak about
these things.

CHORUS True; they who prosper take on airs of vanity.

CASSANDRA Yes, then; he wrestled with me, and he breathed delight.

CHORUS Did you come to the getting of children then, as people do?

CASSANDRA I promised that to Loxias, but I broke my word.

CHORUS Were you already ecstatic in the skills of God?

CASSANDRA Yes; even then I read my city's destinies.

CHORUS So Loxias' wrath did you no harm? How could that be?

CASSANDRA For this my trespass, none believed me ever again.

CHORUS But we do; all that you foretell seems true to us.

CASSANDRA But this is evil, see!
Now once again the pain of grim, true prophecy
shivers my whirling brain in a storm of things foreseen.
Look there, see what is hovering above the house,
so small and young, imaged as in the shadow of dreams,
like children almost, killed by those most dear to them,
and their hands filled with their own flesh, as food to eat.
I see them holding out the inward parts, the vitals,
oh, pitiful, that meat their father tasted of. . . .
I tell you: There is one that plots vengeance for this,
the strengthless lion rolling in his master's bed,
who keeps, ah me, the house against his lord's return;
my lord too, now that I wear the slave's yoke on my
neck.

King of the ships, who tore up Ilium by the roots,
what does he know of this accursed bitch, who licks
his hand, who fawns on him with lifted ears, who like
a secret death shall strike the coward's stroke, nor fail?
No, this is daring when the female shall strike down
the male. What can I call her and be right? What beast
of loathing? Viper double-fanged, or Scylla witch
holed in the rocks and bane of men that range the sea;
smoldering mother of death to smoke relentless hate
on those most dear. How she stood up and howled aloud
and unashamed, as at the breaking point of battle,
in feigned gladness for his salvation from the sea!
What does it matter now if men believe or no?
What is to come will come. And soon you too will stand
beside, to murmur in pity that my words were true.

CHORUS Thyestes' feast upon the flesh of his own children
I understand in terror at the thought, and fear
is on me hearing truth and no tale fabricated.
The rest: I heard it, but wander still far from the course.

CASSANDRA I tell you, you shall look on Agamemnon dead.

CHORUS Peace, peace, poor woman; put those bitter lips to sleep.

CASSANDRA Useless; there is no god of healing in this story.

CHORUS Not if it must be; may it somehow fail to come.

CASSANDRA Prayers, yes; they do not pray; they plan to strike, and kill.

CHORUS What man is it who moves this beastly thing to be?

CASSANDRA What man? You did mistake my divination then.

CHORUS It may be; I could not follow through the schemer's plan.

CASSANDRA Yet I know Greek; I think I know it far too well.

CHORUS And Pythian oracles are Greek, yet hard to read.

CASSANDRA O flame and pain that sweeps me once again! My lord,
Apollo, King of Light, the pain, aye me, the pain!
This is the woman-lioness, who goes to bed
with the wolf, when her proud lion ranges far away,
and she will cut me down; as a wife mixing drugs
she wills to shred the virtue of my punishment
into her bowl of wrath as she makes sharp the blade
against her man, death that he brought a mistress home.
Why do I wear these mockeries upon my body,
this staff of prophecy, these flowers at my throat?
At least I will spoil you before I die. Out, down,
break, damn you! This for all that you have done to me.
Make someone else, not me, luxurious in disaster. . . .
Lo now, this is Apollo who has stripped me here
of my prophetic robes. He watched me all the time
wearing this glory, mocked of all, my dearest ones
who hated me with all their hearts, so vain, so wrong;
called like some gypsy wandering from door to door
beggar, corrupt, half-starved, and I endured it all.
And now the seer has done with me, his prophetess,

and led me into such a place as this, to die.
Lost are my father's altars, but the block is there
to reek with sacrificial blood, my own. We two
must die, yet die not vengeless by the gods. For there
shall come one to avenge us also, born to slay
his mother, and to wreak death for his father's blood.
Outlaw and wanderer, driven far from his own land,
he will come back to cope these stones of inward hate.
For this is a strong oath and sworn by the high gods,
that he shall cast men headlong for his father felled.
Why am I then so pitiful? Why must I weep?
Since once I saw the citadel of Ilium
die as it died, and those who broke the city, doomed
by the gods, fare as they have fared accordingly,
I will go through with it. I too will take my fate.
I call as on the gates of death upon these gates
to pray only for this thing, that the stroke be true,
and that with no convulsion, with a rush of blood
in painless death, I may close up these eyes, and rest.

CHORUS O woman much enduring and so greatly wise,
you have said much. But if this thing you know be true,
this death that comes upon you, how can you, serene,
walk to the altar like a driven ox of God?

CASSANDRA Friends, there is no escape for any longer time.

CHORUS Yet longest left in time is to be honored still.

CASSANDRA The day is here and now; I can not win by flight.

CHORUS Woman, be sure your heart is brave; you can take much.

CASSANDRA None but the unhappy people ever hear such praise.

CHORUS Yet there is a grace on mortals who so nobly die.

CASSANDRA Alas for you, father, and for your lordly sons.
Ah!

CHORUS What now? What terror whirls you backward from the door?

CASSANDRA Foul, foul!

CHORUS What foulness then, unless some horror in the mind?

CASSANDRA That room within reeks with blood like a slaughter house.

CHORUS What then? Only these victims butchered at the hearth.

CASSANDRA There is a breath about it like an open grave.

CHORUS This is no Syrian pride of frankincense you mean.

CASSANDRA So. I am going in, and mourning as I go
my death and Agamemnon's. Let my life be done.
Ah friends,
truly this is no wild bird fluttering at a bush,
nor vain my speech. Bear witness to me when I die,
when falls for me, a woman slain, another woman,
and when a man dies for this wickedly mated man.
Here in my death I claim this stranger's grace of you.

CHORUS Poor wretch, I pity you the fate you see so clear.

CASSANDRA Yet once more will I speak, and not this time my own
death's threnody. I call upon the Sun in prayer
against that ultimate shining when the avengers strike
these monsters down in blood, that they avenge as well
one simple slave who died, a small thing, lightly killed.

Alas, poor men, their destiny. When all goes well
a shadow will overthrow it. If it be unkind
one stroke of a wet sponge wipes all the picture out;
and that is far the most unhappy thing of all.

Cassandra goes slowly into the house.

CHORUS High fortune is a thing slakeless
for mortals. There is no man who shall point
his finger to drive it back from the door
and speak the words: "Come no longer."
Now to this man the blessed ones have given
Priam's city to be captured
and return in the gods' honor.
Must he give blood for generations gone,
die for those slain and in death pile up
more death to come for the blood shed,
what mortal else who hears shall claim
he was born clear of the dark angel?

Agamemnon, inside the house.

Ah, I am struck a deadly blow and deep within!

CHORUS Silence: who cried out that he was stabbed to death within the house?

AGAMEMNON Ah me, again, they struck again. I am wounded twice.

CHORUS How the king cried out aloud to us! I believe the thing is done.
Come, let us put our heads together, try to find some safe way out.

The members of the Chorus go about distractedly, each one speaking in turn.

Listen, let me tell you what I think is best to do.
Let the herald call all citizens to rally here.

No, better to burst in upon them now, at once,
and take them with the blood still running from their blades.

I am with this man and I cast my vote to him.
Act now. This is the perilous and instant time.

Anyone can see it, by these first steps they have taken,
they purpose to be tyrants here upon our city.

Yes, for we waste time, while they trample to the ground
deliberation's honor, and their hands sleep not.

I can not tell which counsel of yours to call my own.
It is the man of action who can plan as well.

I feel as he does; nor can I see how by words
we shall set the dead man back upon his feet again.

Do you mean, to drag our lives out long, that we must yield
to the house shamed, and leadership of such as these?

No, we can never endure that; better to be killed.
Death is a softer thing by far than tyranny.

Shall we, by no more proof than that he cried in pain,
be sure, as by divination, that our lord is dead?

Yes, we should know what is true before we break our rage.
Here is sheer guessing and far different from sure knowledge.

From all sides the voices multiply to make me choose
this course; to learn first how it stands with Agamemnon.

The doors of the palace open, disclosing the bodies of Agamemnon and Cassandra, with Clytaemestra standing over them.

CLYTAEMESTRA Much have I said before to serve necessity,
but I will take no shame now to unsay it all.
How else could I, arming hate against hateful men
disguised in seeming tenderness, fence high the nets
of ruin beyond overleaping? Thus to me
the conflict born of ancient bitterness is not
a thing new thought upon, but pondered deep in time.
I stand now where I struck him down. The thing is done.
Thus have I wrought, and I will not deny it now.
That he might not escape nor beat aside his death,

as fishermen cast their huge circling nets, I spread
deadly abundance of rich robes, and caught him fast.
I struck him twice. In two great cries of agony
he buckled at the knees and fell. When he was down
I struck him the third blow, in thanks and reverence
to Zeus the lord of dead men underneath the ground.
Thus he went down, and the life struggled out of him;
and as he died he spattered me with the dark red
and violent driven rain of bitter savored blood
to make me glad, as gardens stand among the showers
of God in glory at the birthtime of the buds.

These being the facts, elders of Argos assembled here,
be glad, if it be your pleasure; but for me, I glory.
Were it religion to pour wine above the slain,
this man deserved, more than deserved, such sacrament.
He filled our cup with evil things unspeakable
and now himself come home has drunk it to the dregs.

CHORUS We stand here stunned. How can you speak this
way, with mouth
so arrogant, to vaunt above your fallen lord?

CLYTAEMESTRA You try me out as if I were a woman and
vain;
but my heart is not fluttered as I speak before you.
You know it. You can praise or blame me as you wish;
it is all one to me. That man is Agamemnon,
my husband; he is dead; the work of this right hand
that struck in strength of righteousness. And that is that.

CHORUS Woman, what evil thing planted upon the earth
or dragged from the running salt sea could you have
tasted now
to wear such brutality and walk in the people's hate?

You have cast away, you have cut away. You shall go homeless now,
crushed with men's bitterness.

CLYTAEMESTRA Now it is I you doom to be cast out from my city
with men's hate heaped and curses roaring in my ears.
Yet look upon this dead man; you would not cross him once
when with no thought more than as if a beast had died,
when his ranged pastures swarmed with the deep fleece of flocks,
he slaughtered like a victim his own child, my pain
grown into love, to charm away the winds of Thrace.
Were you not bound to hunt him then clear of this soil
for the guilt stained upon him? Yet you hear what I
have done, and lo, you are a stern judge. But I say to you:
go on and threaten me, but know that I am ready,
if fairly you can beat me down beneath your hand,
for you to rule; but if the god grant otherwise,
you shall be taught—too late, for sure—to keep your place.

CHORUS Great your design, your speech is a clamor of pride.
Swung to the red act drives the fury within your brain
signed clear in the splash of blood over your eyes.
Yet to come is stroke given for stroke
vengeless, forlorn of friends.

CLYTAEMESTRA Now hear you this, the right behind my sacrament:
By my child's Justice driven to fulfilment, by
her Wrath and Fury, to whom I sacrificed this man,

the hope that walks my chambers is not traced with fear
while yet Aegisthus makes the fire shine on my hearth,
my good friend, now as always, who shall be for us
the shield of our defiance, no weak thing; while he,
this other, is fallen, stained with this woman you behold,
plaything of all the golden girls at Ilium;
and here lies she, the captive of his spear, who saw
wonders, who shared his bed, the wise in revelations
and loving mistress, who yet knew the feel as well
of the men's rowing benches. Their reward is not
unworthy. He lies there; and she who swanlike cried
aloud her lyric mortal lamentation out
is laid against his fond heart, and to me has given
a delicate excitement to my bed's delight.

CHORUS Oh, that in speed, without pain
and the slow bed of sickness
death could come to us now, death that forever
carries sleep without ending, now that our lord is down,
our shield, kindest of men,
who for a woman's grace suffered so much,
struck down at last by a woman.

Alas, Helen, wild heart
for the multitudes, for the thousand lives
you killed under Troy's shadow,
you alone, to shine in man's memory
as blood flower never to be washed out. Surely a demon
then
of death walked in the house, men's agony.

CLYTAEMESTRA No, be not so heavy, nor yet draw down
in prayer death's ending,
neither turn all wrath against Helen
for men dead, that she alone killed

all those Danaan lives, to work
the grief that is past all healing.

CHORUS Divinity that kneel on this house and the two
strains of the blood of Tantalus,
in the hands and hearts of women you steer
the strength tearing my heart.
Standing above the corpse, obscene
as some carrion crow she sings
the crippled song and is proud.

CLYTAEMESTRA Thus have you set the speech of your lips
straight, calling by name
the spirit thrice glutted that lives in this race.
From him deep in the nerve is given
the love and the blood drunk, that before
the old wound dries, it bleeds again.

CHORUS Surely it is a huge
and heavy spirit bending the house you cry;
alas, the bitter glory
of a doom that shall never be done with;
and all through Zeus, Zeus,
first cause, prime mover.
For what thing without Zeus is done among mortals?
What here is without God's blessing?

O king, my king
how shall I weep for you?
What can I say out of my heart of pity?
Caught in this spider's web you lie,
Your life gasped out in indecent death,
struck prone to this shameful bed
by your lady's hand of treachery
and the stroke twin edged of the iron.

CLYTAEMESTRA Can you claim I have done this?
Speak of me never
more as the wife of Agamemnon.
In the shadow of this corpse's queen
the old stark avenger
of Atreus for his revel of hate
struck down this man,
last blood for the slaughtered children.

CHORUS What man shall testify
your hands are clean of this murder?
How? How? Yet from his father's blood
might swarm some fiend to guide you.
The black ruin that shoulders
through the streaming blood of brothers
strides at last where he shall win requital
for the children who were eaten.

O king, my king
how shall I weep for you?
What can I say out of my heart of pity?
Caught in this spider's web you lie,
your life gasped out in indecent death,
struck prone to this shameful bed
by your lady's hand of treachery
and the stroke twin edged of the iron.

CLYTAEMESTRA No shame, I think, in the death given
this man. And did he not
first of all in this house wreak death
by treachery?
The flower of this man's love and mine,
Iphigeneia of the tears
he dealt with even as he has suffered.

Let his speech in death's house be not loud.
With the sword he struck,
with the sword he paid for his own act.

CHORUS My thoughts are swept away and I go
bewildered.
Where shall I turn the brain's
activity in speed when the house is falling?
There is fear in the beat of the blood rain breaking
wall and tower. The drops come thicker.
Still fate grinds on yet more stones the blade
for more acts of terror.

Earth, my earth, why did you not fold me under
before ever I saw this man lie dead
fenced by the tub in silver?
Who shall bury him? Who shall mourn him?
Shall you dare this who have killed
your lord? Make lamentation,
render the graceless grace to his soul
for huge things done in wickedness?
Who over this great man's grave shall lay
the blessing of tears
worked soberly from a true heart?

CLYTAEMESTRA Not for you to speak of such tendance.
Through us he fell,
by us he died; we shall bury.
There will be no tears in this house for him.
It must be Iphigeneia
his child, who else,
shall greet her father by the whirling stream
and the ferry of tears
to close him in her arms and kiss him.

CHORUS Here is anger for anger. Between them
who shall judge lightly?
The spoiler is robbed; he killed, he has paid.
The truth stands ever beside God's throne
eternal: he who has wrought shall pay; that is law.
Then who shall tear the curse from their blood?
The seed is stiffened to ruin.

CLYTAEMESTRA You see truth in the future
at last. Yet I wish
to seal my oath with the Spirit
in the house: I will endure all things as they stand
now, hard though it be. Hereafter
let him go forth to make bleed with death
and guilt the houses of others.
I will take some small
measure of our riches, and be content
that I swept from these halls
the murder, the sin, and the fury.

Aegisthus enters, followed at a little distance by his armed bodyguard.

AEGISTHUS O splendor and exaltation of this day of doom!
Now I can say once more that the high gods look down
on mortal crimes to vindicate the right at last,
now that I see this man—sweet sight—before me here
sprawled in the tangling nets of fury, to atone
the calculated evil of his father's hand.
For Atreus, this man's father, King of Argolis—
I tell you the clear story—drove my father forth,
Thyestes, his own brother, who had challenged him
in his king's right—forth from his city and his home.
Yet sad Thyestes came again to supplicate

the hearth, and win some grace, in that he was not slain
nor soiled the doorstone of his fathers with blood
spilled.
Not his own blood. But Atreus, this man's godless sire,
angrily hospitable set a feast for him,
in seeming a glad day of fresh meat slain and good
cheer; then served my father his own children's flesh
to feed on. For he carved away the extremities,
hands, feet, and cut the flesh apart, and covered them
served in a dish to my father at his table apart,
who with no thought for the featureless meal before him
ate
that ghastly food whose curse works now before your
eyes.
But when he knew the terrible thing that he had done,
he spat the dead meat from him with a cry, and reeled
spurning the table back to heel with strength the curse:
"Thus crash in ruin all the seed of Pleisthenes."
Out of such acts you see this dead man stricken here,
and it was I, in my right, who wrought this murder, I
third born to my unhappy father, and with him
driven, a helpless baby in arms, to banishment.
Yet I grew up, and justice brought me home again,
till from afar I laid my hands upon this man,
since it was I who pieced together the fell plot.
Now I can die in honor again, if die I must,
having seen him caught in the cords of his just
punishment.

CHORUS Aegisthus, this strong vaunting in distress is vile.
You claim that you deliberately killed the king,
you, and you only, wrought the pity of this death.
I tell you then: There shall be no escape, your head
shall face the stones of anger from the people's hands.

AEGISTHUS So loud from you, stooped to the meanest rowing bench
with the ship's masters lordly on the deck above?
You are old men; well, you shall learn how hard it is
at your age, to be taught how to behave yourselves.
But there are chains, there is starvation with its pain,
excellent teachers of good manners to old men,
wise surgeons and exemplars. Look! Can you not see it?
Lash not at the goads for fear you hit them, and be hurt.

CHORUS So then you, like a woman, waited the war out
here in the house, shaming the master's bed with lust,
and planned against the lord of war this treacherous death?

AEGISTHUS It is just such words as these will make you cry in pain.
Not yours the lips of Orpheus, no, quite otherwise,
whose voice of rapture dragged all creatures in his train.
You shall be dragged, for baby whimperings sobbed out
in rage. Once broken, you will be easier to deal with.

CHORUS How shall you be lord of the men of Argos, you
who planned the murder of this man, yet could not dare
to act it out, and cut him down with your own hand?

AEGISTHUS No, clearly the deception was the woman's part,
and I was suspect, that had hated him so long.
Still with his money I shall endeavor to control
the citizens. The mutinous man shall feel the yoke
drag at his neck, no cornfed racing colt that runs
free traced; but hunger, grim companion of the dark
dungeon shall see him broken to the hand at last.

CHORUS But why, why then, you coward, could you not have slain
your man yourself? Why must it be his wife who killed,
to curse the country and the gods within the ground?
Oh, can Orestes live, be somewhere in sunlight still?
Shall fate grown gracious ever bring him back again
in strength of hand to overwhelm these murderers?

AEGISTHUS You shall learn then, since you stick to stubbornness of mouth and hand.
Up now from your cover, my henchmen: here is work for you to do.

CHORUS Look, they come! Let every man clap fist upon his hilted sword.

AEGISTHUS I too am sword-handed against you; I am not afraid of death.

CHORUS Death you said and death it shall be; we take up the word of fate.

CLYTAEMESTRA No, my dearest, dearest of all men, we have done enough. No more
violence. Here is a monstrous harvest and a bitter reaping time.
There is pain enough already. Let us not be bloody now.
Honored gentlemen of Argos, go to your homes now and give way
to the stress of fate and season. We could not do otherwise
than we did. If this is the end of suffering, we can be content
broken as we are by the brute heel of angry destiny.
Thus a woman speaks among you. Shall men deign to understand?

AEGISTHUS Yes, but think of these foolish lips that blossom into leering gibes,
think of the taunts they spit against me daring destiny and power,
sober opinion lost in insults hurled against my majesty.

CHORUS It was never the Argive way to grovel at a vile man's feet.

AEGISTHUS I shall not forget this; in the days to come I shall be there.

CHORUS Nevermore, if God's hand guiding brings Orestes home again.

AEGISTHUS Exiles feed on empty dreams of hope. I know it. I was one.

CHORUS Have your way, gorge and grow fat, soil justice, while the power is yours.

AEGISTHUS You shall pay, make no mistake, for this misguided insolence.

CHORUS Crow and strut, brave cockerel by your hen; you have no threats to fear.

CLYTAEMESTRA These are howls of impotent rage; forget them, dearest; you and I
have the power; we two shall bring good order to our house at least.

They enter the house. The doors close. All persons leave the stage.

PROMETHEUS BOUND

Translated by David Grene

CHARACTERS

MIGHT

VIOLENCE, *muta persona*

HEPHAESTUS, *the smith*

PROMETHEUS

OCEANOS

IO

HERMES

CHORUS OF THE DAUGHTERS OF OCEANOS

Non-speaking: demons; servants of Zeus

PROMETHEUS BOUND

SCENE *A bare and desolate crag in the Caucasus. Enter Might and Violence, demons, servants of Zeus, and Hephaestus, the smith.*

MIGHT This is the world's limit that we have come to; this is the Scythian country, an untrodden desolation. Hephaestus, it is you that must heed the commands the Father laid upon you to nail this malefactor to the high craggy rocks in fetters unbreakable of adamantine chain. For it was your flower, the brightness of fire that devises all, that he stole and gave to mortal men; this is the sin for which he must pay the gods the penalty—that he may learn to endure and like the sovereignty of Zeus and quit his man-loving disposition.

HEPHAESTUS Might and Violence, in you the command of Zeus has its perfect fulfilment: in you there is nothing to stand in its way. But, for myself, I have not the heart to bind violently a god who is my kin here on this wintry cliff. Yet there is constraint upon me to have the heart for just that, for it is a dangerous thing to treat the Father's words lightly.

High-contriving Son of Themis of Straight Counsel: this is not of your will nor of mine; yet I shall nail you in bonds of indissoluble bronze on this crag far from men. Here you shall hear no voice of mortal; here you shall see no form of mortal. You shall be grilled by the sun's bright fire and change the fair bloom of your skin. You shall be glad when Night comes with her mantle of stars and hides the sun's light; but the sun shall scatter the hoarfrost again at dawn. Always the grievous burden of your torture will be there to wear you down; for he that shall cause it to cease has yet to be born.

Such is the reward you reap of your man-loving disposition. For you, a god, feared not the anger of the gods, but gave honors to mortals beyond what was just. Wherefore you shall mount guard on this unlovely rock, upright, sleepless, not bending the knee. Many a groan and many a lamentation you shall utter, but they shall not serve you. For the mind of Zeus is hard to soften with prayer, and every ruler is harsh whose rule is new.

MIGHT Come, why are you holding back? Why are you pitying in vain? Why is it that you do not hate a god whom the gods hate most of all? Why do you not hate him, since it was your honor that he betrayed to men?

HEPHAESTUS Our kinship has strange power; that, and our life together.

MIGHT Yes. But to turn a deaf ear to the Father's words—how can that be? Do you not fear that more?

HEPHAESTUS You are always pitiless, always full of ruthlessness.

MIGHT There is no good singing dirges over him. Do not labor uselessly at what helps not at all.

HEPHAESTUS O handicraft of mine—that I deeply hate!

MIGHT Why do you hate it? To speak simply, your craft is in no way the author of his present troubles.

HEPHAESTUS Yet would another had had this craft allotted to him.

MIGHT There is nothing without discomfort except the overlordship of the gods. For only Zeus is free.

HEPHAESTUS I know. I have no answer to this.

MIGHT Hurry now. Throw the chain around him that the Father may not look upon your tarrying.

HEPHAESTUS There are the fetters, there: you can see them.

MIGHT Put them on his hands: strong, now with the hammer: strike. Nail him to the rock.

HEPHAESTUS It is being done now. I am not idling at my work.

MIGHT Hammer it more; put in the wedge; leave it loose nowhere. He's a cunning fellow at finding a way even out of hopeless difficulties.

HEPHAESTUS Look now, his arm is fixed immovably!

MIGHT Nail the other safe, that he may learn, for all his cleverness, that he is duller witted than Zeus.

HEPHAESTUS No one, save Prometheus, can justly blame me.

MIGHT Drive the obstinate jaw of the adamantine wedge right through his breast: drive it hard.

HEPHAESTUS Alas, Prometheus, I groan for your sufferings.

MIGHT Are you pitying again? Are you groaning for the enemies of Zeus? Have a care, lest some day you may be pitying yourself.

HEPHAESTUS You see a sight that hurts the eye.

MIGHT I see this rascal getting his deserts. Throw the girth around his sides.

HEPHAESTUS I am forced to do this; do not keep urging me.

MIGHT Yes, I will urge you, and hound you on as well. Get below now, and hoop his legs in strongly.

HEPHAESTUS There now, the task is done. It has not taken long.

MIGHT Hammer the piercing fetters with all your power, for the overseer of our work is severe.

HEPHAESTUS Your looks and the refrain of your tongue are alike.

MIGHT *You* can be softhearted. But do not blame my stubbornness and harshness of temper.

HEPHAESTUS Let us go. He has the harness on his limbs.

MIGHT (*to Prometheus*) Now, play the insolent; now, plunder the gods' privileges and give them to creatures of a day. What drop of your sufferings can mortals spare you? The gods named you wrongly when they called you Forethought; you yourself *need* Forethought to extricate yourself from this contrivance.

Prometheus is left alone on the rock.

PROMETHEUS Bright light, swift-winged winds, springs of the rivers, numberless
laughter of the sea's waves, earth, mother of all, and the all-seeing
circle of the sun: I call upon you to see what I, a god, suffer
at the hands of gods—
see with what kind of torture
worn down I shall wrestle ten thousand
years of time—
such is the despiteful bond that the Prince
has devised against me, the new Prince
of the Blessed Ones. Oh, woe is me!
I groan for the present sorrow,
I groan for the sorrow to come, I groan
questioning when there shall come a time
when He shall ordain a limit to my sufferings.
What am I saying? I have known all before,
all that shall be, and clearly known; to me,
nothing that hurts shall come with a new face.
So must I bear, as lightly as I can,
the destiny that fate has given me;
for I know well against necessity,
against its strength, no one can fight and win.

I cannot speak about my fortune, cannot
hold my tongue either. It was mortal man
to whom I gave great privileges and
for that was yoked in this unyielding harness.

I hunted out the secret spring of fire,
that filled the narthex stem, which when revealed
became the teacher of each craft to men,
a great resource. This is the sin committed
for which I stand accountant, and I pay
nailed in my chains under the open sky.

Ah! Ah!
What sound, what sightless smell approaches me,
God sent, or mortal, or mingled?
Has it come to earth's end
to look on my sufferings,
or what does it wish?
You see me a wretched god in chains,
the enemy of Zeus, hated of all
the gods that enter Zeus' palace hall,
because of my excessive love for Man.

What is that? The rustle
of birds' wings near? The air whispers
with the gentle strokes of wings.
Everything that comes toward me is occasion for fear.

The Chorus, composed of the daughters of Oceanos, enters, the members wearing some formalized representation of wings, so that their general appearance is birdlike.

CHORUS Fear not: this is a company of friends
that comes to your mountain with swift
rivalry of wings.
Hardly have we persuaded our Father's
mind, and the quick-bearing winds
speeded us hither. The sound
of stroke of bronze rang through our cavern
in its depths and it shook from us

shamefaced modesty; unsandaled
we have hastened on our chariot of wings.

PROMETHEUS Alas, children of teeming Tethys and of him
who encircles all the world with stream unsleeping,
Father Ocean,
look, see with what chains
I am nailed on the craggy heights
of this gully to keep a watch
that none would envy me.

CHORUS I see, Prometheus: and a mist of fear and tears
besets my eyes as I see your form
wasting away on these cliffs
in adamantine bonds of bitter shame.
For new are the steersmen that rule Olympus:
and new are the customs by which Zeus rules,
customs that have no law to them,
but what was great before he brings to nothingness.

PROMETHEUS Would that he had hurled me
underneath the earth and underneath
the House of Hades, host to the dead—
yes, down to limitless Tartarus,
yes, though he bound me cruelly
in chains unbreakable,
so neither god nor any other being
might have found joy in gloating over me.
Now as I hang, the plaything of the winds,
my enemies can laugh at what I suffer.

CHORUS Who of the gods is so hard of heart
that he finds joy in this?
Who is that that does not feel
sorrow answering your pain—

save only Zeus? For he malignantly,
always cherishing a mind
that bends not, has subdued the breed
of Uranos, nor shall he cease
until he satisfies his heart,
or someone take the rule from him—that
  hard-to-capture rule—
by some device of subtlety.

PROMETHEUS Yes, there shall come a day for me
when he shall need me, me that now am tortured
in bonds and fetters—he shall need me then,
this president of the Blessed—
to show the new plot whereby he may be spoiled
of his throne and his power.
Then not with honeyed tongues
of persuasion shall he enchant me;
he shall not cow me with his threats
to tell him what I know,
until he free me from my cruel chains
and pay me recompense for what I suffer.

CHORUS You are stout of heart, unyielding
to the bitterness of pain.
You are free of tongue, too free.
It is my mind that piercing fear has fluttered;
your misfortunes frighten me.
Where and when is it fated
to see you reach the term, to see you reach
the harbor free of trouble at the last?
A disposition none can win, a heart
that no persuasions soften—these are his,
the Son of Kronos.

PROMETHEUS I know that he is savage: and his justice

a thing he keeps by his own standard: still
that will of his shall melt to softness yet
when he is broken in the way I know,
and though his temper now is oaken hard
it shall be softened: hastily he'll come
to meet my haste, to join in amity
and union with me—one day he shall come.

CHORUS Reveal it all to us: tell us the story of what the charge was on which Zeus caught you and punished you so cruelly with such dishonor. Tell us, if the telling will not injure you in any way.

PROMETHEUS To speak of this is bitterness. To keep silent bitter no less; and every way is misery.

When first the gods began their angry quarrel,
and god matched god in rising faction, some
eager to drive old Kronos from his throne
that Zeus might rule—the fools!—others again
earnest that Zeus might never be their king—
I then with the best counsel tried to win
the Titans, sons of Uranos and Earth,
but failed. They would have none of crafty schemes
and in their savage arrogance of spirit
thought they would lord it easily by force.
But she that was my mother, Themis, Earth—
she is but one although her names are many—
had prophesied to me how it should be,
even how the fates decreed it: and she said
that "not by strength nor overmastering force
the fates allowed the conquerors to conquer
but by guile only": This is what I told them,
but they would not vouchsafe a glance at me.
Then with those things before me it seemed best

to take my mother and join Zeus' side:
he was as willing as we were:
thanks to my plans the dark receptacle
of Tartarus conceals the ancient Kronos,
him and his allies. These were the services
I rendered to this tyrant and these pains
the payment he has given me in requital.
This is a sickness rooted and inherent
in the nature of a tyranny:
that he that holds it does not trust his friends.

But you have asked on what particular
charge he now tortures me: this I will tell you.
As soon as he ascended to the throne
that was his father's, straightway he assigned
to the several gods their several privileges
and portioned out the power, but to the unhappy
breed of mankind he gave no heed, intending
to blot the race out and create a new.
Against these plans none stood save I: I dared.
I rescued men from shattering destruction
that would have carried them to Hades' house;
and therefore I am tortured on this rock,
a bitterness to suffer, and a pain
to pitiful eyes. I gave to mortal man
a precedence over myself in pity: I
can win no pity: pitiless is he
that thus chastises me, a spectacle
bringing dishonor on the name of Zeus.

CHORUS He would be iron-minded and made of stone, indeed, Prometheus, who did not sympathize with your sufferings. I would not have chosen to see them, and now that I see, my heart is pained.

PROMETHEUS Yes, to my friends I am pitiable to see.

CHORUS Did you perhaps go further than you have told us?

PROMETHEUS I caused mortals to cease foreseeing doom.

CHORUS What cure did you provide them with against that sickness?

PROMETHEUS I placed in them blind hopes.

CHORUS That was a great gift you gave to men.

PROMETHEUS Besides this, I gave them fire.

CHORUS And do creatures of a day now possess bright-faced fire?

PROMETHEUS Yes, and from it they shall learn many crafts.

CHORUS Then these are the charges on which—

PROMETHEUS Zeus tortures me and gives me no respite.

CHORUS Is there no limit set for your pain?

PROMETHEUS None save when it shall seem good to Zeus.

CHORUS How will it ever seem good to him? What hope is there? Do you not see how you have erred? It is not pleasure for me to say that you have erred, and for you it is a pain to hear. But let us speak no more of all this and do you seek some means of deliverance from your trials.

PROMETHEUS It is an easy thing for one whose foot
is on the outside of calamity
to give advice and to rebuke the sufferer.
I have known all that you have said: I knew,
I knew when I transgressed nor will deny it.
In helping man I brought my troubles on me;
but yet I did not think that with such tortures
I should be wasted on these airy cliffs,
this lonely mountain top, with no one near.
But do not sorrow for my present suffering;
alight on earth and hear what is to come
that you may know the whole complete: I beg you
alight and join your sorrow with mine: misfortune
wandering the same track lights now upon one
and now upon another.

CHORUS Willing our ears,
that hear you cry to them, Prometheus,
now with light foot I leave the rushing car
and sky, the holy path of birds, and light
upon this jutting rock: I long
to hear your story to the end.

Enter Oceanos, riding on a hippocamp, or sea-monster.

OCEANOS I come
on a long journey, speeding past the boundaries,
to visit you, Prometheus: with the mind
alone, no bridle needed, I direct
my swift-winged bird; my heart is sore
for your misfortunes; you know that. I think
that it is kinship makes me feel them so.
Besides, apart from kinship, there is no one
I hold in higher estimation: that
you soon shall know and know beside that in me

there is no mere word-kindness: tell me
how I can help you, and you will never say
that you have any friend more loyal to you
than Oceanos.

PROMETHEUS What do I see? Have you, too, come to gape
in wonder at this great display, my torture?
How did you have the courage to come here
to this land, Iron-Mother, leaving the stream
called after you and the rock-roofed, self-established
caverns? Was it to feast your eyes upon
the spectacle of my suffering and join
in pity for my pain? Now look and see
the sight, this friend of Zeus, that helped set up
his tyranny and see what agonies
twist me, by his instructions!

OCEANOS Yes, I see,
Prometheus, and I want, indeed I do,
to advise you for the best, for all your cleverness.
Know yourself and reform your ways to new ways,
for new is he that rules among the gods.
But if you throw about such angry words,
words that are whetted swords, soon Zeus will hear you,
even though his seat in glory is far removed,
and then your present multitude of pains
will seem like child's play. My poor friend, give up
this angry mood of yours and look for means
of getting yourself free of trouble. Maybe
what I say seems to you both old and commonplace;
but this is what you pay, Prometheus, for
that tongue of yours which talked so high and haughty:
you are not yet humble, still you do not yield
to your misfortunes, and you wish, indeed,
to add some more to them; now, if you follow

me as a schoolmaster you will not kick
against the pricks, seeing that he, the King,
that rules alone, is harsh and sends accounts
to no one's audit for the deeds he does.
Now I will go and try if I can free you:
do you be quiet, do not talk so much.
Since your mind is so subtle, don't you know
that a vain tongue is subject to correction?

PROMETHEUS I envy you, that you stand clear of blame,
yet shared and dared in everything with me!
Now let me be, and have no care for me.
Do what you will, Him you will not persuade;
He is not easily won over: look,
take care lest coming here to me should hurt you.

OCEANOS You are by nature better at advising
others than yourself. I take my cue
from deeds, not words. Do not withhold me now
when I am eager to go to Zeus. I'm sure,
I'm sure that he will grant this favor to me,
to free you from your chains.

PROMETHEUS I thank you and will never cease; for loyalty
is not what you are wanting in. Don't trouble,
for you will trouble to no purpose, and no help
to me—if it so be you want to trouble.
No, rest yourself, keep away from this thing;
because I am unlucky I would not,
for that, have everyone unlucky too.
No, for my heart is sore already when
I think about my brothers' fortunes—Atlas,
who stands to westward of the world, supporting
the pillar of earth and heaven on his shoulders,

a load that suits no shoulders; and the earthborn
dweller in caves Cilician, whom I saw
and pitied, hundred-headed, dreadful monster,
fierce Typho, conquered and brought low by force.
Once against all the gods he stood, opposing,
hissing out terror from his grim jaws; his eyes
flashed gorgon glaring lightning as he thought
to sack the sovereign tyranny of Zeus;
but upon him came the unsleeping bolt
of Zeus, the lightning-breathing flame, down rushing,
which cast him from his high aspiring boast.
Struck to the heart, his strength was blasted dead
and burnt to ashes; now a sprawling mass
useless he lies, hard by the narrow seaway
pressed down beneath the roots of Aetna: high
above him on the mountain peak the smith
Hephaestus works at the anvil. Yet one day
there shall burst out rivers of fire, devouring
with savage jaws the fertile, level plains
of Sicily of the fair fruits; such boiling wrath
with weapons of fire-breathing surf, a fiery
unapproachable torrent, shall Typho vomit,
though Zeus' lightning left him but a cinder.
But all of this you know: you do not need me
to be your schoolmaster: reassure yourself
as you know how: this cup I shall drain myself
till the high mind of Zeus shall cease from anger.

OCEANOS Do you not know, Prometheus, that words are healers of the sick temper?

PROMETHEUS Yes, if in season due one soothes the heart with them, not tries violently to reduce the swelling anger.

OCEANOS Tell me, what danger do you see for me in loyalty to you, and courage therein?

PROMETHEUS I see only useless effort and a silly good nature.

OCEANOS Suffer me then to be sick of this sickness, for it is a profitable thing, if one is wise, to seem foolish.

PROMETHEUS This shall seem to be my fault.

OCEANOS Clearly your words send me home again.

PROMETHEUS Yes, lest your doings for me bring you enmity.

OCEANOS His enmity, who newly sits on the all-powerful throne?

PROMETHEUS His is a heart you should beware of vexing.

OCEANOS Your own misfortune will be my teacher, Prometheus.

PROMETHEUS Off with you, then! Begone! Keep your present mind.

OCEANOS These words fall on very responsive ears. Already my four-legged bird is pawing the level track of Heaven with his wings, and he will be glad to bend the knee in his own stable.

CHORUS

Strophe I cry aloud, Prometheus, and lament your bitter fate,

my tender eyes are trickling tears:
their fountains wet my cheek.
This is a tyrant's deed; this is unlovely,
a thing done by a tyrant's private laws,
and with this thing Zeus shows his haughtiness
of temper toward the gods that were of old.

Antistrophe Now all the earth has cried aloud,
lamenting:
now all that was magnificent of old
laments your fall, laments your brethren's fall
as many as in holy Asia hold
their stablished habitation, all lament
in sympathy for your most grievous woes.

Strophe Dwellers in the land of Colchis,
maidens, fearless in the fight,
and the host of Scythia, living
round the lake Maeotis, living
on the edges of the world.

Antistrophe And Arabia's flower of warriors
and the craggy fortress keepers
near Caucasian mountains, fighters
terrible, crying for battle,
brandishing sharp pointed spears.

Strophe One god and one god only I have seen
before this day, in torture and in bonds
unbreakable: he was a Titan,
Atlas, whose strength and might
ever exceeded; now he bends his back
and groans beneath the load of earth and heaven.

Antistrophe The wave cries out as it breaks into surf;

the depth cries out, lamenting you; the dark
Hades, the hollow underneath the world,
sullenly groans below; the springs
of sacred flowing rivers all lament
the pain and pity of your suffering.

PROMETHEUS Do not think that out of pride or stubbornness I hold my peace; my heart is eaten away when I am aware of myself, when I see myself insulted as I am. Who was it but I who in truth dispensed their honors to these new gods? I will say nothing of this; you know it all; but hear what troubles there were among men, how I found them witless and gave them the use of their wits and made them masters of their minds. I will tell you this, not because I would blame men, but to explain the goodwill of my gift. For men at first had eyes but saw to no purpose; they had ears but did not hear. Like the shapes of dreams they dragged through their long lives and handled all things in bewilderment and confusion. They did not know of building houses with bricks to face the sun; they did not know how to work in wood. They lived like swarming ants in holes in the ground, in the sunless caves of the earth. For them there was no secure token by which to tell winter nor the flowering spring nor the summer with its crops; all their doings were indeed without intelligent calculation until I showed them the rising of the stars, and the settings, hard to observe. And further I discovered to them numbering, pre-eminent among subtle devices, and the combining of letters as a means of remembering all things, the Muses' mother, skilled in craft. It was I who first yoked beasts for them in the yokes and made of those beasts the slaves of trace chain and pack saddle that they might be man's substitute in the hardest tasks; and I harnessed to the carriage, so that they loved the rein, horses, the crowning pride of the rich man's luxury. It was I and none other who discovered ships, the sail-driven wagons that the sea buffets. Such were the contrivances that I discovered for men—alas for me! For I myself am without contrivance to rid myself of my present affliction.

CHORUS What you have suffered is indeed terrible. You are all astray and bewildered in your mind, and like a bad doctor that has fallen sick himself, you are cast down and cannot find what sort of drugs would cure your ailment.

PROMETHEUS Hear the rest, and you will marvel even more at the crafts and resources I contrived. Greatest was this: in the former times if a man fell sick he had no defense against the sickness, neither healing food nor drink, nor unguent; but through the lack of drugs men wasted away, until I showed them the blending of mild simples wherewith they drive out all manner of diseases. It was I who arranged all the ways of seercraft, and I first adjudged what things come verily true from dreams; and to men I gave meaning to the ominous cries, hard to interpret. It was I who set in order the omens of the highway and the flight of crooked-taloned birds, which of them were propitious or lucky by nature, and what manner of life each led, and what were their mutual hates, loves, and companionships; also I taught of the smoothness of the vitals and what color they should have to pleasure the gods and the dappled beauty of the gall and the lobe. It was I who burned thighs wrapped in fat and the long shank bone and set mortals on the road to this murky craft. It was I who made visible to men's eyes the flaming signs of the sky that were before dim. So much for these. Beneath the earth, man's hidden blessing, copper, iron, silver, and gold—will anyone claim to have discovered these before I did? No one, I am very sure, who wants to speak truly and to the purpose. One brief word will tell the whole story: all arts that mortals have come from Prometheus.

CHORUS Therefore do not help mortals beyond all expediency while neglecting yourself in your troubles. For I am of good hope that once freed of these bonds you will be no less in power than Zeus.

PROMETHEUS Not yet has fate that brings to fulfilment determined these things to be thus. I must be twisted by ten thousand pangs and agonies, as I now am, to escape my chains at last. Craft is far weaker than necessity.

CHORUS Who then is the steersman of necessity?

PROMETHEUS The triple-formed Fates and the remembering Furies.

CHORUS Is Zeus weaker than these?

PROMETHEUS Yes, for he, too, cannot escape what is fated.

CHORUS What is fated for Zeus besides eternal sovereignty?

PROMETHEUS Inquire of this no further, do not entreat me.

CHORUS This is some solemn secret, I suppose, that you are hiding.

PROMETHEUS Think of some other story: this one it is not yet the season to give tongue to, but it must be hidden with all care; for it is only by keeping it that I will escape my despiteful bondage and my agony.

CHORUS

Strophe May Zeus never, Zeus that all
the universe controls, oppose
his power against my mind:
may I never dallying
be slow to give my worship at
the sacrificial feasts
when the bulls are killed beside
quenchless Father Ocean:
may I never sin in word:
may these precepts still abide
in my mind nor melt away.

Antistrophe It is a sweet thing to draw out
a long, long life in cheerful hopes,
and feed the spirit in the bright
benignity of happiness:
but I shiver when I see you
wasted with ten thousand pains,
all because you did not tremble
at the name of Zeus: your mind
was yours, not his, and at its bidding
you regarded mortal men
too high, Prometheus.

Strophe Kindness that cannot be requited, tell me,
where is the help in that, my friend? What succor
in creatures of a day? You did not see
the feebleness that draws its breath in gasps,
a dreamlike feebleness by which the race
of man is held in bondage, a blind prisoner.
So the plans of men shall never
pass the ordered law of Zeus.

Antistrophe This I have learned while I looked on your pains,
deadly pains, Prometheus.
A dirge for you came to my lips, so different
from the other song I sang to crown your marriage
in honor of your couching and your bath,
upon the day you won her with your gifts
to share your bed—of your own race she was,
Hesione—and so you brought her home.

Enter Io, a girl wearing horns like an ox.

What land is this? what race of men? Who is it
I see here tortured in this rocky bondage?
What is the sin he's paying for? Oh, tell me
to what part of the world my wanderings have brought me.
Oh, Oh, Oh,
there it is again, there again—it stings me,
the gadfly, the ghost of earth-born Argos:
keep it away, keep it away, earth!
I'm frightened when I see the shape of Argos,
Argos the herdsman with ten thousand eyes.
He stalks me with his crafty eyes: he died,
but the earth didn't hide him; still he comes
even from the depths of the Underworld to hunt me:
he drives me starving by the sands of the sea.

The reed-woven pipe drones on in a hum
and drones and drones its sleep-giving strain:
Oh, Oh, Oh,
Where are you bringing me, my far-wandering wanderings?
Son of Kronos, what fault, what fault
did you find in me that you should yoke me

to a harness of misery like this,
that you should torture me so to madness
driven in fear of the gadfly?
Burn me with fire: hide me in earth: cast me away
to monsters of the deep for food: but do not
grudge me the granting of this prayer, King.
Enough have my much wandering wanderings
exercised me: I cannot find
a way to escape my troubles.
Do you hear the voice of the cow-horned maid?

PROMETHEUS Surely I hear the voice, the voice of the maiden, gadfly-haunted, the daughter of Inachus? She set Zeus' heart on fire with love and now she is violently exercised running on courses overlong, driven by Hera's hate.

IO How is it you speak my father's name?
Tell me, who are you? Who are you? Oh,
who are you that so exactly accosts me by name?
You have spoken of the disease that the gods have sent to me
which wastes me away, pricking with goads,
so that I am moving always
tortured and hungry, wild bounding,
quick sped I come,
a victim of jealous plots.
Some have been wretched
before me, but who of these
suffered as I do?
But declare to me clearly
what I have still to suffer: what would avail
against my sickness, what drug would cure it:
Tell me, if you know:
tell me, declare it to the unlucky, wandering maid.

PROMETHEUS I shall tell you clearly all that you would know, weaving you no riddles, but in plain words, as it is just to open the lips to friends. You see before you him that gave fire to men, even Prometheus.

IO O spirit that has appeared as a common blessing to all men, unhappy Prometheus, why are you being punished?

PROMETHEUS I have just this moment ceased from the lamentable tale of my sorrows.

IO Will you then grant me this favor?

PROMETHEUS Say what you are asking for: I will tell you all.

IO Tell who it was that nailed you to the cliff.

PROMETHEUS The plan was the plan of Zeus, and the hand the hand of Hephaestus.

IO And what was the offense of which this is the punishment?

PROMETHEUS It is enough that I have told you a clear story so far.

IO In addition, then, indicate to me what date shall be the limit of my wanderings.

PROMETHEUS Better for you not to know this than know it.

IO I beg you, do not hide from me what I must endure.

PROMETHEUS It is not that I grudge you this favor.

IO Why then delay to tell me all?

PROMETHEUS It is no grudging, but I hesitate to break your spirit.

IO Do not have more thought for me than pleases me myself.

PROMETHEUS Since you are so eager, I must speak; and do you give ear.

CHORUS Not yet: give me, too, a share of pleasure. First let us question her concerning her sickness, and let her tell us of her desperate fortunes. And then let you be our informant for the sorrows that still await her.

PROMETHEUS It is your task, Io, to gratify these spirits, for besides other considerations they are your father's sisters. To make wail and lament for one's ill fortune, when one will win a tear from the audience, is well worthwhile.

IO I know not how I should distrust you: clearly
you shall hear all you want to know from me.
Yet even as I speak I groan in bitterness
for that storm sent by God on me, that ruin
of my beauty; I must sorrow when I think
who sent all this upon me. There were always
night visions that kept haunting me and coming
into my maiden chamber and exhorting
with winning words, "O maiden greatly blessed,
why are you still a maiden, you who might
make marriage with the greatest? Zeus is stricken

with lust for you; he is afire to try
the bed of love with you: do not disdain him.
Go, child, to Lerna's meadow, deep in grass,
to where your father's flocks and cattle stand
that Zeus' eye may cease from longing for you."
With such dreams I was cruelly beset
night after night until I took the courage
to tell my father of my nightly terror.
He sent to Pytho many an embassy
and to Dodona seeking to discover
what deed or word of his might please the god,
but those he sent came back with riddling oracles
dark and beyond the power of understanding.
At last the word came clear to Inachus
charging him plainly that he cast me out
of home and country, drive me out footloose
to wander to the limits of the world;
if he should not obey, the oracle said,
the fire-faced thunderbolt would come from Zeus
and blot out his whole race. These were the oracles
of Loxias, and Inachus obeyed them.
He drove me out and shut his doors against me
with tears on both our parts, but Zeus' bit
compelled him to do this against his will.
Immediately my form and mind were changed
and all distorted; horned, as you see,
pricked on by the sharp biting gadfly, leaping
in frenzied jumps I ran beside the river
Kerchneia, good to drink, and Lerna's spring.
The earth-born herdsman Argos followed me
whose anger knew no limits, and he spied
after my tracks with all his hundred eyes.
Then an unlooked-for doom, descending suddenly,
took him from life: I, driven by the gadfly,
that god-sent scourge, was driven always onward

from one land to another: that is my story.
If you can tell me what remains for me,
tell me, and do not out of pity cozen
with kindly lies: there is no sickness worse
for me than words that to be kind must lie.

CHORUS Hold! Keep away! Alas!
never did I think that such strange
words would come to my ears:
never did I think such intolerable
sufferings, an offense to the eye,
shameful and frightening, so
would chill my soul with a double-edged point.
Alas, Alas, for your fate!
I shudder when I look on Io's fortune.

PROMETHEUS You groan too soon: you are full of fear too soon: wait till you hear besides what is to be.

CHORUS Speak, tell us to the end. For sufferers it is sweet to know beforehand clearly the pain that still remains for them.

PROMETHEUS The first request you made of me you gained
lightly: from her you wished to hear the story
of what she suffered. Now hear what remains,
what sufferings this maid must yet endure
from Hera. Do you listen, child of Inachus,
hear and lay up my words within your heart
that you may know the limits of your journey.
First turn to the sun's rising and walk on
over the fields no plough has broken: then
you will come to the wandering Scythians
who live in wicker houses built above

their well-wheeled wagons; they are an armed people,
armed with the bow that strikes from far away:
do not draw near them; rather let your feet
touch the surf line of the sea where the waves moan,
and cross their country: on your left there live
the Chalybes who work with iron: these
you must beware of; for they are not gentle,
nor people whom a stranger dare approach.
Then you will come to Insolence, a river
that well deserves its name: but cross it not—
it is no stream that you can easily ford—
until you come to Caucasus itself,
the highest mountains, where the river's strength
gushes from its very temples. Cross these peaks,
the neighbors of the stars, and take the road
southward until you reach the Amazons,
the race of women who hate men, who one day
shall live around Thermodon in Themiscyra
where Salmydessos, rocky jaw of the sea,
stands sailor-hating, stepmother of ships.
The Amazons will set you on your way
and gladly: you will reach Cimmeria,
the isthmus, at the narrow gates of the lake.
Leave this with a good heart and cross the channel,
the channel of Maeotis: and hereafter
for all time men shall talk about your crossing,
and they shall call the place for you Cow's-ford.[1]
Leave Europe's mainland then, and go to Asia.

(*To the Chorus*) Do you now think this tyrant of the gods
is hard in all things without difference?
He was a god and sought to lie in love
with this girl who was mortal, and on her

[1] Cow's-ford: Bosporus.

he brought this curse of wandering: bitter indeed
you found your marriage with this suitor, maid.
Yet you must think of all that I have told you
as still only in prelude.

IO Oh, Oh!

PROMETHEUS Again, you are crying and lamenting: what will you do when you hear of the evils to come?

CHORUS Is there still something else to her sufferings of which you will speak?

PROMETHEUS A wintry sea of agony and ruin.

IO What good is life to me then? Why do I not throw myself at once from some rough crag, to strike the ground and win a quittance of all my troubles? It would be better to die once for all than suffer all one's days.

PROMETHEUS You would ill bear my trials, then, for whom Fate reserves no death. Death would be a quittance of trouble: but for me there is no limit of suffering set till Zeus fall from power.

IO Can Zeus ever fall from power?

PROMETHEUS You would be glad to see that catastrophe, I think.

IO Surely, since Zeus is my persecutor.

PROMETHEUS Then know that this shall be.

IO Who will despoil him of his sovereign scepter?

PROMETHEUS His own witless plans.

IO How? Tell me, if there is no harm to telling.

PROMETHEUS He shall make a marriage that shall hurt him.

IO With god or mortal? Tell me, if you may say it.

PROMETHEUS Why ask what marriage? That is not to be spoken.

IO Is it his wife shall cast him from his throne?

PROMETHEUS She shall bear him a son mightier than his father.

IO Has he no possibility of escaping this downfall?

PROMETHEUS None, save through my release from these chains.

IO But who will free you, against Zeus' will?

PROMETHEUS Fate has determined that it be one of your descendants.

IO What, shall a child of mine bring you free?

PROMETHEUS Yes, in the thirteenth generation.

IO Your prophecy has now passed the limits of understanding.

PROMETHEUS Then also do not seek to learn your trials.

IO Do not offer me a boon and then withhold it.

PROMETHEUS I offer you then one of two stories.

IO Which? Tell me and give me the choice.

PROMETHEUS I will: choose that I tell you clearly either what remains for you or the one that shall deliver me.

CHORUS Grant her one and grant me the other and do not deny us the tale. Tell her what remains of her wanderings: tell us of the one that shall deliver you. That is what I desire.

PROMETHEUS Since you have so much eagerness, I will not refuse to tell you all that you have asked me.
First to you, Io, I shall tell the tale
of your sad wanderings, rich in groans—inscribe
the story in the tablets of your mind.
When you shall cross the channel that divides
Europe from Asia, turn to the rising sun,
to the burnt plains, sun-scorched; cross by the edge
of the foaming sea till you come to Gorgona
to the flat stretches of Kisthene's country.
There live the ancient maids, children of Phorcys:
these swan-formed hags, with but one common eye,
single-toothed monsters, such as nowhere else
the sun's rays look on nor the moon by night.
Near are their winged sisters, the three Gorgons,
with snakes to bind their hair up, mortal-hating:
nor mortal that but looks on them shall live:
these are the sentry guards I tell you of.
Here, too, of yet another gruesome sight,
the sharp-toothed hounds of Zeus, that have no bark,
the vultures—them take heed of—and the host

of one-eyed Arimaspians, horse-riding,
that live around the spring which flows with gold,
the spring of Pluto's river: go not near them.
A land far off, a nation of black men,
these you shall come to, men who live hard by
the fountain of the sun where is the river
Aethiops—travel by his banks along
to a waterfall where from the Bibline hills
Nile pours his holy waters, pure to drink.
This river shall be your guide to the triangular
land of the Nile and there, by Fate's decree,
there, Io, you shall find your distant home,
a colony for you and your descendants.
If anything of this is still obscure
or difficult ask me again and learn
clearly: I have more leisure than I wish.

CHORUS If there is still something left for you to tell her of her ruinous wanderings, tell it; but if you have said everything, grant us the favor we asked and tell us the story too.

PROMETHEUS The limit of her wanderings complete
she now has heard: but so that she may know
that she has not been listening to no purpose
I shall recount what she endured before
she came to us here: this I give as pledge,
a witness to the good faith of my words.
The great part of the story I omit
and come to the very boundary of your travels.
When you had come to the Molossian plains
around the sheer back of Dodona where
is the oracular seat of Zeus Thesprotian,
the talking oaks, a wonder past belief,
by them full clearly, in no riddling terms,

you were hailed glorious wife of Zeus that shall be:
does anything of this wake pleasant memories?
Then, goaded by the gadfly, on you hastened
to the great gulf of Rhea by the track
at the side of the sea: but in returning course
you were storm-driven back: in time to come
that inlet of the sea shall bear your name
and shall be called Ionian, a memorial
to all men of your journeying: these are proofs
for you, of how far my mind sees something farther
than what is visible: for what is left,
to you and you this I shall say in common,
taking up again the track of my old tale.
There is a city, furthest in the world,
Canobos, near the mouth and issuing point
of the Nile: there Zeus shall make you sound of mind
touching you with a hand that brings no fear,
and through that touch alone shall come your healing.
You shall bear Epaphos, dark of skin, his name
recalling Zeus' touch and his begetting.
This Epaphos shall reap the fruit of all
the land that is watered by the broad flowing Nile.
From him five generations, and again
to Argos they shall come, against their will,
in number fifty, women, flying from
a marriage with their kinsfolk: but these kinsfolk
their hearts with lust aflutter like the hawks
barely outdistanced by the doves will come
hunting a marriage that the law forbids:
the god shall grudge the men these women's bodies,
and the Pelasgian earth shall welcome them
in death: for death shall claim them in a fight
where women strike in the dark, a murderous vigil.
Each wife shall rob her husband of his life
dipping in blood her two-edged sword: even so

may Love come, too, upon my enemies.
But one among these girls shall love beguile
from killing her bedfellow, blunting her purpose:
and she shall make her choice—to bear the name
of coward and not murder: this girl,
she shall in Argos bear a race of kings.
To tell this clearly needs a longer story,
but from her seed shall spring a man renowned
for archery, and he shall set me free.
Such was the prophecy which ancient Themis
my Titan mother opened up to me;
but how and by what means it shall come true
would take too long to tell, and if you heard
the knowledge would not profit you.

IO Eleleu, eleleu
It creeps on me again, the twitching spasm,
the mind-destroying madness, burning me up
and the gadfly's sting goads me on—
steel point by no fire tempered—
and my heart in its fear knocks on my breast.
There's a dazing whirl in my eyes as I run
out of my course by the madness driven,
the crazy frenzy; my tongue ungoverned
babbles, the words in a muddy flow strike
on the waves of the mischief I hate, strike wild
without aim or sense.

CHORUS
Strophe A wise man indeed he was
that first in judgment weighed this word
and gave it tongue: the best by far
it is to marry in one's rank and station:
let no one working with her hands aspire
to marriage with those lifted high in pride
because of wealth, or of ancestral glory.

Antistrophe Never, never may you see me,
Fates majestic, drawing nigh
the bed of Zeus, to share it with the kings:
nor ever may I know a heavenly wooer:
I dread such things beholding
Io's sad virginity
ravaged, ruined; bitter wandering
hers because of Hera's wrath.

Epode When a match has equal partners
then I fear not: may the eye
inescapable of the mighty
gods not look on me.
That is a fight that none can fight: a fruitful
source of fruitlessness: I would not
know what I could do: I cannot
see the hope when Zeus is angry
of escaping him.

PROMETHEUS Yet shall this Zeus, for all his pride of heart
be humble yet: such is the match he plans,
a marriage that shall drive him from his power
and from his throne, out of the sight of all.
So shall at last the final consummation
be brought about of Father Kronos' curse
which he, driven from his ancient throne, invoked
against the son deposing him: no one
of all the gods save I alone can tell
a way to escape this mischief: I alone
know it and how. So let him confidently
sit on his throne and trust his heavenly thunder
and brandish in his hand his fiery bolt.
Nothing shall all of this avail against
a fall intolerable, a dishonored end.
So strong a wrestler Zeus is now equipping
against himself, a monster hard to fight.

This enemy shall find a plan to best
the thunderbolt, a thunderclap to best
the thunderclap of Zeus: and he shall shiver
Poseidon's trident, curse of sea and land.
So, in his crashing fall shall Zeus discover
how different are rule and slavery.

CHORUS You voice your wishes for the god's destruction.

PROMETHEUS They are my wishes, yet shall come to pass.

CHORUS Must we expect someone to conquer Zeus?

PROMETHEUS Yes; he shall suffer worse than I do now.

CHORUS Have you no fear of uttering such words?

PROMETHEUS Why should I fear, since death is not my fate?

CHORUS But he might give you pain still worse than this.

PROMETHEUS Then let him do so; all this I expect.

CHORUS Wise are the worshipers of Adrasteia.

PROMETHEUS Worship him, pray; flatter whatever king
is king today; but I care less than nothing
for Zeus. Let him do what he likes,
let him be king for his short time: he shall not
be king for long.
Look, here is Zeus' footman,
this fetch-and-carry messenger of him,
the New King. Certainly he has come here
with news for us.

HERMES You, subtle-spirit, you
bitterly overbitter, you that sinned
against the immortals, giving honor to
the creatures of a day, you thief of fire:
the Father has commanded you to say
what marriage of his is this you brag about
that shall drive him from power—and declare it
in clear terms and no riddles. You, Prometheus,
do not cause me a double journey; these

Pointing to the chains.

will prove to you that Zeus is not softhearted.

PROMETHEUS Your speech is pompous sounding, full of pride,
as fits the lackey of the gods. You are young
and young your rule and you think that the tower
in which you live is free from sorrow: from it
have I not seen two tyrants thrown? the third,
who now is king, I shall yet live to see him
fall, of all three most suddenly, most dishonored.
Do you think I will crouch before your gods,
—so new—and tremble? I am far from that.
Hasten away, back on the road you came.
You shall learn nothing that you ask of me.

HERMES Just such the obstinacy that brought you here,
to this self-willed calamitous anchorage.

PROMETHEUS Be sure of this: when I set my misfortune
against your slavery, I would not change.

HERMES It is better, I suppose, to be a slave
to this rock, than Zeus' trusted messenger.

PROMETHEUS Thus must the insolent show their insolence!

HERMES I think you find your present lot too soft.

PROMETHEUS Too soft? I would my enemies had it then,
and you are one of those I count as such.

HERMES Oh, you would blame me too for your calamity?

PROMETHEUS In a single word, I am the enemy
of all the gods that gave me ill for good.

HERMES Your words declare you mad, and mad indeed.

PROMETHEUS Yes, if it's madness to detest my foes.

HERMES No one could bear you in success.

PROMETHEUS Alas!

HERMES Alas! *Zeus* does not know that word.

PROMETHEUS Time in its aging course teaches all things.

HERMES But you have not yet learned a wise discretion.

PROMETHEUS True: or I would not speak so to a servant.

HERMES It seems you will not grant the Father's wish.

PROMETHEUS I should be glad, indeed, to requite his kindness!

HERMES You mock me like a child!

PROMETHEUS And are you not
a child, and sillier than a child, to think
that I should tell you anything? There is not
a torture or an engine wherewithal
Zeus can induce me to declare these things,
till he has loosed me from these cruel shackles.
So let him hurl his smoky lightning flame,
and throw in turmoil all things in the world
with white-winged snowflakes and deep bellowing
thunder beneath the earth: me he shall not
bend by all this to tell him who is fated
to drive him from his tyranny.

HERMES Think, here and now, if this seems to your
interest.

PROMETHEUS I have already thought—and laid my plans.

HERMES Bring your proud heart to know a true
discretion—
O foolish spirit—in the face of ruin.

PROMETHEUS You vex me by these senseless adjurations,
senseless as if you were to advise the waves.
Let it not cross your mind that I will turn
womanish-minded from my fixed decision
or that I shall entreat the one I hate
so greatly, with a woman's upturned hands,
to loose me from my chains: I am far from that.

HERMES I have said too much already—so I think—
and said it to no purpose: you are not softened:
your purpose is not dented by my prayers.
You are a colt new broken, with the bit
clenched in its teeth, fighting against the reins,

and bolting. You are far too strong and confident
in your weak cleverness. For obstinacy
standing alone is the weakest of all things
in one whose mind is not possessed by wisdom.
Think what a storm, a triple wave of ruin
will rise against you, if you will not hear me,
and no escape for you. First this rough crag
with thunder and the lightning bolt the Father
shall cleave asunder, and shall hide your body
wrapped in a rocky clasp within its depth;
a tedious length of time you must fulfil
before you see the light again, returning.
Then Zeus' winged hound, the eagle red,
shall tear great shreds of flesh from you, a feaster
coming unbidden, every day: your liver
bloodied to blackness will be his repast.
And of this pain do not expect an end
until some god shall show himself successor
to take your tortures for himself and willing
go down to lightless Hades and the shadows
of Tartarus' depths. Bear this in mind
and so determine. This is no feigned boast
but spoken with too much truth. The mouth of Zeus
does not know how to lie, but every word
brings to fulfilment. Look, you, and reflect
and never think that obstinacy is better
than prudent counsel.

CHORUS Hermes seems to us
to speak not altogether out of season.
He bids you leave your obstinacy and seek
a wise good counsel. Hearken to him. Shame
it were for one so wise to fall in error.

PROMETHEUS Before he told it me I knew this message:

but there is no disgrace in suffering
at an enemy's hand, when you hate mutually.
So let the curling tendril of the fire
from the lightning bolt be sent against me: let
the air be stirred with thunderclaps, the winds
in savage blasts convulsing all the world.
Let earth to her foundations shake, yes to her root,
before the quivering storm: let it confuse
the paths of heavenly stars and the sea's waves
in a wild surging torrent: this my body
let Him raise up on high and dash it down
into black Tartarus with rigorous
compulsive eddies: death he cannot give me.

HERMES These are a madman's words, a madman's plan:
is there a missing note in this mad harmony?
is there a slack chord in his madness? You,
you, who are so sympathetic with his troubles,
away with you from here, quickly away!
lest you should find your wits stunned by the thunder
and its hard defending roar.

CHORUS Say something else
different from this: give me some other counsel
that I will listen to: this word of yours
for all its instancy is not for us.
How dare you bid us practice baseness? We
will bear along with him what we must bear.
I have learned to hate all traitors: there is no
disease I spit on more than treachery.

HERMES Remember then my warning before the act:
when you are trapped by ruin don't blame fortune.
don't say that Zeus has brought you to calamity
that you could not foresee: do not do this:

but blame yourselves: now you know what you're
doing:
and with this knowledge neither suddenly
nor secretly your own want of good sense
has tangled you in the net of ruin, past
all hope of rescue.

PROMETHEUS Now it is words no longer: now in very
truth
the earth is staggered: in its depths the thunder
bellows resoundingly, the fiery tendrils
of the lightning flash light up, and whirling clouds
carry the dust along: all the winds' blasts
dance in a fury one against the other
in violent confusion: earth and sea
are one, confused together: such is the storm
that comes against me manifestly from Zeus
to work its terrors. O Holy mother mine,
O Sky that circling brings the light to all,
you see me, how I suffer, how unjustly.

SOPHOCLES

OEDIPUS THE KING

Translated by David Grene

CHARACTERS

OEDIPUS, *king of Thebes*
JOCASTA, *his wife*
CREON, *his brother-in-law*
TEIRESIAS, *an old blind prophet*
PRIEST
FIRST MESSENGER, *a shepherd from Corinth*
SECOND MESSENGER
HERDSMAN, *formerly in the service of Laius*
CHORUS OF THEBAN ELDERS

Non-speaking: a crowd of children; servants of Oedipus; a boy attendant of Teiresias; Antigone and Ismene, daughters of Oedipus and Jocasta

OEDIPUS THE KING

SCENE *In front of the palace of Oedipus at Thebes. To the right of the stage near the altar stands the Priest with a crowd of children. Oedipus emerges from the central door.*

OEDIPUS Children, young sons and daughters of old Cadmus,
why do you sit here with your suppliant crowns?
The town is heavy with a mingled burden
of sounds and smells, of groans and hymns and incense;
I did not think it fit that I should hear
of this from messengers but came myself—
I, Oedipus, whom all men call the Great.

He turns to the Priest.

You're old and they are young; come, speak for them.
What do you fear or want, that you sit here
suppliant? Indeed I'm willing to give all
that you may need; I would be very hard
should I not pity suppliants like these.

PRIEST O ruler of my country, Oedipus,
you see our company around the altar;
you see our ages; some of us, like these,
who cannot yet fly far, and some of us
heavy with age; these children are the chosen
among the young, and I the priest of Zeus.
Within the marketplace sit others crowned
with suppliant garlands, at the double shrine

of Pallas and the temple where Ismenus
gives oracles by fire. King, you yourself
have seen our city reeling like a wreck
already; it can scarcely lift its prow
out of the depths, out of the bloody surf.
A blight is on the fruitful plants of the earth,
a blight is on the cattle in the fields,
a blight is on our women that no children
are born to them; a god that carries fire,
a deadly pestilence, is on our town,
strikes us and spares not, and the house of Cadmus
is emptied of its people while black Death
grows rich in groaning and in lamentation.
We have not come as suppliants to this altar
because we thought of you as of a god,
but rather judging you the first of men
in all the chances of this life and when
we mortals have to do with more than man.
You came and by your coming saved our city,
freed us from tribute which we paid of old
to the Sphinx, cruel singer. This you did
in virtue of no knowledge we could give you,
in virtue of no teaching; it was God
that aided you, men say, and you are held
with God's assistance to have saved our lives.
Now Oedipus, Greatest in all men's eyes,
here falling at your feet we all entreat you,
find us some strength for rescue.
Perhaps you'll hear a wise word from some god,
perhaps you will learn something from a man
(for I have seen that for the skilled of practice
the outcome of their counsels live the most).
Noblest of men, go, and raise up our city,
go—and give heed. For now this land of ours

calls you its savior since you saved it once.
So, let us never speak about your reign
as of a time when first our feet were set
secure on high, but later fell to ruin.
Raise up our city, save it and raise it up.
Once you have brought us luck with happy omen;
be no less now in fortune.
If you will rule this land, as now you rule it,
better to rule it full of men than empty.
For neither tower nor ship is anything
when empty, and none live in it together.

OEDIPUS I pity you, children. You have come full of longing,
but I have known the story before you told it
only too well. I know you are all sick,
yet there is not one of you, sick though you are,
that is as sick as I myself.
Your several sorrows each have single scope
and touch but one of you. My spirit groans
for city and myself and you at once.
You have not roused me like a man from sleep;
know that I have given many tears to this,
gone many ways wandering in thought,
but as I thought I found only one remedy
and that I took. I sent Menoeceus' son
Creon, Jocasta's brother, to Apollo,
to his Pythian temple,
that he might learn there by what act or word
I could save this city. As I count the days,
it vexes me what ails him; he is gone
far longer than he needed for the journey.
But when he comes, then, may I prove a villain,
if I shall not do all the god commands.

PRIEST Thanks for your gracious words. Your servants here
signal that Creon is this moment coming.

OEDIPUS His face is bright. O holy Lord Apollo,
grant that his news too may be bright for us
and bring us safety.

PRIEST It is happy news,
I think, for else his head would not be crowned
with sprigs of fruitful laurel.

OEDIPUS We will know soon,
he's within hail. Lord Creon, my good brother,
what is the word you bring us from the god?

Creon enters.

CREON A good word—for things hard to bear themselves,
if in the final issue all is well,
I count complete good fortune.

OEDIPUS What do you mean?
What you have said so far
leaves me uncertain whether to trust or fear.

CREON If you will hear my news before these others
I am ready to speak, or else to go within.

OEDIPUS Speak it to all;
the grief I bear, I bear it more for these
than for my own heart.

CREON I will tell you, then,
what I heard from the god.
King Phoebus in plain words commanded us
to drive out a pollution from our land,
pollution grown ingrained within the land;
drive it out, said the god, not cherish it,
till it's past cure.

OEDIPUS What is the rite
of purification? How shall it be done?

CREON By banishing a man, or expiation
of blood by blood, since it is murder-guilt
which holds our city in this destroying storm.

OEDIPUS Who is this man whose fate the god pronounces?

CREON My lord, before you piloted the state
we had a king called Laius.

OEDIPUS I know of him by hearsay. I have not seen him.

CREON The god commanded clearly: let someone
punish with force this dead man's murderers.

OEDIPUS Where are they in the world? Where would a trace
of this old crime be found? It would be hard
to guess where.

CREON The clue is in this land;
that which is sought is found;
the unheeded thing escapes:
so said the god.

OEDIPUS Was it at home,
or in the country that death came upon him,
or in another country traveling?

CREON He went, he said himself, upon an embassy,
but never returned when he set out from home.

OEDIPUS Was there no messenger, no fellow traveler
who knew what happened? Such a one might tell
something of use.

CREON They were all killed save one. He fled in terror,
and he could tell us nothing in clear terms
of what he knew, nothing, but one thing only.

OEDIPUS What was it?
If we could even find a slim beginning
in which to hope, we might discover much.

CREON This man said that the robbers they encountered
were many and the hands that did the murder
were many; it was no man's single power.

OEDIPUS How could a robber dare a deed like this
were he not helped with money from the city,
money and treachery?

CREON That indeed was thought.
But Laius was dead, and in our trouble
there was none to help.

OEDIPUS What trouble was so great to hinder you
inquiring out the murder of your king?

CREON The riddling Sphinx induced us to neglect
mysterious crimes and rather seek solution
of troubles at our feet.

OEDIPUS I will bring this to light again. King Phoebus
fittingly took this care about the dead,
and you too fittingly.
And justly you will see in me an ally,
a champion of my country and the god.
For when I drive pollution from the land
I will not serve a distant friend's advantage,
but act in my own interest. Whoever
he was that killed the king may readily
wish to dispatch me with his murderous hand;
so helping the dead king I help myself.

Come, children, take your suppliant boughs and go;
up from the altars now. Call the assembly
and let it meet upon the understanding
that I'll do everything. God will decide
whether we prosper or remain in sorrow.

PRIEST Rise, children—it was this we came to seek,
which of himself the king now offers us.
May Phoebus who gave us the oracle
come to our rescue and stay the plague.

Exeunt all but the Chorus.

CHORUS
Strophe What is the sweet spoken word of God from
the shrine of Pytho rich in gold
that has come to glorious Thebes?

I am stretched on the rack of doubt, and terror and trembling hold
my heart, O Delian Healer, and I worship full of fears
for what doom you will bring to pass, new or renewed in the revolving years.
Speak to me, immortal voice,
child of golden Hope.

Antistrophe First I call on you, Athena, deathless daughter of Zeus,
and Artemis, Earth Upholder,
who sits in the midst of the marketplace in the throne which men call Fame,
and Phoebus, the Far Shooter, three averters of Fate,
come to us now, if ever before, when ruin rushed upon the state,
you drove destruction's flame away
out of our land.

Strophe Our sorrows defy number;
all the ship's timbers are rotten;
taking of thought is no spear for the driving away of the plague.
There are no growing children in this famous land;
there are no women bearing the pangs of childbirth.
You may see them one with another, like birds swift on the wing,
quicker than fire unmastered,
speeding away to the coast of the Western God.

Antistrophe In the unnumbered deaths
of its people the city dies;
those children that are born lie dead on the naked earth
unpitied, spreading contagion of death; and grey-haired mothers and wives

everywhere stand at the altar's edge, suppliant, moaning;
the hymn to the healing god rings out but with it the
wailing voices are blended.
From these our sufferings grant us, O golden Daughter
of Zeus,
glad-faced deliverance.

Strophe There is no clash of brazen shields but our fight
is with the War God,
a War God ringed with the cries of men, a savage god
who burns us;
grant that he turn in racing course backward out of our
country's bounds
to the great palace of Amphitrite or where the waves of
the Thracian sea
deny the stranger safe anchorage.
Whatsoever escapes the night
at last the light of day revisits;
so smite the War God, Father Zeus,
beneath your thunderbolt,
for you are the Lord of the Lightning, the lightning that
carries fire.

Antistrophe And your unconquered arrow shafts,
winged by the golden-corded bow,
Lycean King, I beg to be at our side for help;
and the gleaming torches of Artemis with which she
scours the Lycean hills,
and I call on the god with the turban of gold, who gave
his name to this country of ours,
the Bacchic God with the wind-flushed face,
Evian One, who travel
with the Maenad company,
combat the god that burns us
with your torch of pine;

for the god that is our enemy is a god unhonored among
the gods.

Oedipus returns.

OEDIPUS For what you ask me—if you will hear my
words,
and hearing welcome them and fight the plague,
you will find strength and lightening of your load.

Hark to me; what I say to you, I say
as one that is a stranger to the story
as stranger to the deed. For I would not
be far upon the track if I alone
were tracing it without a clue. But now,
since after all was finished, I became
a citizen among you, citizens—
now I proclaim to all the men of Thebes:
who so among you knows the murderer
by whose hand Laius, son of Labdacus,
died—I command him to tell everything
to me—yes, though he fears himself to take the blame
on his own head; for bitter punishment
he shall have none, but leave this land unharmed.
Or if he knows the murderer, another,
a foreigner, still let him speak the truth.
For I will pay him and be grateful, too.
But if you shall keep silence, if perhaps
some one of you, to shield a guilty friend,
or for his own sake shall reject my words—
hear what I shall do then:
I forbid that man, whoever he be, my land,
my land where I hold sovereignty and throne;
and I forbid any to welcome him
or cry him greeting or make him a sharer

in sacrifice or offering to the gods,
or give him water for his hands to wash.
I command all to drive him from their homes,
since he is our pollution, as the oracle
of Pytho's god proclaimed him now to me.
So I stand forth a champion of the god
and of the man who died.
Upon the murderer I invoke this curse—
whether he is one man and all unknown,
or one of many—may he wear out his life
in misery to miserable doom!
If with my knowledge he lives at my hearth,
I pray that I myself may feel my curse.
On you I lay my charge to fulfill all this
for me, for the god, and for this land of ours,
destroyed and blighted, by the god forsaken.

Even were this no matter of God's ordinance,
it would not fit you so to leave it lie,
unpurified, since a good man is dead,
and one that was a king. Search it out.
Since I am now the holder of his office,
and have his bed and wife that once was his,
and had his line not been unfortunate
we would have common children—(fortune leaped
upon his head)—because of all these things,
I fight in his defense as for my father,
and I shall try all means to take the murderer
of Laius the son of Labdacus
the son of Polydorus and before him
of Cadmus and before him of Agenor.
Those who do not obey me, may the gods
grant no crops springing from the ground they plow
nor children to their women! May a fate
like this, or one still worse than this consume them!

For you whom these words please, the other Thebans,
may Justice as your ally and all the gods
live with you, blessing you now and forever!

CHORUS As you have held me to my oath, I speak:
I neither killed the king nor can declare
the killer; but since Phoebus set the quest
it is his part to tell who the man is.

OEDIPUS Right; but to put compulsion on the gods
against their will—no man can do that.

CHORUS May I then say what I think second best?

OEDIPUS If there's a third best, too, spare not to tell it.

CHORUS I know that what the Lord Teiresias
sees, is most often what the Lord Apollo
sees. If you should inquire of this from him
you might find out most clearly.

OEDIPUS Even in this my actions have not been sluggard.
On Creon's word I have sent two messengers,
and why the prophet is not here already
I have been wondering.

CHORUS His skill apart,
there is besides only an old faint story.

OEDIPUS What is it?
I look at every story.

CHORUS It was said
that he was killed by certain wayfarers.

OEDIPUS I heard that, too, but no one saw the killer.

CHORUS Yet, if he has a share of fear at all,
his courage will not stand firm, hearing your curse.

OEDIPUS The man who in the doing did not shrink
will fear no word.

CHORUS Here comes his prosecutor:
led by your men the godly prophet comes
in whom alone of mankind truth is native.

Enter Teiresias, led by a little boy.

OEDIPUS Teiresias, you are versed in everything,
things teachable and things not to be spoken,
things of the heaven and earth-creeping things.
You have no eyes, but in your mind you know
with what a plague our city is afflicted.
My lord, in you alone we find a champion,
in you alone one that can rescue us.
Perhaps you have not heard the messengers;
but Phoebus sent in answer to our sending
an oracle, declaring that our freedom
from this disease would only come when we
should learn the names of those who killed King Laius,
and kill them or expel from our country.
Do not begrudge us oracles from birds,
or any other way of prophecy
within your skill; save yourself and the city,
save me; redeem the debt of our pollution
that lies on us because of this dead man.
We are in your hands; pains are most nobly taken
to help another when you have means and power.

TEIRESIAS Alas, how terrible is wisdom when
it brings no profit to the man that's wise!
This I knew well, but had forgotten it,
else I would not have come here.

OEDIPUS What is this?
How sad you are now you have come!

TEIRESIAS Let me
go home. It will be easiest for us both
to bear our several destinies to the end
if you will follow my advice.

OEDIPUS You'd rob us
of this your gift of prophecy? You talk
as one who had no care for law nor love
for Thebes who reared you.

TEIRESIAS Yes, but I see that even your own words
miss the mark; therefore I must fear for mine.

OEDIPUS For God's sake if you know of anything,
do not turn from us; all of us kneel to you,
all of us here, your suppliants.

TEIRESIAS All of you here know nothing. I will not
bring to the light of day my troubles, mine—
rather than call them yours.

OEDIPUS What do you mean?
You know of something but refuse to speak.
Would you betray us and destroy the city?

TEIRESIAS I will not bring this pain upon us both,
neither on you nor on myself. Why is it

you question me and waste your labor? I
will tell you nothing.

OEDIPUS You would provoke a stone! Tell us, you villain,
tell us, and do not stand there quietly
unmoved and balking at the issue.

TEIRESIAS You blame my temper but you do not see
your own that lives within you; it is me
you chide.

OEDIPUS Who would not feel his temper rise
at words like these with which you shame our city?

TEIRESIAS Of themselves things will come, although I
hide them
and breathe no word of them.

OEDIPUS Since they will come
tell them to me.

TEIRESIAS I will say nothing further.
Against this answer let your temper rage
as wildly as you will.

OEDIPUS Indeed I am
so angry I shall not hold back a jot
of what I think. For I would have you know
I think you were complotter of the deed
and doer of the deed save in so far
as for the actual killing. Had you had eyes
I would have said alone you murdered him.

TEIRESIAS Yes? Then I warn you faithfully to keep
the letter of your proclamation and

from this day forth to speak no word of greeting
to these nor me; you are the land's pollution.

OEDIPUS How shamelessly you started up this taunt!
How do you think you will escape?

TEIRESIAS I have.
I have escaped; the truth is what I cherish
and that's my strength.

OEDIPUS And who has taught you truth?
Not your profession surely!

TEIRESIAS You have taught me,
for you have made me speak against my will.

OEDIPUS Speak what? Tell me again that I may learn it better.

TEIRESIAS Did you not understand before or would you provoke me into speaking?

OEDIPUS I did not grasp it,
not so to call it known. Say it again.

TEIRESIAS I say you are the murderer of the king
whose murderer you seek.

OEDIPUS Not twice you shall
say calumnies like this and stay unpunished.

TEIRESIAS Shall I say more to tempt your anger more?

OEDIPUS As much as you desire; it will be said
in vain.

TEIRESIAS I say that with those you love best
you live in foulest shame unconsciously
and do not see where you are in calamity.

OEDIPUS Do you imagine you can always talk
like this, and live to laugh at it hereafter?

TEIRESIAS Yes, if the truth has anything of strength.

OEDIPUS It has, but not for you; it has no strength
for you because you are blind in mind and ears
as well as in your eyes.

TEIRESIAS You are a poor wretch
to taunt me with the very insults which
everyone soon will heap upon yourself.

OEDIPUS Your life is one long night so that you cannot
hurt me or any other who sees the light.

TEIRESIAS It is not fate that I should be your ruin,
Apollo is enough; it is his care
to work this out.

OEDIPUS Was this your own design
or Creon's?

TEIRESIAS Creon is no hurt to you,
but you are to yourself.

OEDIPUS Wealth, sovereignty and skill outmatching skill
for the contrivance of an envied life!
Great store of jealousy fill your treasury chests,
if my friend Creon, friend from the first and loyal,
thus secretly attacks me, secretly

desires to drive me out and secretly
suborns this juggling, trick-devising quack,
this wily beggar who has only eyes
for his own gains, but blindness in his skill.
For, tell me, where have you seen clear, Teiresias,
with your prophetic eyes? When the dark singer,
the Sphinx, was in your country, did you speak
word of deliverance to its citizens?
And yet the riddle's answer was not the province
of a chance comer. It was a prophet's task
and plainly you had no such gift of prophecy
from birds nor otherwise from any god
to glean a word of knowledge. But I came,
Oedipus, who knew nothing, and I stopped her.
I solved the riddle by my wit alone.
Mine was no knowledge got from birds. And now
you would expel me,
because you think that you will find a place
by Creon's throne. I think you will be sorry,
both you and your accomplice, for your plot
to drive me out. And did I not regard you
as an old man, some suffering would have taught you
that what was in your heart was treason.

CHORUS We look at this man's words and yours, my king,
and we find both have spoken them in anger.
We need no angry words but only thought
how we may best hit the god's meaning for us.

TEIRESIAS If you are king, at least I have the right
no less to speak in my defense against you.
Of that much I am master. I am no slave
of yours, but Loxias', and so I shall not
enroll myself with Creon for my patron.
Since you have taunted me with being blind,

here is my word for you.
You have your eyes but see not where you are
in sin, nor where you live, nor whom you live with.
Do you know who your parents are? Unknowing,
you are an enemy to kith and kin
in death, beneath the earth, and in this life.
A deadly footed, double striking curse,
from father and mother both, shall drive you forth
out of this land, with darkness on your eyes,
that now have such straight vision. Shall there be
a place will not be harbor to your cries,
a corner of Cithaeron will not ring
in echo to your cries, soon, soon—
when you shall learn the secret of your marriage,
which steered you to a haven in this house—
haven no haven, after lucky voyage?
And of the multitude of other evils
establishing a grim equality
between you and your children, you know nothing.
So, muddy with contempt my words and Creon's!
Misery shall grind no man as it will you.

OEDIPUS Is it endurable that I should hear
such words from him? Go and a curse go with you!
Quick, home with you! Out of my house at once!

TEIRESIAS I would not have come either had you not called me.

OEDIPUS I did not know then you would talk like a fool—
or it would have been long before I called you.

TEIRESIAS I am a fool then, as it seems to you—
but to the parents who have bred you, wise.

OEDIPUS What parents? Stop! Who are they of all the world?

TEIRESIAS This day will show your birth and will destroy you.

OEDIPUS How needlessly your riddles darken everything.

TEIRESIAS But it's in riddle answering you are strongest.

OEDIPUS Yes. Taunt me where you will find me great.

TEIRESIAS It is this very luck that has destroyed you.

OEDIPUS I do not care, if it has saved this city.

TEIRESIAS Well, I will go. Come, boy, lead me away.

OEDIPUS Yes, lead him off. So long as you are here,
you'll be a stumbling block and a vexation;
once gone, you will not trouble me again.

TEIRESIAS I have said
what I came here to say not fearing your
countenance: there is no way you can hurt me.
I tell you, king, this man, this murderer
(whom you have long declared you are in search of,
indicting him in threatening proclamation
as murderer of Laius)—he is here.
In name he is a stranger among citizens,
but soon he will be shown to be a citizen,
true native Theban, and he'll have no joy
of the discovery: blindness for sight
and beggary for riches his exchange,
he shall go journeying to a foreign country

tapping his way before him with a stick.
He shall be proved father and brother both
to his own children in his house; to her
that gave him birth, a son and husband both;
a fellow sower in his father's bed
with that same father that he murdered.
Go within, reckon that out, and if you find me
mistaken, say I have no skill in prophecy.

Exeunt separately Teiresias and Oedipus.

CHORUS

Strophe Who is the man proclaimed
by Delphi's prophetic rock
as the bloody handed murderer,
the doer of deeds that none dare name?
Now is the time for him to run
with a stronger foot
than Pegasus,
for the child of Zeus leaps in arms upon him
with fire and the lightning bolt,
and terribly close on his heels
are the Fates that never miss.

Antistrophe Lately from snowy Parnassus
clearly the voice flashed forth,
bidding each Theban track him down,
the unknown murderer.
In the savage forests he lurks and in
the caverns like
the mountain bull.
He is sad and lonely, and lonely his feet
that carry him far from the navel of earth;
but its prophecies, ever living,
flutter around his head.

Strophe The augur has spread confusion,
terrible confusion;
I do not approve what was said,
nor can I deny it.
I do not know what to say;
I am in a flutter of foreboding;
I never heard in the present
nor past of a quarrel between
the sons of Labdacus and Polybus,
that I might bring as proof
in attacking the popular fame
of Oedipus, seeking
to take vengeance for undiscovered
death in the line of Labdacus.

Antistrophe Truly Zeus and Apollo are wise
and in human things all knowing;
but amongst men there is no
distinct judgment, between the prophet
and me—which of us is right.
One man may pass another in wisdom
but I would never agree
with those that find fault with the king
till I should see the word
proved right beyond doubt. For once
in visible form the Sphinx
came on him and all of us
saw his wisdom and in that test
he saved the city. So he will not be condemned by my
mind.

Enter Creon.

CREON Citizens, I have come because I heard
deadly words spread about me, that the king

accuses me. I cannot take that from him.
If he believes that in these present troubles
he has been wronged by me in word or deed
I do not want to live on with the burden
of such a scandal on me. The report
injures me doubly and most vitally—
for I'll be called a traitor to my city
and traitor also to my friends and you.

CHORUS Perhaps it was a sudden gust of anger
that forced that insult from him, and no judgment.

CREON But did he say that it was in compliance
with schemes of mine that the seer told him lies?

CHORUS Yes, he said that, but why, I do not know.

CREON Were his eyes straight in his head? Was his mind right
when he accused me in this fashion?

CHORUS I do not know; I have no eyes to see
what princes do. Here comes the king himself.

Enter Oedipus.

OEDIPUS You, sir, how is it you come here? Have you so much
brazen-faced daring that you venture in
my house although you are proved manifestly
the murderer of that man, and though you tried,
openly, highway robbery of my crown?
For God's sake, tell me what you saw in me,
what cowardice or what stupidity,
that made you lay a plot like this against me?

Did you imagine I should not observe
the crafty scheme that stole upon me or
seeing it, take no means to counter it?
Was it not stupid of you to make the attempt,
to try to hunt down royal power without
the people at your back or friends? For only
with the people at your back or money can
the hunt end in the capture of a crown.

CREON Do you know what you're doing? Will you listen
to words to answer yours, and then pass judgment?

OEDIPUS You're quick to speak, but I am slow to grasp
you,
for I have found you dangerous—and my foe.

CREON First of all hear what I shall say to that.

OEDIPUS At least don't tell me that you are not guilty.

CREON If you think obstinacy without wisdom
a valuable possession, you are wrong.

OEDIPUS And you are wrong if you believe that one,
a criminal, will not be punished only
because he is my kinsman.

CREON This is but just—
but tell me, then, of what offense I'm guilty?

OEDIPUS Did you or did you not urge me to send
to this prophetic mumbler?

CREON I did indeed,
and I shall stand by what I told you.

OEDIPUS How long ago is it since Laius. . . .

CREON What about Laius? I don't understand.

OEDIPUS Vanished?—died?—was murdered?

CREON It is long,
a long, long time to reckon.

OEDIPUS Was this prophet
in the profession then?

CREON He was, and honored
as highly as he is today.

OEDIPUS At that time did he say a word about me?

CREON Never, at least when I was near him.

OEDIPUS You never made a search for the dead man?

CREON We searched, indeed, but never learned of anything.

OEDIPUS Why did our wise old friend not say this then?

CREON I don't know; and when I know nothing, I usually hold my tongue.

OEDIPUS You know this much,
and can declare this much if you are loyal.

CREON What is it? If I know, I'll not deny it.

OEDIPUS That he would not have said that I killed Laius
had he not met you first.

CREON You know yourself
whether he said this, but I demand that I
should hear as much from you as you from me.

OEDIPUS Then hear—I'll not be proved a murderer.

CREON Well, then. You're married to my sister.

OEDIPUS Yes,
that I am not disposed to deny.

CREON You rule
this country giving her an equal share
in the government?

OEDIPUS Yes, everything she wants
she has from me.

CREON And I, as thirdsman to you,
am rated as the equal of you two?

OEDIPUS Yes, and it's there you've proved yourself false friend.

CREON Not if you will reflect on it as I do.
Consider, first, if you think anyone
would choose to rule and fear—rather than rule
and sleep untroubled by a fear—if power
were equal in both cases. I, at least,
I was not born with such a frantic yearning
to be a king—but to do what kings do.
And so it is with everyone who has learned
wisdom and self-control. As it stands now,
the prizes are all mine—and without fear.
But if I were the king myself, I must

do much that went against the grain.
How should despotic rule seem sweeter to me
than painless power and an assured authority?
I am not so besotted yet that I
want other honors than those that come with profit.
Now every man's my pleasure; every man greets me;
now those who are your suitors fawn on me—
success for them depends upon my favor.
Why should I let all this go to win that?
My mind would not be traitor if it's wise;
I am no treason lover, of my nature,
nor would I ever dare to join a plot.
Prove what I say. Go to the oracle
at Pytho and inquire about the answers,
if they are as I told you. For the rest,
if you discover I laid any plot
together with the seer, kill me, I say,
not only by your vote but by my own.
But do not charge me on obscure opinion
without some proof to back it. It's not just
lightly to count your knaves as honest men,
nor honest men as knaves. To throw away
an honest friend is, as it were, to throw
your life away, which a man loves the best.
In time you will know all with certainty;
time is the only test of honest men,
one day is space enough to know a rogue.

CHORUS His words are wise, king, if one fears to fall.
Those who are quick of temper are not safe.

OEDIPUS When he that plots against me secretly
moves quickly, I must quickly counterplot.
If I wait, taking no decisive measure,
his business will be done and mine be spoiled.

CREON What do you want to do then? Banish me?

OEDIPUS No, certainly; kill you, not banish you.[1]

CREON I do not think that you've your wits about you.

OEDIPUS For my own interests, yes.

CREON But for mine, too,
you should think equally.

OEDIPUS You are a rogue.

CREON Suppose you do not understand?

OEDIPUS But yet
I must be ruler.

CREON Not if you rule badly.

OEDIPUS O city, city!

CREON I too have some share
in the city; it is not yours alone.

CHORUS Stop, my lords! Here—and in the nick of time
I see Jocasta coming from the house;
with her help lay the quarrel that now stirs you.

[1] Two lines omitted here owing to the confusion in the dialogue consequent on the loss of a third line. The lines as they stand in Jebb's edition (1902) are:

OEDIPUS That you may show what manner of thing is envy.
CREON You speak as one that will not yield or trust.
OEDIPUS [Lost line]

Enter Jocasta.

JOCASTA For shame! Why have you raised this foolish squabbling
brawl? Are you not ashamed to air your private
griefs when the country's sick? Go in, you, Oedipus,
and you, too, Creon, into the house. Don't magnify
your nothing troubles.

CREON Sister, Oedipus,
your husband, thinks he has the right to do
terrible wrongs—he has but to choose between
two terrors: banishing or killing me.

OEDIPUS He's right, Jocasta; for I find him plotting
with knavish tricks against my person.

CREON That God may never bless me! May I die
accursed, if I have been guilty of
one tittle of the charge you bring against me!

JOCASTA I beg you, Oedipus, trust him in this,
spare him for the sake of this his oath to God,
for my sake, and the sake of those who stand here.

CHORUS Be gracious, be merciful,
we beg of you.

OEDIPUS In what would you have me yield?

CHORUS He has been no silly child in the past.
He is strong in his oath now.
Spare him.

OEDIPUS Do you know what you ask?

CHORUS Yes.

OEDIPUS Tell me then.

CHORUS He has been your friend before all men's eyes; do not cast him away dishonored on an obscure conjecture.

OEDIPUS I would have you know that this request of yours
really requests my death or banishment.

CHORUS May the Sun God, king of gods, forbid! May I die without God's blessing, without friends' help, if I had any such thought. But my spirit is broken by my unhappiness for my wasting country; and this would but add troubles amongst ourselves to the other troubles.

OEDIPUS Well, let him go then—if I must die ten times for it,
or be sent out dishonored into exile.
It is your lips that prayed for him I pitied,
not his; wherever he is, I shall hate him.

CREON I see you sulk in yielding and you're dangerous
when you are out of temper; natures like yours
are justly heaviest for themselves to bear.

OEDIPUS Leave me alone! Take yourself off, I tell you.

CREON I'll go, you have not known me, but they have,
and they have known my innocence.

Exit.

CHORUS Won't you take him inside, lady?

JOCASTA Yes, when I've found out what was the matter.

CHORUS There was some misconceived suspicion of a story, and on the other side the sting of injustice.

JOCASTA So, on both sides?

CHORUS Yes.

JOCASTA What was the story?

CHORUS I think it best, in the interests of the country, to leave it where it ended.

OEDIPUS You see where you have ended, straight of judgment
although you are, by softening my anger.

CHORUS Sir, I have said before and I say again—be sure that I would have been proved a madman, bankrupt in sane council, if I should put you away, you who steered the country I love safely when she was crazed with troubles. God grant that now, too, you may prove a fortunate guide for us.

JOCASTA Tell me, my lord, I beg of you, what was it that roused your anger so?

OEDIPUS Yes, I will tell you.
I honor you more than I honor them.
It was Creon and the plots he laid against me.

JOCASTA Tell me—if you can clearly tell the quarrel—

OEDIPUS Creon says
that I'm the murderer of Laius.

JOCASTA Of his own knowledge or on information?

OEDIPUS He sent this rascal prophet to me, since
he keeps his own mouth clean of any guilt.

JOCASTA Do not concern yourself about this matter;
listen to me and learn that human beings
have no part in the craft of prophecy.
Of that I'll show you a short proof.
There was an oracle once that came to Laius—
I will not say that it was Phoebus' own,
but it was from his servants—and it told him
that it was fate that he should die a victim
at the hands of his own son, a son to be born
of Laius and me. But, see now, he,
the king, was killed by foreign highway robbers
at a place where three roads meet—so goes the story;
and for the son—before three days were out
after his birth King Laius pierced his ankles
and by the hands of others cast him forth
upon a pathless hillside. So Apollo
failed to fulfill his oracle to the son,
that he should kill his father, and to Laius
also proved false in that the thing he feared,
death at his son's hands, never came to pass.
So clear in this case were the oracles,
so clear and false. Give them no heed, I say;
what God discovers need of, easily
he shows to us himself.

OEDIPUS O dear Jocasta,
as I hear this from you, there comes upon me
a wandering of the soul—I could run mad.

JOCASTA What trouble is it, that you turn again
and speak like this?

OEDIPUS I thought I heard you say
that Laius was killed at a crossroads.

JOCASTA Yes, that was how the story went and still
that word goes round.

OEDIPUS Where is this place, Jocasta,
where he was murdered?

JOCASTA Phocis is the country
and the road splits there, one of two roads from Delphi,
another comes from Daulia.

OEDIPUS How long ago is this?

JOCASTA The news came to the city just before
you became king and all men's eyes looked to you.
What is it, Oedipus, that's in your mind?

OEDIPUS What have you designed, O Zeus, to do with
me?

JOCASTA What is the thought that troubles your heart?

OEDIPUS Don't ask me yet—tell me of Laius—
How did he look? How old or young was he?

JOCASTA He was a tall man and his hair was grizzled
already—nearly white—and in his form
not unlike you.

OEDIPUS O God, I think I have
called curses on myself in ignorance.

JOCASTA What do you mean? I am terrified
when I look at you.

OEDIPUS I have a deadly fear
that the old seer had eyes. You'll show me more
if you can tell me one more thing.

JOCASTA I will.
I'm frightened—but if I can understand,
I'll tell you all you ask.

OEDIPUS How was his company?
Had he few with him when he went this journey,
or many servants, as would suit a prince?

JOCASTA In all there were but five, and among them
a herald; and one carriage for the king.

OEDIPUS It's plain—it's plain—who was it told you this?

JOCASTA The only servant that escaped safe home.

OEDIPUS Is he at home now?

JOCASTA No, when he came home again
and saw you king and Laius was dead,
he came to me and touched my hand and begged
that I should send him to the fields to be
my shepherd and so he might see the city
as far off as he might. So I
sent him away. He was an honest man,
as slaves go, and was worthy of far more
than what he asked of me.

OEDIPUS Oh, how I wish that he could come back
quickly!

JOCASTA He can. Why is your heart so set on this?

OEDIPUS O dear Jocasta, I am full of fears
that I have spoken far too much; and therefore
I wish to see this shepherd.

JOCASTA He will come;
but, Oedipus, I think I'm worthy too
to know what it is that disquiets you.

OEDIPUS It shall not be kept from you, since my mind
has gone so far with its forebodings. Whom
should I confide in rather than you, who is there
of more importance to me who have passed
through such a fortune?
Polybus was my father, king of Corinth,
and Merope, the Dorian, my mother.
I was held greatest of the citizens
in Corinth till a curious chance befell me
as I shall tell you—curious, indeed,
but hardly worth the store I set upon it.
There was a dinner and at it a man,
a drunken man, accused me in his drink
of being bastard. I was furious
but held my temper under for that day.
Next day I went and taxed my parents with it;
they took the insult very ill from him,
the drunken fellow who had uttered it.
So I was comforted for their part, but
still this thing rankled always, for the story
crept about widely. And I went at last
to Pytho, though my parents did not know.
But Phoebus sent me home again unhonored
in what I came to learn, but he foretold
other and desperate horrors to befall me,
that I was fated to lie with my mother,

and show to daylight an accursed breed
which men would not endure, and I was doomed
to be murderer of the father that begot me.
When I heard this I fled, and in the days
that followed I would measure from the stars
the whereabouts of Corinth—yes, I fled
to somewhere where I should not see fulfilled
the infamies told in that dreadful oracle.
And as I journeyed I came to the place
where, as you say, this king met with his death.
Jocasta, I will tell you the whole truth.
When I was near the branching of the crossroads,
going on foot, I was encountered by
a herald and a carriage with a man in it,
just as you tell me. He that led the way
and the old man himself wanted to thrust me
out of the road by force. I became angry
and struck the coachman who was pushing me.
When the old man saw this he watched his moment,
and as I passed he struck me from his carriage,
full on the head with his two-pointed goad.
But he was paid in full and presently
my stick had struck him backward from the car
and he rolled out of it. And then I killed them
all. If it happened there was any tie
of kinship twixt this man and Laius,
who is then now more miserable than I,
what man on earth so hated by the gods,
since neither citizen nor foreigner
may welcome me at home or even greet me,
but drive me out-of-doors? And it is I,
I and no other have so cursed myself.
And I pollute the bed of him I killed
by the hands that killed him. Was I not born evil?
Am I not utterly unclean? I had to fly

and in my banishment not even see
my kindred nor set foot in my own country,
or otherwise my fate was to be yoked
in marriage with my mother and kill my father,
Polybus who begot me and had reared me.
Would not one rightly judge and say that on me
these things were sent by some malignant god?
Oh, no, no, no—O holy majesty
of God on high, may I not see that day!
May I be gone out of men's sight before
I see the deadly taint of this disaster
come upon me.

CHORUS Sir, we too fear these things. But until you see this man face to face and hear his story, hope.

OEDIPUS Yes, I have just this much of hope—to wait until the herdsman comes.

JOCASTA And when he comes, what do you want with him?

OEDIPUS I'll tell you; if I find that his story is the same as yours, I at least will be clear of this guilt.

JOCASTA Why, what so particularly did you learn from my story?

OEDIPUS You said that he spoke of highway *robbers* who killed Laius. Now if he uses the same number, it was not I who killed him. One man cannot be the same as many. But if he speaks of a man traveling alone, then clearly the burden of the guilt inclines toward me.

JOCASTA Be sure, at least, that this was how he told the

story. He cannot unsay it now, for everyone in the city heard it—not I alone. But, Oedipus, even if he diverges from what he said then, he shall never prove that the murder of Laius squares rightly with the prophecy—for Loxias declared that the king should be killed by his own son. And that poor creature did not kill him surely—for he died himself first. So as far as prophecy goes, henceforward I shall not look to the right hand or the left.

OEDIPUS Right. But yet, send someone for the peasant to bring him here; do not neglect it.

JOCASTA I will send quickly. Now let me go indoors. I will do nothing except what pleases you.

Exeunt.

CHORUS

Strophe May destiny ever find me
pious in word and deed
prescribed by the laws that live on high:
laws begotten in the clear air of heaven,
whose only father is Olympus;
no mortal nature brought them to birth,
no forgetfulness shall lull them to sleep;
for God is great in them and grows not old.

Antistrophe Insolence breeds the tyrant, insolence
if it is glutted with a surfeit, unseasonable, unprofitable,
climbs to the rooftop and plunges
sheer down to the ruin that must be,
and there its feet are no service.
But I pray that the god may never
abolish the eager ambition that profits the state.
For I shall never cease to hold the god as our protector.

Strophe If a man walks with haughtiness
of hand or word and gives no heed
to Justice and the shrines of gods
despises—may an evil doom
smite him for his ill-starred pride of heart!—
if he reaps gains without justice
and will not hold from impiety
and his fingers itch for untouchable things.
When such things are done, what man shall contrive
to shield his soul from the shafts of the god?
When such deeds are held in honor,
why should I honor the gods in the dance?

Antistrophe No longer to the holy place,
to the navel of earth I'll go
to worship, nor to Abae
nor to Olympia,
unless the oracles are proved to fit,
for all men's hands to point at.
O Zeus, if you are rightly called
the sovereign lord, all-mastering,
let this not escape you nor your ever-living power!
The oracles concerning Laius
are old and dim and men regard them not.
Apollo is nowhere clear in honor; God's service perishes.

Enter Jocasta, carrying garlands.

JOCASTA Princes of the land, I have had the thought to go
to the gods' temples, bringing in my hand
garlands and gifts of incense, as you see.
For Oedipus excites himself too much
at every sort of trouble, not conjecturing,
like a man of sense, what will be from what was,
but he is always at the speaker's mercy,
when he speaks terrors. I can do no good

by my advice, and so I came as suppliant
to you, Lycaean Apollo, who are nearest.
These are the symbols of my prayer and this
my prayer: grant us escape free of the curse.
Now when we look to him we are all afraid;
he's pilot of our ship and he is frightened.

Enter Messenger.

MESSENGER Might I learn from you, sirs, where is the house of Oedipus? Or best of all, if you know, where is the king himself?

CHORUS This is his house and he is within doors. This lady is his wife and mother of his children.

MESSENGER God bless you, lady, and God bless your household! God bless Oedipus' noble wife!

JOCASTA God bless you, sir, for your kind greeting! What do you want of us that you have come here? What have you to tell us?

MESSENGER Good news, lady. Good for your house and for your husband.

JOCASTA What is your news? Who sent you to us?

MESSENGER I come from Corinth and the news I bring will give you pleasure. Perhaps a little pain too.

JOCASTA What is this news of double meaning?

MESSENGER The people of the Isthmus will choose Oedipus to be their king. That is the rumor there.

JOCASTA But isn't their king still old Polybus?

MESSENGER No. He is in his grave. Death has got him.

JOCASTA Is that the truth? Is Oedipus' father dead?

MESSENGER May I die myself if it be otherwise!

JOCASTA (*to a servant*) Be quick and run to the king with the news! O oracles of the gods, where are you now? It was from this man Oedipus fled, lest he should be his murderer! And now he is dead, in the course of nature, and not killed by Oedipus.

Enter Oedipus.

OEDIPUS Dearest Jocasta, why have you sent for me?

JOCASTA Listen to this man and when you hear reflect what is the outcome of the holy oracles of the gods.

OEDIPUS Who is he? What is his message for me?

JOCASTA He is from Corinth and he tells us that your father, Polybus, is dead and gone.

OEDIPUS What's this you say, sir? Tell me yourself.

MESSENGER Since this is the first matter you want clearly told: Polybus has gone down to death. You may be sure of it.

OEDIPUS By treachery or sickness?

MESSENGER A small thing will put old bodies asleep.

OEDIPUS So he died of sickness, it seems—poor old man!

MESSENGER Yes, and of age—the long years he had
measured.

OEDIPUS Ha! Ha! O dear Jocasta, why should one
look to the Pythian hearth? Why should one look
to the birds screaming overhead? They prophesied
that I should kill my father! But he's dead,
and hidden deep in earth, and I stand here
who never laid a hand on spear against him—
unless perhaps he died of longing for me,
and thus I am his murderer. But they,
the oracles, as they stand—he's taken them
away with him, they're dead as he himself is,
and worthless.

JOCASTA That I told you before now.

OEDIPUS You did, but I was misled by my fear.

JOCASTA Then lay no more of them to heart, not one.

OEDIPUS But surely I must fear my mother's bed?

JOCASTA Why should man fear since chance is all in all
for him, and he can clearly foreknow nothing?
Best to live lightly, as one can, unthinkingly.
As to your mother's marriage bed—don't fear it.
Before this, in dreams too, as well as oracles,
many a man has lain with his own mother.
But he to whom such things are nothing bears
his life most easily.

OEDIPUS All that you say would be said perfectly

if she were dead; but since she lives I must
still fear, although you talk so well, Jocasta.

JOCASTA Still in your father's death there's light of comfort?

OEDIPUS Great light of comfort; but I fear the living.

MESSENGER Who is the woman that makes you afraid?

OEDIPUS Merope, old man, Polybus' wife.

MESSENGER What about her frightens the queen and you?

OEDIPUS A terrible oracle, stranger, from the gods.

MESSENGER Can it be told? Or does the sacred law
forbid another to have knowledge of it?

OEDIPUS Oh, no! Once on a time Loxias said
that I should lie with my own mother and
take on my hands the blood of my own father.
And so for these long years I've lived away
from Corinth; it has been to my great happiness;
but yet it's sweet to see the face of parents.

MESSENGER This was the fear which drove you out of Corinth?

OEDIPUS Old man, I did not wish to kill my father.

MESSENGER Why should I not free you from this fear, sir,
since I have come to you in all goodwill?

OEDIPUS You would not find me thankless if you did.

MESSENGER Why, it was just for this I brought the news—
to earn your thanks when you had come safe home.

OEDIPUS No, I will never come near my parents.

MESSENGER Son,
it's very plain you don't know what you're doing.

OEDIPUS What do you mean, old man? For God's sake, tell me.

MESSENGER If your homecoming is checked by fears like these.

OEDIPUS Yes, I'm afraid that Phoebus may prove right.

MESSENGER The murder and the incest?

OEDIPUS Yes, old man;
that is my constant terror.

MESSENGER Do you know
that all your fears are empty?

OEDIPUS How is that,
if they are father and mother and I their son?

MESSENGER Because Polybus was no kin to you in blood.

OEDIPUS What, was not Polybus my father?

MESSENGER No more than I but just so much.

OEDIPUS How can
my father be my father as much as one
that's nothing to me?

MESSENGER Neither he nor I
begat you.

OEDIPUS Why then did he call me son?

MESSENGER A gift he took you from these hands of mine.

OEDIPUS Did he love so much what he took from another's hand?

MESSENGER His childlessness before persuaded him.

OEDIPUS Was I a child you bought or found when I was given to him?

MESSENGER On Cithaeron's slopes
in the twisting thickets you were found.

OEDIPUS And why
were you a traveler in those parts?

MESSENGER I was
in charge of mountain flocks.

OEDIPUS You were a shepherd?
A hireling vagrant?

MESSENGER Yes, but at least at that time
the man that saved your life, son.

OEDIPUS What ailed me when you took me in your arms?

MESSENGER In that your ankles should be witnesses.

OEDIPUS Why do you speak of that old pain?

MESSENGER I loosed you;
the tendons of your feet were pierced and fettered—

OEDIPUS My swaddling clothes brought me a rare disgrace.

MESSENGER So that from this you're called your present name.

OEDIPUS Was this my father's doing or my mother's?
For God's sake, tell me.

MESSENGER I don't know, but he
who gave you to me has more knowledge than I.

OEDIPUS You yourself did not find me then? You took me from someone else?

MESSENGER Yes, from another shepherd.

OEDIPUS Who was he? Do you know him well enough to tell?

MESSENGER He was called Laius' man.

OEDIPUS You mean the king who reigned here in the old days?

MESSENGER Yes, he was that man's shepherd.

OEDIPUS Is he alive
still, so that I could see him?

MESSENGER You who live here
would know that best.

OEDIPUS Do any of you here
know of this shepherd whom he speaks about
in town or in the fields? Tell me. It's time
that this was found out once for all.

CHORUS I think he is none other than the peasant
whom you have sought to see already; but
Jocasta here can tell us best of that.

OEDIPUS Jocasta, do you know about this man
whom we have sent for? Is he the man he mentions?

JOCASTA Why ask of whom he spoke? Don't give it heed;
nor try to keep in mind what has been said.
It will be wasted labor.

OEDIPUS With such clues
I could not fail to bring my birth to light.

JOCASTA I beg you—do not hunt this out—I beg you,
if you have any care for your own life.
What I am suffering is enough.

OEDIPUS Keep up
your heart, Jocasta. Though I'm proved a slave,
thrice slave, and though my mother is thrice slave,
you'll not be shown to be of lowly lineage.

JOCASTA Oh, be persuaded by me, I entreat you;
do not do this.

OEDIPUS I will not be persuaded to let be
the chance of finding out the whole thing clearly.

JOCASTA It is because I wish you well that I
give you this counsel—and it's the best counsel.

OEDIPUS Then the best counsel vexes me, and has
for some while since.

JOCASTA O Oedipus, God help you!
God keep you from the knowledge of who you are!

OEDIPUS Here, someone, go and fetch the shepherd for
me;
and let her find her joy in her rich family!

JOCASTA O Oedipus, unhappy Oedipus!
that is all I can call you, and the last thing
that I shall ever call you.

Exit.

CHORUS Why has the queen gone, Oedipus, in wild
grief rushing from us? I am afraid that trouble
will break out of this silence.

OEDIPUS Break out what will! I at least shall be
willing to see my ancestry, though humble.
Perhaps she is ashamed of my low birth,
for she has all a woman's high-flown pride.
But I account myself a child of Fortune,
beneficent Fortune, and I shall not be
dishonored. She's the mother from whom I spring;
the months, my brothers, marked me, now as small,
and now again as mighty. Such is my breeding,
and I shall never prove so false to it,
as not to find the secret of my birth.

CHORUS

Strophe If I am a prophet and wise of heart
you shall not fail, Cithaeron,
by the limitless sky, you shall not!—
to know at tomorrow's full moon
that Oedipus honors you,
as native to him and mother and nurse at once;
and that you are honored in dancing by us, as finding favor in sight of our king.
Apollo, to whom we cry, find these things pleasing!

Antistrophe Who was it bore you, child? One of
the long-lived nymphs who lay with Pan—
the father who treads the hills?
Or was she a bride of Loxias, your mother? The grassy slopes
are all of them dear to him. Or perhaps Cyllene's king
or the Bacchants' god that lives on the tops
of the hills received you a gift from some
one of the Helicon Nymphs, with whom he mostly plays?

Enter an old man, led by Oedipus' servants.

OEDIPUS If someone like myself who never met him
may make a guess—I think this is the herdsman,
whom we were seeking. His old age is consonant
with the other. And besides, the men who bring him
I recognize as my own servants. You
perhaps may better me in knowledge since
you've seen the man before.

CHORUS You can be sure
I recognize him. For if Laius
had ever an honest shepherd, this was he.

OEDIPUS You, sir, from Corinth, I must ask you first, is this the man you spoke of?

MESSENGER This is he before your eyes.

OEDIPUS Old man, look here at me and tell me what I ask you. Were you ever a servant of King Laius?

HERDSMAN I was— no slave he bought but reared in his own house.

OEDIPUS What did you do as work? How did you live?

HERDSMAN Most of my life was spent among the flocks.

OEDIPUS In what part of the country did you live?

HERDSMAN Cithaeron and the places near to it.

OEDIPUS And somewhere there perhaps you knew this man?

HERDSMAN What was his occupation? Who?

OEDIPUS This man here, have you had any dealings with him?

HERDSMAN No— not such that I can quickly call to mind.

MESSENGER That is no wonder, master. But I'll make him remember what he does not know. For I know, that he well knows the country of Cithaeron, how he with two flocks, I with one kept company for three years—each year half a year—from spring till autumn time and then when winter came I drove my flocks to our fold home again and he to Laius' steadings. Well—am I right or not in what I said we did?

HERDSMAN You're right—although it's a long time ago.

MESSENGER Do you remember giving me a child
to bring up as my foster child?

HERDSMAN What's this?
Why do you ask this question?

MESSENGER Look old man,
here he is—here's the man who was that child!

HERDSMAN Death take you! Won't you hold your tongue?

OEDIPUS No, no,
do not find fault with him, old man. Your words
are more at fault than his.

HERDSMAN O best of masters,
how do I give offense?

OEDIPUS When you refuse
to speak about the child of whom he asks you.

HERDSMAN He speaks out of his ignorance, without meaning.

OEDIPUS If you'll not talk to gratify me, you
will talk with pain to urge you.

HERDSMAN Oh, please, sir,
don't hurt an old man, sir.

OEDIPUS (*to the servants*) Here, one of you,
twist his hands behind him.

HERDSMAN Why, God help me, why?
What do you want to know?

OEDIPUS You gave a child
to him—the child he asked you of?

HERDSMAN I did.
I wish I'd died the day I did.

OEDIPUS You will
unless you tell me truly.

HERDSMAN And I'll die
far worse if I should tell you.

OEDIPUS This fellow
is bent on more delays, as it would seem.

HERDSMAN Oh, no, no! I have told you that I gave it.

OEDIPUS Where did you get this child from? Was it your
own or did you get it from another?

HERDSMAN Not
my own at all; I had it from someone.

OEDIPUS One of these citizens? or from what house?

HERDSMAN O master, please—I beg you, master, please
don't ask me more.

OEDIPUS You're a dead man if I ask you again.

HERDSMAN It was one of the children of Laius.

OEDIPUS A slave? Or born in wedlock?

HERDSMAN O God, I am on the brink of frightful speech.

OEDIPUS And I of frightful hearing. But I must hear.

HERDSMAN The child was called his child; but she within, your wife would tell you best how all this was.

OEDIPUS *She* gave it to you?

HERDSMAN Yes, she did, my lord.

OEDIPUS To do what with it?

HERDSMAN Make away with it.

OEDIPUS She was so hard—its mother?

HERDSMAN Aye, through fear of evil oracles.

OEDIPUS Which?

HERDSMAN They said that he should kill his parents.

OEDIPUS How was it that you gave it away to this old man?

HERDSMAN O master,
I pitied it, and thought that I could send it
off to another country and this man
was from another country. But he saved it
for the most terrible troubles. If you are
the man he says you are, you're bred to misery.

OEDIPUS Oh! Oh! Oh! they will all come,
all come out clearly! Light of the sun, let me
look upon you no more after today!
I who first saw the light bred of a match
accursed, and accursed in my living
with them I lived with, cursed in my killing.

Exeunt all but the Chorus.

CHORUS
Strophe O generations of men, how I
count you as equal with those who live
not at all!
What man, what man on earth wins more
of happiness than a seeming
and after that turning away?
Oedipus, you are my pattern of this,
Oedipus, you and your fate!
Luckless Oedipus, whom of all men
I envy not at all.

Antistrophe In as much as he shot his bolt
beyond the others and won the prize
of happiness complete—
O Zeus—and killed and reduced to nought
the hooked taloned maid of the riddling speech,
standing a tower against death for my land:
hence he was called my king and hence

was honored the highest of all
honors; and hence he ruled
in the great city of Thebes.

Strophe But now whose tale is more miserable?
Who is there lives with a savager fate?
Whose troubles so reverse his life as his?

O Oedipus, the famous prince
for whom a great haven
the same both as father and son
sufficed for generation,
how, Oh, how have the furrows plowed
by your father endured to bear you, poor wretch,
and hold their peace so long?

Antistrophe Time who sees all has found you out
against your will; judges your marriage accursed,
begetter and begot at one in it.

O child of Laius,
would I had never seen you.
I weep for you and cry
a dirge of lamentation.

To speak directly, I drew my breath
from you at the first and so now I lull
my mouth to sleep with your name.

Enter Second Messenger.

SECOND MESSENGER O princes always honored by our country,
what deeds you'll hear of and what horrors see,
what grief you'll feel, if you as true born Thebans

care for the house of Labdacus' sons.
Phasis nor Ister cannot purge this house,
I think, with all their streams, such things
it hides, such evils shortly will bring forth
into the light, whether they will or not;
and troubles hurt the most
when they prove self-inflicted.

CHORUS What we had known before did not fall short
of bitter groaning's worth; what's more to tell?

SECOND MESSENGER Shortest to hear and tell—our glorious queen
Jocasta's dead.

CHORUS Unhappy woman! How?

SECOND MESSENGER By her own hand. The worst of what was done
you cannot know. You did not see the sight.
Yet in so far as I remember it
you'll hear the end of our unlucky queen.
When she came raging into the house she went
straight to her marriage bed, tearing her hair
with both her hands, and crying upon Laius
long dead—"Do you remember, Laius,
that night long past which bred a child for us
to send you to your death and leave
a mother making children with her son?"
And then she groaned and cursed the bed in which
she brought forth husband by her husband, children
by her own child, an infamous double bond.
How after that she died I do not know—
for Oedipus distracted us from seeing.

He burst upon us shouting and we looked
to him as he paced frantically around,
begging us always: "Give me a sword, I say,
to find this wife no wife, this mother's womb,
this field of double sowing whence I sprang
and where I sowed my children!" As he raved
some god showed him the way—none of us there.
Bellowing terribly and led by some
invisible guide he rushed on the two doors—
wrenching the hollow bolts out of their sockets,
he charged inside. There, there, we saw his wife
hanging, the twisted rope around her neck.
When he saw her, he cried out fearfully
and cut the dangling noose. Then, as she lay,
poor woman, on the ground, what happened after,
was terrible to see. He tore the brooches—
the gold-chased brooches fastening her robe—
away from her and lifting them up high
dashed them on his own eyeballs, shrieking out
such things as: "They will never see the crime
I have committed or had done upon me!"
"Dark eyes, now in the days to come look on
forbidden faces, do not recognize
those whom you long for"—with such imprecations
he struck his eyes again and yet again
with the brooches. And the bleeding eyeballs gushed
and stained his beard—no sluggish oozing drops
but a black rain and bloody hail poured down.

So it has broken—and not on one head
but troubles mixed for husband and for wife.
The fortune of the days gone by was true
good fortune—but today groans and destruction
and death and shame—of all ills can be named
not one is missing.

CHORUS Is he now in any ease from pain?

SECOND MESSENGER He shouts
for someone to unbar the doors and show him
to all the men of Thebes, his father's killer,
his mother's—no I cannot say the word,
it is unholy—for he'll cast himself
out of the land, he says, and not remain
to bring a curse upon his house, the curse
he called upon it in his proclamation. But
he wants for strength, aye, and someone to guide him;
his sickness is too great to bear. You, too,
will be shown that. The bolts are opening.
Soon you will see a sight to waken pity
even in the horror of it.

Enter the blinded Oedipus.

CHORUS This is a terrible sight for men to see!
I never found a worse!
Poor wretch, what madness came upon you!
What evil spirit leaped upon your life
to your ill-luck—a leap beyond man's strength!
Indeed I pity you, but I cannot
look at you, though there's much I want to ask
and much to learn and much to see.
I shudder at the sight of you.

OEDIPUS Oh! Oh!
where am I going? Where is my voice
borne on the wind to and fro?
Spirit, how far have you sprung?

CHORUS To a terrible place whereof men's ears
may not hear, nor their eyes behold it.

OEDIPUS Darkness!
Horror of darkness enfolding, resistless,
unspeakable visitant sped by an ill wind in haste!
madness and stabbing pain and memory
of evil deeds I have done!

CHORUS In such misfortunes it's no wonder
if double weighs the burden of your grief.

OEDIPUS My friend,
you are the only one steadfast, the only one that attends
on me;
you still stay nursing the blind man.
Your care is not unnoticed. I can know
your voice, although this darkness is my world.

CHORUS Doer of dreadful deeds, how did you dare
so far to do despite to your own eyes?
what spirit urged you to it?

OEDIPUS It was Apollo, friends, Apollo,
that brought this bitter bitterness, my sorrows to
completion.
But the hand that struck me
was none but my own.
Why should I see
whose vision showed me nothing sweet to see?

CHORUS These things are as you say.

OEDIPUS What can I see to love?
What greeting can touch my ears with joy?
Take me away, and haste—to a place out of the way!
Take me away, my friends, the greatly miserable,
the most accursed, whom God too hates
above all men on earth!

CHORUS Unhappy in your mind and your misfortune,
would I had never known you!

OEDIPUS Curse on the man who took
the cruel bonds from off my legs, as I lay in the field.
He stole me from death and saved me,
no kindly service.
Had I died then
I would not be so burdensome to friends.

CHORUS I, too, could have wished it had been so.

OEDIPUS Then I would not have come
to kill my father and marry my mother infamously.
Now I am godless and child of impurity,
begetter in the same seed that created my wretched self.
If there is any ill worse than ill,
that is the lot of Oedipus.

CHORUS I cannot say your remedy was good;
you would be better dead than blind and living.

OEDIPUS What I have done here was best done—don't tell me
otherwise, do not give me further counsel.
I do not know with what eyes I could look
upon my father when I die and go
under the earth, nor yet my wretched mother—
those two to whom I have done things deserving
worse punishment than hanging. Would the sight
of children, bred as mine are, gladden me?
No, not these eyes, never. And my city,
its towers and sacred places of the gods,
of these I robbed my miserable self
when I commanded all to drive *him* out,

the criminal since proved by God impure
and of the race of Laius.
To this guilt I bore witness against myself—
with what eyes shall I look upon my people?
No. If there were a means to choke the fountain
of hearing I would not have stayed my hand
from locking up my miserable carcase,
seeing and hearing nothing; it is sweet
to keep our thoughts out of the range of hurt.

Cithaeron, why did you receive me? Why
having received me did you not kill me straight?
And so I had not shown to men my birth.

O Polybus and Corinth and the house,
the old house that I used to call my father's—
what fairness you were nurse to, and what foulness
festered beneath! Now I am found to be
a sinner and a son of sinners. Crossroads,
and hidden glade, oak and the narrow way
at the crossroads, that drank my father's blood
offered you by my hands, do you remember
still what I did as you looked on, and what
I did when I came here? O marriage, marriage!
you bred me and again when you had bred
bred children of your child and showed to men
brides, wives and mothers and the foulest deeds
that can be in this world of ours.

Come—it's unfit to say what is unfit
to do. I beg of you in God's name hide me
somewhere outside your country, yes, or kill me,
or throw me into the sea, to be forever
out of your sight. Approach and deign to touch me
for all my wretchedness, and do not fear.
No man but I can bear my evil doom.

CHORUS Here Creon comes in fit time to perform
or give advice in what you ask of us.
Creon is left sole ruler in your stead.

OEDIPUS Creon! Creon! What shall I say to him?
How can I justly hope that he will trust me?
In what is past I have been proved towards him
an utter liar.

Enter Creon.

CREON Oedipus, I've come
not so that I might laugh at you nor taunt you
with evil of the past. But if you still
are without shame before the face of men
reverence at least the flame that gives all life,
our Lord the Sun, and do not show unveiled
to him pollution such that neither land
nor holy rain nor light of day can welcome.
(*to a servant*) Be quick and take him in. It is most decent
that only kin should see and hear the troubles
of kin.

OEDIPUS I beg you, since you've torn me from
my dreadful expectations and have come
in a most noble spirit to a man
that has used you vilely—do a thing for me.
I shall speak for your own good, not for my own.

CREON What do you need that you would ask of me?

OEDIPUS Drive me from here with all the speed you can
to where I may not hear a human voice.

CREON Be sure, I would have done this had not I
wished first of all to learn from the god the course
of action I should follow.

OEDIPUS But his word
has been quite clear to let the parricide,
the sinner, die.

CREON Yes, that indeed was said.
But in the present need we had best discover
what we should do.

OEDIPUS And will you ask about
a man so wretched?

CREON Now even you will trust
the god.

OEDIPUS So. I command you—
and will beseech you—
to her that lies inside that house give burial
as you would have it; she is yours and rightly
you will perform the rites for her. For me—
never let this my father's city have me
living a dweller in it. Leave me live
in the mountains where Cithaeron is, that's called
my mountain, which my mother and my father
while they were living would have made my tomb.
So I may die by their decree who sought
indeed to kill me. Yet I know this much:
no sickness and no other thing will kill me.
I would not have been saved from death if not
for some strange evil fate. Well, let my fate
go where it will.

Creon, you need not care
about my sons; they're men and so wherever
they are, they will not lack a livelihood.
But my two girls—so sad and pitiful—
whose table never stood apart from mine,
and everything I touched they always shared—
O Creon, have a thought for them! And most
I wish that you might suffer me to touch them
and sorrow with them.

Enter Antigone and Ismene, Oedipus' two daughters.

O my lord! O true noble Creon! Can I
really be touching them, as when I saw?
What shall I say?
Yes, I can hear them sobbing—my two darlings!
and Creon has had pity and has sent me
what I loved most?
Am I right?

CREON You're right: it was I gave you this
because I knew from old days how you loved them
as I see now.

OEDIPUS God bless you for it, Creon,
and may God guard you better on your road
than he did me!
O children,
where are you? Come here, come to my hands,
a brother's hands which turned your father's eyes,
those bright eyes you knew once, to what you see,
a father seeing nothing, knowing nothing,
begetting you from his own source of life.

I weep for you—I cannot see your faces—
I weep when I think of the bitterness
there will be in your lives, how you must live
before the world. At what assemblages
of citizens will you make one? To what
gay company will you go and not come home
in tears instead of sharing in the holiday?
And when you're ripe for marriage, who will he be,
the man who'll risk to take such infamy
as shall cling to my children, to bring hurt
on them and those that marry with them? What
curse is not there? "Your father killed his father
and sowed the seed where he had sprung himself
and begot you out of the womb that held him."
These insults you will hear. Then who will marry you?
No one, my children; clearly you are doomed
to waste away in barrenness unmarried.
Son of Menoeceus, since you are all the father
left these two girls, and we, their parents, both
are dead to them—do not allow them to wander
like beggars, poor and husbandless.
They are of your own blood.
And do not make them equal with myself
in wretchedness; for you can see them now—
so young, so utterly alone, save for you only.
Touch my hand, noble Creon, and say yes.
If you were older, children, and were wiser,
there's much advice I'd give you. But as it is,
let this be what you pray: give me a life
wherever there is opportunity
to live, and better life than was my father's.

CREON Your tears have had enough of scope; now go within the house.

OEDIPUS I must obey, though bitter of heart.

CREON In season, all is good.

OEDIPUS Do you know on what conditions I obey?

CREON You tell me them,
and I shall know them when I hear.

OEDIPUS That you shall send me out
to live away from Thebes.

CREON That gift you must ask of the god.

OEDIPUS But I'm now hated by the gods.

CREON So quickly you'll obtain your prayer.

OEDIPUS You consent then?

CREON What I do not mean, I do not use to say.

OEDIPUS Now lead me away from here.

CREON Let go the children, then, and come.

OEDIPUS Do not take them from me.

CREON Do not seek to be master in everything,
for the things you mastered did not follow you
throughout your life.

CHORUS (*As Creon and Oedipus go out*) You that live in my
ancestral Thebes, behold this Oedipus—

him who knew the famous riddles and was a man most masterful;
not a citizen who did not look with envy on his lot—
see him now and see the breakers of misfortune swallow him!
Look upon that last day always. Count no mortal happy till
he has passed the final limit of his life secure from pain.

ANTIGONE

Translated by Elizabeth Wyckoff

CHARACTERS

ANTIGONE, ISMENE — *daughters of Oedipus and Jocasta*

CREON, *king of Thebes*

EURYDICE, *his wife*

HAEMON, *his son*

TEIRESIAS, *an old blind prophet*

GUARD, *set to watch the corpse of Polyneices*

MESSENGER

CHORUS OF THEBAN ELDERS

Non-speaking: guards; attendants

ANTIGONE

SCENE *Thebes, before the royal palace. Antigone and Ismene emerge from its great central door.*

ANTIGONE My sister, my Ismene, do you know
of any suffering from our father sprung
that Zeus does not achieve for us survivors?
There's nothing grievous, nothing free from doom,
not shameful, not dishonored, I've not seen.
Your sufferings and mine.
And now, what of this edict which they say
the commander has proclaimed to the whole people?
Have you heard anything? Or don't you know
that the foes' trouble comes upon our friends?

ISMENE I've heard no word, Antigone, of our friends.
Not sweet nor bitter, since that single moment
when we two lost two brothers
who died on one day by a double blow.
And since the Argive army went away
this very night, I have no further news
of fortune or disaster for myself.

ANTIGONE I knew it well, and brought you from the house
for just this reason, that you alone may hear.

ISMENE What is it? Clearly some news has clouded you.

ANTIGONE It has indeed. Creon will give the one

of our two brothers honor in the tomb;
the other none.
Eteocles, with just entreatment treated,
as law provides he has hidden under earth
to have full honor with the dead below.
But Polyneices' corpse who died in pain,
they say he has proclaimed to the whole town
that none may bury him and none bewail,
but leave him unwept, untombed, a rich sweet sight
for the hungry birds' beholding.
Such orders they say the worthy Creon gives
to you and me—yes, yes, I say to *me*—
and that he's coming to proclaim it clear
to those who know it not.
Further: he has the matter so at heart
that anyone who dares attempt the act
will die by public stoning in the town.
So there you have it and you soon will show
if you are noble, or fallen from your descent.

ISMENE If things have reached this stage, what can I do,
poor sister, that will help to make or mend?

ANTIGONE Think, will you share my labor and my act.

ISMENE What will you risk? And where is your intent?

ANTIGONE Will you take up that corpse along with me?

ISMENE To bury him you mean, when it's forbidden?

ANTIGONE My brother, and yours, though you may wish
he were not.
I never shall be found to be his traitor.

ISMENE O hard of mind! When Creon spoke against it!

ANTIGONE It's not for him to keep me from my own.

ISMENE Alas! Remember, sister, how our father
perished abhorred, ill-famed.
Himself with his own hand, through his own curse
destroyed both eyes.
Remember next his mother and his wife
finishing life in the shame of the twisted strings.
And third two brothers on a single day,
poor creatures, murdering, a common doom
each with his arm accomplished on the other.
And now look at the two of us alone.
We'll perish terribly if we force law
and try to cross the royal vote and power.
We must remember that we two are women
so not to fight with men.
And that since we are subject to strong power
we must hear these orders, or any that may be worse.
So I shall ask of them beneath the earth
forgiveness, for in these things I am forced,
and shall obey the men in power. I know
that wild and futile action makes no sense.

ANTIGONE I wouldn't urge it. And if now you wished
to act, you wouldn't please me as a partner.
Be what you want to; but that man shall I
bury. For me, the doer, death is best.
Friend shall I lie with him, yes, friend with friend,
when I have dared the crime of piety.
Longer the time in which to please the dead
than that for those up here.
There shall I lie forever. You may see fit
to keep from honor what the gods have honored.

ISMENE I shall do no dishonor. But to act
against the citizens. I cannot.

ANTIGONE That's your protection. Now I go, to pile
the burial-mound for him, my dearest brother.

ISMENE O my poor sister. How I fear for you!

ANTIGONE For me, don't borrow trouble. Clear your fate.

ISMENE At least give no one warning of this act;
you keep it hidden, and I'll do the same.

ANTIGONE Dear God! Denounce me. I shall hate you more
if silent, not proclaiming this to all.

ISMENE You have a hot mind over chilly things.

ANTIGONE I know I please those whom I most should please.

ISMENE If but you can. You crave what can't be done.

ANTIGONE And so, when strength runs out, I shall give over.

ISMENE Wrong from the start, to chase what cannot be.

ANTIGONE If that's your saying, I shall hate you first,
and next the dead will hate you in all justice.
But let me and my own ill-counseling
suffer this terror. I shall suffer nothing
as great as dying with a lack of grace.

ISMENE Go, since you want to. But know this: you go
senseless indeed, but loved by those who love you.

Ismene returns to the palace; Antigone leaves by one of the side entrances. The Chorus now enters from the other side.

CHORUS Sun's own radiance, fairest light ever shone on
the gates of Thebes,
then did you shine, O golden day's
eye, coming over Dirce's stream,
on the Man who had come from Argos with all his
armor
running now in headlong fear as you shook his bridle
free.

He was stirred by the dubious quarrel of Polyneices.
So, screaming shrill,
like an eagle over the land he flew,
covered with white-snow wing,
with many weapons,
with horsehair crested helms.

He who had stood above our halls, gaping about our
seven gates,
with that circle of thirsting spears.
Gone, without our blood in his jaws,
before the torch took hold on our tower crown.
Rattle of war at his back; hard the fight for the dragon's
foe.

The boasts of a proud tongue are for Zeus to hate.
So seeing them streaming on
in insolent clangor of gold,
he struck with hurling fire him who rushed

for the high wall's top,
to cry conquest abroad.

Swinging, striking the earth he fell
fire in hand, who in mad attack,
had raged against us with blasts of hate.
He failed. He failed of his aim.
For the rest great Ares dealt his blows about,
first in the war team.

The captains stationed at seven gates
fought with seven and left behind
their brazen arms as an offering
to Zeus who is turner of battle.
All but those wretches, sons of one man,
one mother's sons, who sent their spears
each against each and found the share
of a common death together.

Great-named Victory comes to us
answering Thebe's warrior joy.
Let us forget the wars just done
and visit the shrines of the gods.
All, with night-long dance which Bacchus will lead,
who shakes Thebe's acres.

Creon enters from the palace.

Now here he comes, the king of the land,
Creon, Menoeceus' son,
newly named by the gods' new fate.
What plan that beats about his mind
has made him call this council session,
sending his summons to all?

CREON My friends, the very gods who shook the state
with mighty surge have set it straight again.
So now I sent for you, chosen from all,
first that I knew you constant in respect
to Laius' royal power; and again
when Oedipus had set the state to rights,
and when he perished, you were faithful still
in mind to the descendants of the dead.
When they two perished by a double fate,
on one day struck and striking and defiled
each by his own hand, now it comes that I
hold all the power and the royal throne
through close connection with the perished men.
You cannot learn of any man the soul,
the mind, and the intent until he shows
his practice of the government and law.
For I believe that who controls the state
and does not hold to the best plans of all,
but locks his tongue up through some kind of fear,
that he is worst of all who are or were.
And he who counts another greater friend
than his own fatherland, I put him nowhere.
So I—may Zeus all-seeing always know it—
could not keep silent as disaster crept
upon the town, destroying hope of safety.
Nor could I count the enemy of the land
friend to myself, not I who know so well
that she it is who saves us, sailing straight,
and only so can we have friends at all.
With such good rules shall I enlarge our state.
And now I have proclaimed their brother-edict.
In the matter of the sons of Oedipus,
citizens, know: Eteocles who died,
defending this our town with champion spear,

is to be covered in the grave and granted
all holy rites we give the noble dead.
But his brother Polyneices—whom I name
the exile who came back and sought to burn
his fatherland, the gods who were his kin,
who tried to gorge on blood he shared, and lead
the rest of us as slaves—
it is announced that no one in this town
may give him burial or mourn for him.
Leave him unburied, leave his corpse disgraced,
a dinner for the birds and for the dogs.
Such is my mind. Never shall I, myself,
honor the wicked and reject the just.
The man who is well-minded to the state
from me in death and life shall have his honor.

CHORUS This resolution, Creon, is your own,
in the matter of the traitor and the true.
For you can make such rulings as you will
about the living and about the dead.

CREON Now you be sentinels of the decree.

CHORUS Order some younger man to take this on.

CREON Already there are watchers of the corpse.

CHORUS What other order would you give us, then?

CREON Not to take sides with any who disobey.

CHORUS No fool is fool as far as loving death.

CREON Death is the price. But often we have known
men to be ruined by the hope of profit.

Enter, from the side, the Guard.

GUARD Lord, I can't claim that I am out of breath
from rushing here with light and hasty step,
for I had many haltings in my thought
making me double back upon my road.
My mind kept saying many things to me:
"Why go where you will surely pay the price?"
"Fool, are you halting? And if Creon learns
from someone else, how shall you not be hurt?"
Turning this over, on I dilly-dallied.
And so a short trip turns itself to long.
Finally, though, my coming here won out.
If what I say is nothing, still I'll say it.
For I come clutching to one single hope
that I can't suffer what is not my fate.

CREON What is it that brings on this gloom of yours?

GUARD I want to tell you first about myself.
I didn't do it, didn't see who did it.
It isn't right for me to get in trouble.

CREON Your aim is good. You fence the fact around.
It's clear you have some shocking news to tell.

GUARD Terrible tidings make for long delays.

CREON Speak out the story, and then get away.

GUARD I'll tell you. Someone left the corpse just now,
burial all accomplished, thirsty dust
strewn on the flesh, the ritual complete.

CREON What are you saying? What man has dared to do it?

GUARD I wouldn't know. There were no marks of picks,
no grubbed-out earth. The ground was dry and hard,
no trace of wheels. The doer left no sign.
When the first fellow on the day-shift showed us,
we all were sick with wonder.
For he was hidden, not inside a tomb,
light dust upon him, enough to turn the curse,
no wild beast's track, nor track of any hound
having been near, nor was the body torn.
We roared bad words about, guard against guard,
and came to blows. No one was there to stop us.
Each man had done it, nobody had done it
so as to prove it on him—we couldn't tell.
We were prepared to hold to red-hot iron,
to walk through fire, to swear before the gods
we hadn't done it, hadn't shared the plan,
when it was plotted or when it was done.
And last, when all our sleuthing came out nowhere,
one fellow spoke, who made our heads to droop
low toward the ground. We couldn't disagree.
We couldn't see a chance of getting off.
He said we had to tell you all about it.
We couldn't hide the fact.
So he won out. The lot chose poor old me
to win the prize. So here I am unwilling,
quite sure you people hardly want to see me.
Nobody likes the bringer of bad news.

CHORUS Lord, while he spoke, my mind kept on debating.
Isn't this action possibly a god's?

CREON Stop now, before you fill me up with rage,
or you'll prove yourself insane as well as old.
Unbearable, your saying that the gods
take any kindly forethought for this corpse.
Would it be they had hidden him away,
honoring his good service, his who came
to burn their pillared temples and their wealth,
even their land, and break apart their laws?
Or have you seen them honor wicked men?
It isn't so.
No, from the first there were some men in town
who took the edict hard, and growled against me,
who hid the fact that they were rearing back,
not rightly in the yoke, no way my friends.
These are the people—Oh, it's clear to me—
who have bribed these men and brought about the deed.
No current custom among men as bad
as silver currency. This destroys the state;
this drives men from their homes; this wicked teacher
drives solid citizens to acts of shame.
It shows men how to practice infamy
and know the deeds of all unholiness.
Every least hireling who helped in this
brought about then the sentence he shall have.
But further, as I still revere great Zeus,
understand this, I tell you under oath,
if you don't find the very man whose hands
buried the corpse, bring him for me to see,
not death alone shall be enough for you
till living, hanging, you make clear the crime.
For any future grabbings you'll have learned
where to get pay, and that it doesn't pay
to squeeze a profit out of every source.
For you'll have felt that more men come to doom
through dirty profits than are kept by them.

GUARD May I say something? Or just turn and go?

CREON Aren't you aware your speech is most unwelcome?

GUARD Does it annoy your hearing or your mind?

CREON Why are you out to allocate my pain?

GUARD The doer hurts your mind. I hurt your ears.

CREON You are a quibbling rascal through and through.

GUARD But anyhow I never did the deed.

CREON And you the man who sold your mind for money!

GUARD Oh!
How terrible to guess, and guess at lies!

CREON Go pretty up your guesswork. If you don't
show me the doers you will have to say
that wicked payments work their own revenge.

GUARD Indeed, I pray he's found, but yes or no,
taken or not as luck may settle it,
you won't see me returning to this place.
Saved when I neither hoped nor thought to be,
I owe the gods a mighty debt of thanks.

Creon enters the palace. The Guard leaves by the way he came.

CHORUS Many the wonders but nothing walks stranger than man.
This thing crosses the sea in the winter's storm,

making his path through the roaring waves.
And she, the greatest of gods, the earth—
ageless she is, and unwearied—he wears her away
as the plows go up and down from year to year
and his mules turn up the soil.

Gay nations of birds he snares and leads,
wild beast tribes and the salty brood of the sea,
with the twisted mesh of his nets, this clever man.
He controls with craft the beasts of the open air,
walkers on hills. The horse with his shaggy mane
he holds and harnesses, yoked about the neck,
and the strong bull of the mountain.

Language, and thought like the wind
and the feelings that make the town,
he has taught himself, and shelter against the cold,
refuge from rain. He can always help himself.
He faces no future helpless. There's only death
that he cannot find an escape from. He has contrived
refuge from illnesses once beyond all cure.

Clever beyond all dreams
the inventive craft that he has
which may drive him one time or another to well or ill.
When he honors the laws of the land and the gods'
  sworn right
high indeed is his city; but stateless the man
who dares to dwell with dishonor. Not by my fire,
never to share my thoughts, who does these things.

The Guard enters with Antigone.

My mind is split at this awful sight.
I know her. I cannot deny

Antigone is here.
Alas, the unhappy girl,
her unhappy father's child.
Oh, what is the meaning of this?
It cannot be you that they bring
for breaking the royal law,
caught in open shame.

GUARD This is the woman who has done the deed.
We caught her at the burying. Where's the king?

Creon enters.

CHORUS Back from the house again just when he's needed.

CREON What must I measure up to? What has happened?

GUARD Lord, one should never swear off anything.
Afterthought makes the first resolve a liar.
I could have vowed I wouldn't come back here
after your threats, after the storm I faced.
But joy that comes beyond the wildest hope
is bigger than all other pleasure known.
I'm here, though I swore not to be, and bring
this girl. We caught her burying the dead.
This time we didn't need to shake the lots;
mine was the luck, all mine.
So now, lord, take her, you, and question her
and prove her as you will. But I am free.
And I deserve full clearance on this charge.

CREON Explain the circumstance of the arrest.

GUARD She was burying the man. You have it all.

CREON Is this the truth? And do you grasp its meaning?

GUARD I saw her burying the very corpse
you had forbidden. Is this adequate?

CREON How was she caught and taken in the act?

GUARD It was like this: when we got back again
struck with those dreadful threatenings of yours,
we swept away the dust that hid the corpse.
We stripped it back to slimy nakedness.
And then we sat to windward on the hill
so as to dodge the smell.
We poked each other up with growling threats
if anyone was careless of his work.
For some time this went on, till it was noon.
The sun was high and hot. Then from the earth
up rose a dusty whirlwind to the sky,
filling the plain, smearing the forest-leaves,
clogging the upper air. We shut our eyes,
sat and endured the plague the gods had sent.
So the storm left us after a long time.
We saw the girl. She cried the sharp and shrill
cry of a bitter bird which sees the nest
bare where the young birds lay.
So this same girl, seeing the body stripped,
cried with great groanings, cried a dreadful curse
upon the people who had done the deed.
Soon in her hands she brought the thirsty dust,
and holding high a pitcher of wrought bronze
she poured the three libations for the dead.
We saw this and surged down. We trapped her fast;
and she was calm. We taxed her with the deeds
both past and present. Nothing was denied.
And I was glad, and yet I took it hard.

One's own escape from trouble makes one glad;
but bringing friends to trouble is hard grief.
Still, I care less for all these second thoughts
than for the fact that I myself am safe.

CREON You there, whose head is drooping to the ground,
do you admit this, or deny you did it?

ANTIGONE I say I did it and I don't deny it.

CREON (*to the Guard*) Take yourself off wherever you wish to go
free of a heavy charge.
(*to Antigone*) You—tell me not at length but in a word.
You knew the order not to do this thing?

ANTIGONE I knew, of course I knew. The word was plain.

CREON And still you dared to overstep these laws?

ANTIGONE For me it was not Zeus who made that order.
Nor did that Justice who lives with the gods below
mark out such laws to hold among mankind.
Nor did I think your orders were so strong
that you, a mortal man, could overrun
the gods' unwritten and unfailing laws.
Not now, nor yesterday's, they always live,
and no one knows their origin in time.
So not through fear of any man's proud spirit
would I be likely to neglect these laws,
draw on myself the gods' sure punishment.
I knew that I must die; how could I not?
even without your warning. If I die
before my time, I say it is a gain.

Who lives in sorrows many as are mine
how shall he not be glad to gain his death?
And so, for me to meet this fate, no grief.
But if I left that corpse, my mother's son,
dead and unburied I'd have cause to grieve
as now I grieve not.
And if you think my acts are foolishness
the foolishness may be in a fool's eye.

CHORUS The girl is bitter. She's her father's child.
She cannot yield to trouble; nor could he.

CREON These rigid spirits are the first to fall.
The strongest iron, hardened in the fire,
most often ends in scraps and shatterings.
Small curbs bring raging horses back to terms.
Slave to his neighbor, who can think of pride?
This girl was expert in her insolence
when she broke bounds beyond established law.
Once she had done it, insolence the second,
to boast her doing, and to laugh in it.
I am no man and she the man instead
if she can have this conquest without pain.
She is my sister's child, but were she child
of closer kin than any at my hearth,
she and her sister should not so escape
their death and doom. I charge Ismene too.
She shared the planning of this burial.
Call her outside. I saw her in the house,
maddened, no longer mistress of herself.
The sly intent betrays itself sometimes
before the secret plotters work their wrong.
I hate it too when someone caught in crime
then wants to make it seem a lovely thing.

ANTIGONE Do you want more than my arrest and death?

CREON No more than that. For that is all I need.

ANTIGONE Why are you waiting? Nothing that you say
fits with my thought. I pray it never will.
Nor will you ever like to hear my words.
And yet what greater glory could I find
than giving my own brother funeral?
All these would say that they approved my act
did fear not mute them.
(A king is fortunate in many ways,
and most, that he can act and speak at will.)

CREON None of these others see the case this way.

ANTIGONE They see, and do not say. You have them cowed.

CREON And you are not ashamed to think alone?

ANTIGONE No, I am not ashamed. When was it shame
to serve the children of my mother's womb?

CREON It was not your brother who died against him, then?

ANTIGONE Full brother, on both sides, my parents' child.

CREON Your act of grace, in his regard, is crime.

ANTIGONE The corpse below would never say it was.

CREON When you honor him and the criminal just alike?

ANTIGONE It was a brother, not a slave, who died.

CREON Died to destroy this land the other guarded.

ANTIGONE Death yearns for equal law for all the dead.

CREON Not that the good and bad draw equal shares.

ANTIGONE Who knows that this is holiness below?

CREON Never the enemy, even in death, a friend.

ANTIGONE I cannot share in hatred, but in love.

CREON Then go down there, if you must love, and love the dead. No woman rules me while I live.

Ismene is brought from the palace under guard.

CHORUS Look there! Ismene is coming out.
She loves her sister and mourns,
with clouded brow and bloodied cheeks,
tears on her lovely face.

CREON You, lurking like a viper in the house,
who sucked me dry. I looked the other way
while twin destruction planned against the throne.
Now tell me, do you say you shared this deed?
Or will you swear you didn't even know?

ISMENE I did the deed, if she agrees I did.
I am accessory and share the blame.

ANTIGONE Justice will not allow this. You did not wish for a part, nor did I give you one.

ISMENE You are in trouble, and I'm not ashamed
to sail beside you into suffering.

ANTIGONE Death and the dead, they know whose act it was.
I cannot love a friend whose love is words.

ISMENE Sister, I pray, don't fence me out from honor,
from death with you, and honor done the dead.

ANTIGONE Don't die along with me, nor make your own
that which you did not do. My death's enough.

ISMENE When you are gone what life can be my friend?

ANTIGONE Love Creon. He's your kinsman and your care.

ISMENE Why hurt me, when it does yourself no good?

ANTIGONE I also suffer, when I laugh at you.

ISMENE What further service can I do you now?

ANTIGONE To save yourself. I shall not envy you.

ISMENE Alas for me! Am I outside your fate?

ANTIGONE Yes. For you chose to live when I chose death.

ISMENE At least I was not silent. You were warned.

ANTIGONE Some will have thought you wiser. Some will not.

ISMENE And yet the blame is equal for us both.

ANTIGONE Take heart. You live. My life died long ago.
And that has made me fit to help the dead.

CREON One of these girls has shown her lack of sense
just now. The other had it from her birth.

ISMENE Yes, lord. When people fall in deep distress
their native sense departs, and will not stay.

CREON You chose your mind's distraction when you chose
to work out wickedness with this wicked girl.

ISMENE What life is there for me to live without her?

CREON Don't speak of her. For she is here no more.

ISMENE But will you kill your own son's promised bride?

CREON Oh, there are other furrows for his plow.

ISMENE But where the closeness that has bound these two?

CREON Not for my sons will I choose wicked wives.

ISMENE Dear Haemon, your father robs you of your rights.

CREON You and your marriage trouble me too much.

ISMENE You will take away his bride from your own son?

CREON Yes. Death will help me break this marriage off.

CHORUS It seems determined that the girl must die.

CREON You helped determine it. Now, no delay!
Slaves, take them in. They must be women now.
No more free running.
Even the bold will fly when they see Death
drawing in close enough to end their life.

Antigone and Ismene are taken inside.

CHORUS Fortunate they whose lives have no taste of pain.
For those whose house is shaken by the gods
escape no kind of doom. It extends to all the kin
like the wave that comes when the winds of Thrace
run over the dark of the sea.
The black sand of the bottom is brought from the depth;
the beaten capes sound back with a hollow cry.

Ancient the sorrow of Labdacus' house, I know.
Dead men's grief comes back, and falls on grief.
No generation can free the next.
One of the gods will strike. There is no escape.
So now the light goes out
for the house of Oedipus, while the bloody knife
cuts the remaining root. Folly and Fury have done this.

What madness of man, O Zeus, can bind your power?
Not sleep can destroy it who ages all,
nor the weariless months the gods have set. Unaged in
time
Monarch you rule of Olympus' gleaming light.
Near time, far future, and the past,
one law controls them all:
any greatness in human life brings doom.

Wandering hope brings help to many men.
But others she tricks from their giddy loves,
and her quarry knows nothing until he has walked into flame.
Word of wisdom it was when someone said,
"The bad becomes the good
to him a god would doom."
Only briefly is that one from under doom.

Haemon enters from the side.

Here is your one surviving son.
Does he come in grief at the fate of his bride,
in pain that he's tricked of his wedding?

CREON Soon we shall know more than a seer could tell us.
Son, have you heard the vote condemned your bride?
And are you here, maddened against your father,
or are we friends, whatever I may do?

HAEMON My father, I am yours. You keep me straight
with your good judgment, which I shall ever follow.
Nor shall a marriage count for more with me
than your kind leading.

CREON There's my good boy. So should you hold at heart
and stand behind your father all the way.
It is for this men pray they may beget
households of dutiful obedient sons,
who share alike in punishing enemies,
and give due honor to their father's friends.
Whoever breeds a child that will not help
what has he sown but trouble for himself,

and for his enemies laughter full and free?
Son, do not let your lust mislead your mind,
all for a woman's sake, for well you know
how cold the thing he takes into his arms
who has a wicked woman for his wife.
What deeper wounding than a friend no friend?
Oh, spit her forth forever, as your foe.
Let the girl marry somebody in Hades.
Since I have caught her in the open act,
the only one in town who disobeyed,
I shall not now proclaim myself a liar,
but kill her. Let her sing her song of Zeus
who guards the kindred.
If I allow disorder in my house
I'd surely have to license it abroad.
A man who deals in fairness with his own,
he can make manifest justice in the state.
But he who crosses law, or forces it,
or hopes to bring the rulers under him,
shall never have a word of praise from me.
The man the state has put in place must have
obedient hearing to his least command
when it is right, and even when it's not.
He who accepts this teaching I can trust,
ruler, or ruled, to function in his place,
to stand his ground even in the storm of spears,
a mate to trust in battle at one's side.
There is no greater wrong than disobedience.
This ruins cities, this tears down our homes,
this breaks the battlefront in panic-rout.
If men live decently it is because
discipline saves their very lives for them.
So I must guard the men who yield to order,
not let myself be beaten by a woman.
Better, if it must happen, that a man

should overset me.
I won't be called weaker than womankind.

CHORUS We think—unless our age is cheating us—
that what you say is sensible and right.

HAEMON Father, the gods have given men good sense,
the only sure possession that we have.
I couldn't find the words in which to claim
that there was error in your late remarks.
Yet someone else might bring some further light.
Because I am your son I must keep watch
on all men's doing where it touches you,
their speech, and most of all, their discontents.
Your presence frightens any common man
from saying things you would not care to hear.
But in dark corners I have heard them say
how the whole town is grieving for this girl,
unjustly doomed, if ever woman was,
to die in shame for glorious action done.
She would not leave her fallen, slaughtered brother
there, as he lay, unburied, for the birds
and hungry dogs to make an end of him.
Isn't her real desert a golden prize?
This is the undercover speech in town.
Father, your welfare is my greatest good.
What loveliness in life for any child
outweighs a father's fortune and good fame?
And so a father feels his children's faring.
Then, do not have one mind, and one alone
that only your opinion can be right.
Whoever thinks that he alone is wise,
his eloquence, his mind, above the rest,
come the unfolding, shows his emptiness.
A man, though wise, should never be ashamed

of learning more, and must unbend his mind.
Have you not seen the trees beside the torrent,
the ones that bend them saving every leaf,
while the resistant perish root and branch?
And so the ship that will not slacken sail,
the sheet drawn tight, unyielding, overturns.
She ends the voyage with her keel on top.
No, yield your wrath, allow a change of stand.
Young as I am, if I may give advice,
I'd say it would be best if men were born
perfect in wisdom, but that failing this
(which often fails) it can be no dishonor
to learn from others when they speak good sense.

CHORUS Lord, if your son has spoken to the point
you should take his lesson. He should do the same.
Both sides have spoken well.

CREON At my age I'm to school my mind by his?
This boy instructor is my master, then?

HAEMON I urge no wrong. I'm young, but you should watch
my actions, not my years, to judge of me.

CREON A loyal action, to respect disorder?

HAEMON I wouldn't urge respect for wickedness.

CREON You don't think she is sick with that disease?

HAEMON Your fellow-citizens maintain she's not.

CREON Is the town to tell me how I ought to rule?

HAEMON Now there you speak just like a boy yourself.

CREON Am I to rule by other mind than mine?

HAEMON No city is property of a single man.

CREON But custom gives possession to the ruler.

HAEMON You'd rule a desert beautifully alone.

CREON (*to the Chorus*) It seems he's firmly on the woman's side.

HAEMON If you're a woman. It is you I care for.

CREON Wicked, to try conclusions with your father.

HAEMON When you conclude unjustly, so I must.

CREON Am I unjust, when I respect my office?

HAEMON You tread down the gods' due. Respect is gone.

CREON Your mind is poisoned. Weaker than a woman!

HAEMON At least you'll never see me yield to shame.

CREON Your whole long argument is but for her.

HAEMON And you, and me, and for the gods below.

CREON You shall not marry her while she's alive.

HAEMON Then she shall die. Her death will bring another.

CREON Your boldness has made progress. Threats, indeed!

HAEMON No threat, to speak against your empty plan.

CREON Past due, sharp lessons for your empty brain.

HAEMON If you weren't father, I should call you mad.

CREON Don't flatter me with "father," you woman's slave.

HAEMON You wish to speak but never wish to hear.

CREON You think so? By Olympus, you shall not
revile me with these tauntings and go free.
Bring out the hateful creature; she shall die
full in his sight, close at her bridegroom's side.

HAEMON Not at my side her death, and you will not
ever lay eyes upon my face again.
Find other friends to rave with after this.

Haemon leaves, by one of the side entrances.

CHORUS Lord, he has gone with all the speed of rage.
When such a man is grieved his mind is hard.

CREON Oh, let him go, plan superhuman action.
In any case the girls shall not escape.

CHORUS You plan for both the punishment of death?

CREON Not her who did not do it. You are right.

CHORUS And what death have you chosen for the other?

CREON To take her where the foot of man comes not.
There shall I hide her in a hollowed cave,
living, and leave her just so much to eat
as clears the city from the guilt of death.
There, if she prays to Death, the only god
of her respect, she may manage not to die.
Or she may learn at last and even then
how much too much her labor for the dead.

Creon returns to the palace.

CHORUS Love unconquered in fight, Love who falls on our havings.
You rest in the bloom of a girl's unwithered face.
You cross the sea, you are known in the wildest lairs.
Not the immortal gods can fly,
nor men of a day. Who has you within him is mad.

You twist the minds of the just. Wrong they pursue and are ruined.
You made this quarrel of kindred before us now.
Desire looks clear from the eyes of a lovely bride:
power as strong as the founded world.
For there is the goddess at play with whom no man can fight.

Antigone is brought from the palace under guard.

Now I am carried beyond all bounds.
My tears will not be checked.
I see Antigone depart
to the chamber where all men sleep.

ANTIGONE Men of my fathers' land, you see me go
my last journey. My last sight of the sun,
then never again. Death who brings all to sleep
takes me alive to the shore
of the river underground.
Not for me was the marriage hymn, nor will anyone
start the song
at a wedding of mine. Acheron is my mate.

CHORUS With praise as your portion you go
in fame to the vault of the dead.
Untouched by wasting disease,
not paying the price of the sword,
of your own motion you go.
Alone among mortals will you descend
in life to the house of Death.

ANTIGONE Pitiful was the death that stranger died,
our queen once, Tantalus' daughter. The rock
it covered her over, like stubborn ivy it grew.
Still, as she wastes, the rain
and snow companion her.
Pouring down from her mourning eyes comes the water
that soaks the stone.
My own putting to sleep a god has planned like hers.

CHORUS God's child and god she was.
We are born to death.
Yet even in death you will have your fame,
to have gone like a god to your fate,
in living and dying alike.

ANTIGONE Laughter against me now. In the name of our
fathers' gods,

could you not wait till I went? Must affront be thrown in my face?
O city of wealthy men,
I call upon Dirce's spring,
I call upon Thebe's grove in the armored plain,
to be my witnesses, how with no friend's mourning,
by what decree I go to the fresh-made prison-tomb.
Alive to the place of corpses, an alien still,
never at home with the living nor with the dead.

CHORUS You went to the furthest verge
of daring, but there you found
the high foundation of justice, and fell.
Perhaps you are paying your father's pain.

ANTIGONE You speak of my darkest thought, my pitiful father's fame,
spread through all the world, and the doom that haunts our house,
the royal house of Thebes.
My mother's marriage bed.
Destruction where she lay with her husband-son,
my father. These are my parents and I their child.
I go to stay with them. My curse is to die unwed.
My brother, you found your fate when you found your bride,
found it for me as well. Dead, you destroy my life.

CHORUS You showed respect for the dead.
So we for you: but power
is not to be thwarted so.
Your self-sufficiency has brought you down.

ANTIGONE Unwept, no wedding song, unfriended, now I go

the road laid down for me.
No longer shall I see this holy light of the sun.
No friend to bewail my fate.

Creon enters from the palace.

CREON When people sing the dirge for their own deaths
ahead of time, nothing will break them off
if they can hope that this will buy delay.
Take her away at once, and open up
the tomb I spoke of. Leave her there alone.
There let her choose: death, or a buried life.
No stain of guilt upon us in this case,
but she is exiled from our life on earth.

ANTIGONE O tomb, O marriage chamber, hollowed out
house that will watch forever, where I go.
To my own people, who are mostly there;
Persephone has taken them to her.
Last of them all, ill-fated past the rest,
shall I descend, before my course is run.
Still when I get there I may hope to find
I come as a dear friend to my dear father,
to you, my mother, and my brother too.
All three of you have known my hand in death.
I washed your bodies, dressed them for the grave,
poured out the last libation at the tomb.
Last, Polyneices knows the price I pay
for doing final service to his corpse.
And yet the wise will know my choice was right.
Had I had children or their father dead,
I'd let them moulder. I should not have chosen
in such a case to cross the state's decree.
What is the law that lies behind these words?
One husband gone, I might have found another,

or a child from a new man in first child's place,
but with my parents hid away in death,
no brother, ever, could spring up for me.
Such was the law by which I honored you.
But Creon thought the doing was a crime,
a dreadful daring, brother of my heart.
So now he takes and leads me out by force.
No marriage bed, no marriage song for me,
and since no wedding, so no child to rear.
I go, without a friend, struck down by fate,
live to the hollow chambers of the dead.
What divine justice have I disobeyed?
Why, in my misery, look to the gods for help?
Can I call any of them my ally?
I stand convicted of impiety,
the evidence my pious duty done.
Should the gods think that this is righteousness,
in suffering I'll see my error clear.
But if it is the others who are wrong
I wish them no greater punishment than mine.

CHORUS The same tempest of mind
as ever, controls the girl.

CREON Therefore her guards shall regret
the slowness with which they move.

ANTIGONE That word comes close to death.

CREON You are perfectly right in that.

ANTIGONE O town of my fathers in Thebe's land,
O gods of our house.
I am led away at last.
Look, leaders of Thebes,

I am last of your royal line.
Look what I suffer, at whose command,
because I respected the right.

Antigone is led away. The slow procession should begin during the preceding passage.

CHORUS Danaë suffered too.
She went from the light to the brass-built room,
chamber and tomb together. Like you, poor child,
she was of great descent, and more, she held and kept
the seed of the golden rain which was Zeus.
Fate has terrible power.
You cannot escape it by wealth or war.
No fort will keep it out, no ships outrun it.

Remember the angry king,
son of Dryas, who raged at the god and paid,
pent in a rock-walled prison. His bursting wrath
slowly went down. As the terror of madness went,
he learned of his frenzied attack on the god.
Fool, he had tried to stop
the dancing women possessed of God,
the fire of Dionysus, the songs and flutes.

Where the dark rocks divide
sea from sea in Thrace
is Salmydessus whose savage god
beheld the terrible blinding wounds
dealt to Phineus' sons by their father's wife.
Dark the eyes that looked to avenge their mother.
Sharp with her shuttle she struck, and blooded her
hands.

Wasting they wept their fate,
settled when they were born

to Cleopatra, unhappy queen.
She was a princess too, of an ancient house,
reared in the cave of the wild north wind, her father.
Half a goddess but, child, she suffered like you.

Enter, from the side Teiresias, the blind prophet, led by a boy attendant.

TEIRESIAS Elders of Thebes, we two have come one road,
two of us looking through one pair of eyes.
This is the way of walking for the blind.

CREON Teiresias, what news has brought you here?

TEIRESIAS I'll tell you. You in turn must trust the prophet.

CREON I've always been attentive to your counsel.

TEIRESIAS And therefore you have steered this city straight.

CREON So I can say how helpful you have been.

TEIRESIAS But now you are balanced on a razor's edge.

CREON What is it? How I shudder at your words!

TEIRESIAS You'll know, when you hear the signs that I have marked.
I sat where every bird of heaven comes
in my old place of augury, and heard
bird cries I'd never known. They screeched about
goaded by madness, inarticulate.
I marked that they were tearing one another
with claws of murder. I could hear the wing beats.
I was afraid, so straight away I tried

burnt sacrifice upon the flaming altar.
No fire caught my offerings. Slimy ooze
dripped on the ashes, smoked and sputtered there.
Gall burst its bladder, vanished into vapor;
the fat dripped from the bones and would not burn.
These are the omens of the rites that failed,
as my boy here has told me. He's my guide
as I am guide to others.
Why has this sickness struck against the state?
Through your decision.
All of the altars of the town are choked
with leavings of the dogs and birds; their feast
was on that fated, fallen Polyneices.
So the gods will have no offering from us,
not prayer, nor flame of sacrifice. The birds
will not cry out a sound I can distinguish,
gorged with the greasy blood of that dead man.
Think of these things, my son. All men may err,
but error once committed he's no fool
nor yet unfortunate who gives up his stiffness
and cures the trouble he has fallen in.
Stubbornness and stupidity are twins.
Yield to the dead. Why goad him where he lies?
What use to kill the dead a second time?
I speak for your own good. And I am right.
Learning from a wise counselor is not pain
if what he speaks are profitable words.

CREON Old man, you all, like bowmen at a mark,
have bent your bows at me. I've had my share
of seers. I've been an item in your accounts.
Make profit, trade in Lydian silver-gold,
pure gold of India; that's your chief desire.
But you will never cover up that corpse.
Not if the very eagles tear their food

from him, and leave it at the throne of Zeus.
I wouldn't give him up for burial
in fear of that pollution. For I know
no mortal being can pollute the gods.
O old Teiresias, human beings fall;
the clever ones the farthest, when they plead
a shameful case so well in hope of profit.

TEIRESIAS Alas!
What man can tell me, has he thought at all . . .

CREON What hackneyed saw is coming from your lips?

TEIRESIAS How better than all wealth is sound good counsel.

CREON And so is folly worse than anything.

TEIRESIAS And you're infected with that same disease.

CREON I'm reluctant to be uncivil to a seer . . .

TEIRESIAS You're that already. You have said I lie.

CREON Well, the whole crew of seers are money-mad.

TEIRESIAS And the whole tribe of tyrants grab at gain.

CREON Do you realize you are talking to a king?

TEIRESIAS I know. Who helped you save this town you hold?

CREON You're a wise seer, but you love wickedness.

TEIRESIAS You'll bring me to speak the unspeakable, very soon.

CREON Well, speak it out. But do not speak for profit.

TEIRESIAS No, there's no profit in my words for you.

CREON You'd better realize that you can't deliver
my mind, if you should sell it, to the buyer.

TEIRESIAS Know well, the sun will not have rolled its course
many more days, before you come to give
corpse for these corpses, child of your own loins.
For you've confused the upper and lower worlds.
You sent a life to settle in a tomb;
you keep up here that which belongs below
the corpse unburied, robbed of its release.
Not you, nor any god that rules on high
can claim him now.
You rob the nether gods of what is theirs.
So the pursuing horrors lie in wait
to track you down. The Furies sent by Hades
and by all gods will even you with your victims.
Now say that I am bribed! At no far time
shall men and women wail within your house.
And all the cities that you fought in war
whose sons had burial from wild beasts, or dogs,
or birds that brought the stench of your great wrong
back to each hearth, they move against you now.
A bowman, as you said, I send my shafts,
now you have moved me, straight. You'll feel the wound.
Boy, take me home now. Let him spend his rage

on younger men, and learn to calm his tongue,
and keep a better mind than now he does.

Exit.

CHORUS Lord, he has gone. Terrible prophecies!
And since the time when I first grew gray hair
his sayings to the city have been true.

CREON I also know this. And my mind is torn.
To yield is dreadful. But to stand against him—
dreadful to strike my spirit to destruction.

CHORUS Now you must come to counsel, and take advice.

CREON What must I do? Speak, and I shall obey.

CHORUS Go free the maiden from that rocky house.
Bury the dead who lies in readiness.

CREON This is your counsel? You would have me yield?

CHORUS Quick as you can. The gods move very fast
when they bring ruin on misguided men.

CREON How hard, abandonment of my desire.
But I can fight necessity no more.

CHORUS Do it yourself. Leave it to no one else.

CREON I'll go at once. Come, followers, to your work.
You that are here round up the other fellows.
Take axes with you, hurry to that place

that overlooks us.
Now my decision has been overturned
shall I, who bound her, set her free myself.
I've come to fear it's best to hold the laws
of old tradition to the end of life.

Exit.

CHORUS God of the many names, Semele's golden child,
child of Olympian thunder, Italy's lord.
Lord of Eleusis, where all men come
to mother Demeter's plain.
Bacchus, who dwell in Thebes,
by Ismenus' running water,
where wild Bacchic women are at home,
on the soil of the dragon seed.

Seen in the glaring flame, high on the double mount,
with the nymphs of Parnassus at play on the hill,
seen by Kastalia's flowing stream.
You come from the ivied heights,
from green Euboea's shore.
In immortal words we cry
your name, Lord, who watch the ways,
the many ways of Thebes.

This is your city, honored beyond the rest,
the town of your mother's miracle-death.
Now, as we wrestle our grim disease,
come with healing step from Parnassus' slope
or over the moaning sea.

Leader in dance of the fire-pulsing stars,
overseer of the voices of night,
child of Zeus, be manifest,

with due companionship of Maenad maids
whose cry is but your name.

Enter one of those who left with Creon, as Messenger.

MESSENGER Neighbors of Cadmus, and Amphion's house,
there is no kind of state in human life
which I now dare to envy or to blame.
Luck sets it straight, and luck she overturns
the happy or unhappy day by day.
No prophecy can deal with men's affairs.
Creon was envied once, as I believe,
for having saved this city from its foes
and having got full power in this land.
He steered it well. And he had noble sons.
Now everything is gone.
Yes, when a man has lost all happiness,
he's not alive. Call him a breathing corpse.
Be very rich at home. Live as a king.
But once your joy has gone, though these are left
they are smoke's shadow to lost happiness.

CHORUS What is the grief of princes that you bring?

MESSENGER They're dead. The living are responsible.

CHORUS Who died? Who did the murder? Tell us now.

MESSENGER Haemon is gone. One of his kin drew blood.

CHORUS But whose arm struck? His father's or his own?

MESSENGER He killed himself. His blood is on his father.

CHORUS Seer, all too true the prophecy you told!

MESSENGER This is the state of things. Now make your plans.

Enter, from the palace, Eurydice.

CHORUS Eurydice is with us now, I see.
Creon's poor wife. She may have come by chance.
She may have heard something about her son.

EURYDICE I heard your talk as I was coming out
to greet the goddess Pallas with my prayer.
And as I moved the bolts that held the door
I heard of my own sorrow.
I fell back fainting in my women's arms.
But say again just what the news you bring.
I, whom you speak to, have known grief before.

MESSENGER Dear lady, I was there, and I shall tell,
leaving out nothing of the true account.
Why should I make it soft for you with tales
to prove myself a liar? Truth is right.
I followed your husband to the plain's far edge,
where Polyneices' corpse was lying still
unpitied. The dogs had torn him all apart.
We prayed the goddess of all journeyings,
and Pluto, that they turn their wrath to kindness,
we gave the final purifying bath,
then burned the poor remains on new-cut boughs,
and heaped a high mound of his native earth.
Then turned we to the maiden's rocky bed,
death's hollow marriage chamber.
But, still far off, one of us heard a voice
in keen lament by that unblest abode.
He ran and told the master. As Creon came

he heard confusion crying. He groaned and spoke:
"Am I a prophet now, and do I tread
the saddest of all roads I ever trod?
My son's voice crying! Servants, run up close,
stand by the tomb and look, push through the crevice
where we built the pile of rock, right to the entry.
Find out if that is Haemon's voice I hear
or if the gods are tricking me indeed."
We obeyed the order of our mournful master.
In the far corner of the tomb we saw
her, hanging by the neck, caught in a noose
of her own linen veiling.
Haemon embraced her as she hung, and mourned
his bride's destruction, dead and gone below,
his father's actions, the unfated marriage.
When Creon saw him, he groaned terribly,
and went toward him, and called him with lament:
"What have you done, what plan have you caught up,
what sort of suffering is killing you?
Come out, my child, I do beseech you, come!"
The boy looked at him with his angry eyes,
spat in his face and spoke no further word.
He drew his sword, but as his father ran,
he missed his aim. Then the unhappy boy,
in anger at himself, leaned on the blade.
It entered, half its length, into his side.
While he was conscious he embraced the maiden,
holding her gently. Last, he gasped out blood,
red blood on her white cheek.
Corpse on a corpse he lies. He found his marriage.
Its celebration in the halls of Hades.
So he has made it very clear to men
that to reject good counsel is a crime.

Eurydice returns to the house.

CHORUS What do you make of this? The queen has gone
in silence. We know nothing of her mind.

MESSENGER I wonder at her, too. But we can hope
that she has gone to mourn her son within
with her own women, not before the town.
She knows discretion. She will do no wrong.

CHORUS I am not sure. This muteness may portend
as great disaster as a loud lament.

MESSENGER I will go in and see if some deep plan
hides in her heart's wild pain. You may be right.
There can be heavy danger in mute grief.

The Messenger goes into the house. Creon enters with his attendants. They are carrying Haemon's body on a bier.

CHORUS But look, the king draws near.
His own hand brings
the witness of his crime,
the doom he brought on himself.

CREON O crimes of my wicked heart,
harshness bringing death.
You see the killer, you see the kin he killed.
My planning was all unblest.
Son, you have died too soon.
Oh, you have gone away
through my fault, not your own.

CHORUS You have learned justice, though it comes too late.

CREON Yes, I have learned in sorrow. It was a god who struck,

who has weighted my head with disaster; he drove me
to wild strange ways,
his heavy heel on my joy.
O sorrows, sorrows of men.

Re-enter the Messenger, from a side door of the palace.

MESSENGER Master, you hold one sorrow in your hands
but you have more, stored up inside the house.

CREON What further suffering can come on me?

MESSENGER Your wife has died. The dead man's mother in
deed,
poor soul, her wounds are fresh.

CREON Hades, harbor of all,
you have destroyed me now.
Terrible news to hear, horror the tale you tell.
I was dead, and you kill me again.
Boy, did I hear you right?
Did you say the queen was dead,
slaughter on slaughter heaped?

The central doors of the palace begin to open.

CHORUS Now you can see. Concealment is all over.

The doors are open, and the corpse of Eurydice is revealed.

CREON My second sorrow is here. Surely no fate remains
which can strike me again. Just now, I held my son in
my arms.
And now I see her dead.
Woe for the mother and son!

MESSENGER There, by the altar, dying on the sword,
her eyes fell shut. She wept her older son
who died before, and this one. Last of all
she cursed you as the killer of her children.

CREON I am mad with fear. Will no one strike
and kill me with cutting sword?
Sorrowful, soaked in sorrow to the bone!

MESSENGER Yes, for she held you guilty in the death
of him before you, and the elder dead.

CREON How did she die?

MESSENGER Struck home at her own heart
when she had heard of Haemon's suffering.

CREON This is my guilt, all mine. I killed you, I say it
clear.
Servants, take me away, out of the sight of men.
I who am nothing more than nothing now.

CHORUS Your plan is good—if any good is left.
Best to cut short our sorrow.

CREON Let me go, let me go. May death come quick,
bringing my final day.
Oh, let me never see tomorrow's dawn.

CHORUS That is the future's. We must look to now.
What will be is in other hands than ours.

CREON All my desire was in that prayer of mine.

CHORUS Pray not again. No mortal can escape
the doom prepared for him.

CREON Take me away at once, the frantic man who killed
my son, against my meaning. I cannot rest.
My life is warped past cure. My fate has struck me down.

Creon and his attendants enter the house.

CHORUS Our happiness depends
on wisdom all the way.
The gods must have their due.
Great words by men of pride
bring greater blows upon them.
So wisdom comes to the old.

EURIPIDES

MEDEA

Translated by Rex Warner

CHARACTERS

MEDEA, *princess of Colchis and wife of Jason*

JASON, *son of Aeson, king of Iolcus*

TWO CHILDREN, *sons of Medea and Jason*

CREON, *king of Corinth*

AEGEUS, *king of Athens*

NURSE TO MEDEA

TUTOR TO MEDEA'S CHILDREN

MESSENGER

CHORUS OF CORINTHIAN WOMEN

Non-speaking: attendants of Creon; attendants of Jason; servants of Medea

MEDEA

SCENE *In front of Medea's house in Corinth. Enter from the house Medea's nurse.*

NURSE How I wish the Argo never had reached the land
Of Colchis, skimming through the blue Symplegades,
Nor ever had fallen in the glades of Pelion
The smitten fir-tree to furnish oars for the hands
Of heroes who in Pelias' name attempted
The Golden Fleece! For then my mistress Medea
Would not have sailed for the towers of the land of Iolcus,
Her heart on fire with passionate love for Jason;
Nor would she have persuaded the daughters of Pelias
To kill their father, and now be living here
In Corinth with her husband and children. She gave
Pleasure to the people of her land of exile,
And she herself helped Jason in every way.
This is indeed the greatest salvation of all—
For the wife not to stand apart from the husband.
But now there's hatred everywhere. Love is diseased.
For, deserting his own children and my mistress,
Jason has taken a royal wife to his bed,
The daughter of the ruler of this land, Creon.
And poor Medea is slighted, and cries aloud on the
Vows they made to each other, the right hands clasped
In eternal promise. She calls upon the gods to witness
What sort of return Jason has made to her love.
She lies without food and gives herself up to suffering,
Wasting away every moment of the day in tears.

So it has gone since she knew herself slighted by him.
Not stirring an eye, not moving her face from the
ground,
No more than either a rock or surging sea water
She listens when she is given friendly advice.
Except that sometimes she twists back her white neck
and
Moans to herself, calling out on her father's name,
And her land, and her home betrayed when she came
away with
A man who now is determined to dishonor her.
Poor creature, she has discovered by her sufferings
What it means to one not to have lost one's own
country.
She has turned from the children and does not like to see
them.
I am afraid she may think of some dreadful thing,
For her heart is violent. She will never put up with
The treatment she is getting. I know and fear her
Lest she may sharpen a sword and thrust to the heart,
Stealing into the palace where the bed is made,
Or even kill the king and the new-wedded groom,
And thus bring a greater misfortune on herself.
She's a strange woman. I know it won't be easy
To make an enemy of her and come off best.
But here the children come. They have finished playing.
They have no thought at all of their mother's trouble.
Indeed it is not usual for the young to grieve.

Enter from the right the slave who is the tutor to Medea's two small children. The children follow him.

TUTOR You old retainer of my mistress' household,
Why are you standing here all alone in front of the
Gates and moaning to yourself over your misfortune?
Medea could not wish you to leave her alone.

NURSE Old man, and guardian of the children of Jason,
If one is a good servant, it's a terrible thing
When one's master's luck is out; it goes to one's heart.
So I myself have got into such a state of grief
That a longing stole over me to come outside here
And tell the earth and air of my mistress' sorrows.

TUTOR Has the poor lady not yet given up her crying?

NURSE Given up? She's at the start, not halfway through her tears.

TUTOR Poor fool—if I may call my mistress such a name—
How ignorant she is of trouble more to come.

NURSE What do you mean, old man? You needn't fear to speak.

TUTOR Nothing. I take back the words which I used just now.

NURSE Don't, by your beard, hide this from me, your fellow-servant.
If need be, I'll keep quiet about what you tell me.

TUTOR I heard a person saying, while I myself seemed
Not to be paying attention, when I was at the place
Where the old draught-players sit, by the holy fountain,
That Creon, ruler of the land, intends to drive
These children and their mother in exile from Corinth.
But whether what he said is really true or not
I do not know. I pray that it may not be true.

NURSE And will Jason put up with it that his children
Should suffer so, though he's no friend to their mother?

TUTOR Old ties give place to new ones. As for Jason, he
No longer has a feeling for this house of ours.

NURSE It's black indeed for us, when we add new to old
Sorrows before even the present sky has cleared.

TUTOR But you be silent, and keep all this to yourself.
It is not the right time to tell our mistress of it.

NURSE Do you hear, children, what a father he is to you?
I wish he were dead—but no, he is still my master.
Yet certainly he has proved unkind to his dear ones.

TUTOR What's strange in that? Have you only just discovered
That everyone loves himself more than his neighbor?
Some have good reason, others get something out of it.
So Jason neglects his children for the new bride.

NURSE Go indoors, children. That will be the best thing.
And you, keep them to themselves as much as possible.
Don't bring them near their mother in her angry mood.
For I've seen her already blazing her eyes at them
As though she meant some mischief and I am sure that
She'll not stop raging until she has struck at someone.
May it be an enemy and not a friend she hurts!

Medea is heard inside the house.

MEDEA Ah, wretch! Ah, lost in my sufferings,
I wish, I wish I might die.

NURSE What did I say, dear children? Your mother
Frets her heart and frets it to anger.

Run away quickly into the house,
And keep well out of her sight.
Don't go anywhere near, but be careful
Of the wildness and bitter nature
Of that proud mind.
Go now! Run quickly indoors.
It is clear that she soon will put lightning
In that cloud of her cries that is rising
With a passion increasing. Oh, what will she do,
Proud-hearted and not to be checked on her course,
A soul bitten into with wrong?

The Tutor takes the children into the house.

MEDEA Ah, I have suffered
What should be wept for bitterly. I hate you,
Children of a hateful mother. I curse you
And your father. Let the whole house crash.

NURSE Ah, I pity you, you poor creature.
How can your children share in their father's
Wickedness? Why do you hate them? O children,
How much I fear that something may happen!
Great people's tempers are terrible, always
Having their own way, seldom checked,
Dangerous they shift from mood to mood.
How much better to have been accustomed
To live on equal terms with one's neighbors.
I would like to be safe and grow old in a
Humble way. What is moderate sounds best,
Also in practice *is* best for everyone.
Greatness brings no profit to people.
God indeed, when in anger, brings
Greater ruin to great men's houses.

Enter, on the right, a Chorus of Corinthian women. They have come to inquire about Medea and to attempt to console her.

CHORUS I heard the voice, I heard the cry
Of Colchis' wretched daughter.
Tell me, mother, is she not yet
At rest? Within the double gates
Of the court I heard her cry. I am sorry
For the sorrow of this home. Oh, say, what has
happened?

NURSE There is no home. It's over and done with.
Her husband holds fast to his royal wedding,
While she, my mistress, cries out her eyes
There in her room, and takes no warmth from
Any word of any friend.

MEDEA Oh, I wish
That lightning from heaven would split my head open.
Oh, what use have I now for life?
I would find my release in death
And leave hateful existence behind me.

CHORUS O God and Earth and Heaven!
Did you hear what a cry was that
Which the sad wife sings?
Poor foolish one, why should you long
For that appalling rest?
The final end of death comes fast.
No need to pray for that.
Suppose your man gives honor
To another woman's bed.
It often happens. Don't be hurt.
God will be your friend in this.

You must not waste away
Grieving too much for him who shared your bed.

MEDEA Great Themis, lady Artemis, behold
The things I suffer, though I made him promise,
My hateful husband. I pray that I may see him,
Him and his bride and all their palace shattered
For the wrong they dare to do me without cause.
Oh, my father! Oh, my country! In what dishonor
I left you, killing my own brother for it.

NURSE Do you hear what she says, and how she cries
On Themis, the goddess of Promises, and on Zeus,
Whom we believe to be the Keeper of Oaths?
Of this I am sure, that no small thing
Will appease my mistress's anger.

CHORUS Will she come into our presence?
Will she listen when we are speaking
To the words we say?
I wish she might relax her rage
And temper of her heart.
My willingness to help will never
Be wanting to my friends.
But go inside and bring her
Out of the house to us,
And speak kindly to her: hurry,
Before she wrongs her own.
This passion of hers moves to something great.

NURSE I will, but I doubt if I'll manage
To win my mistress over.
But still I'll attempt it to please you.
Such a look she will flash on her servants
If any comes near with a message,

Like a lioness guarding her cubs.
It is right, I think, to consider
Both stupid and lacking in foresight
Those poets of old who wrote songs
For revels and dinners and banquets,
Pleasant sounds for men living at ease;
But none of them all has discovered
How to put to an end with their singing
Or musical instruments grief,
Bitter grief, from which death and disaster
Cheat the hopes of a house. Yet how good
If music could cure men of this! But why raise
To no purpose the voice at a banquet? For *there* is
Already abundance of pleasure for men
With a joy of its own.

The Nurse goes into the house.

CHORUS I heard a shriek that is laden with sorrow.
Shrilling out her hard grief she cries out
Upon him who betrayed both her bed and her marriage.
Wronged, she calls on the gods,
On the justice of Zeus, the oath sworn,
Which brought her away
To the opposite shore of the Greeks
Through the gloomy salt straits to the gateway
Of the salty unlimited sea.

Medea, attended by servants, comes out of the house.

MEDEA Women of Corinth, I have come outside to you
Lest you should be indignant with me; for I know
That many people are overproud, some when alone,
And others when in company. And those who live
Quietly, as I do, get a bad reputation.

For a just judgment is not evident in the eyes
When a man at first sight hates another, before
Learning his character, being in no way injured;
And a foreigner especially must adapt himself.
I'd not approve of even a fellow-countryman
Who by pride and want of manners offends his
  neighbors.
But on me this thing has fallen so unexpectedly,
It has broken my heart. I am finished. I let go
All my life's joy. My friends, I only want to die.
It was everything to me to think well of one man,
And he, my own husband, has turned out wholly vile.
Of all things which are living and can form a judgment
We women are the most unfortunate creatures.
Firstly, with an excess of wealth it is required
For us to buy a husband and take for our bodies
A master; for not to take one is even worse.
And now the question is serious whether we take
A good or bad one; for there is no easy escape
For a woman, nor can she say no to her marriage.
She arrives among new modes of behavior and manners,
And needs prophetic power, unless she has learned at
  home,
How best to manage him who shares the bed with her.
And if we work out all this well and carefully,
And the husband lives with us and lightly bears his yoke,
Then life is enviable. If not, I'd rather die.
A man, when he's tired of the company in his home,
Goes out of the house and puts an end to his boredom
And turns to a friend or companion of his own age.
But we are forced to keep our eyes on one alone.
What they say of us is that we have a peaceful time
Living at home, while they do the fighting in war.
How wrong they are! I would very much rather stand
Three times in the front of battle than bear one child.

Yet what applies to me does not apply to you.
You have a country. Your family home is here.
You enjoy life and the company of your friends.
But I am deserted, a refugee, thought nothing of
By my husband—something he won in a foreign land.
I have no mother or brother, nor any relation
With whom I can take refuge in this sea of woe.
This much then is the service I would beg from you:
If I can find the means or devise any scheme
To pay my husband back for what he has done to me—
Him and his father-in-law and the girl who married him—
Just to keep silent. For in other ways a woman
Is full of fear, defenseless, dreads the sight of cold
Steel; but, when once she is wronged in the matter of love,
No other soul can hold so many thoughts of blood.

CHORUS This I will promise. You are in the right, Medea,
In paying your husband back. I am not surprised at you
For being sad.
But look! I see our king Creon
Approaching. He will tell us of some new plan.

Enter, from the right, Creon, with attendants.

CREON You, with that angry look, so set against your husband,
Medea, I order you to leave my territories
An exile, and take along with you your two children,
And not to waste time doing it. It is my decree,
And I will see it done. I will not return home
Until you are cast from the boundaries of my land.

MEDEA Oh, this is the end for me. I am utterly lost.

Now I am in the full force of the storm of hate
And have no harbor from ruin to reach easily.
Yet still, in spite of it all, I'll ask the question:
What is your reason, Creon, for banishing me?

CREON I am afraid of you—why should I dissemble it?—
Afraid that you may injure my daughter mortally.
Many things accumulate to support my feeling.
You are a clever woman, versed in evil arts,
And are angry at having lost your husband's love.
I hear that you are threatening, so they tell me,
To do something against my daughter and Jason
And me, too. I shall take my precautions first.
I tell you, I prefer to earn your hatred now
Than to be soft-hearted and afterward regret it.

MEDEA This is not the first time, Creon. Often previously
Through being considered clever I have suffered much.
A person of sense ought never to have his children
Brought up to be more clever than the average.
For, apart from cleverness bringing them no profit,
It will make them objects of envy and ill-will.
If you put new ideas before the eyes of fools
They'll think you foolish and worthless into the bargain;
And if you are thought superior to those who have
Some reputation for learning, you will become hated.
I have some knowledge myself of how this happens;
For being clever, I find that some will envy me,
Others object to me. Yet all my cleverness
Is not so much.
Well, then, are you frightened, Creon,
That I should harm you? There is no need. It is not
My way to transgress the authority of a king.
How have you injured me? You gave your daughter away

To the man you wanted. Oh, certainly I hate
My husband, but you, I think, have acted wisely;
Nor do I grudge it you that your affairs go well.
May the marriage be a lucky one! Only let me
Live in this land. For even though I have been wronged,
I will not raise my voice, but submit to my betters.

CREON What you say sounds gentle enough. Still in my heart
I greatly dread that you are plotting some evil,
And therefore I trust you even less than before.
A sharp-tempered woman, or, for that matter, a man,
Is easier to deal with than the clever type
Who holds her tongue. No. You must go. No need for more
Speeches. The thing is fixed. By no manner of means
Shall you, an enemy of mine, stay in my country.

MEDEA I beg you. By your knees, by your new-wedded girl.

CREON Your words are wasted. You will never persuade me.

MEDEA Will you drive me out, and give no heed to my prayers?

CREON I will, for I love my family more than you.

MEDEA O my country! How bitterly now I remember you!

CREON I love my country too—next after my children.

MEDEA Oh, what an evil to men is passionate love!

CREON That would depend on the luck that goes along with it.

MEDEA O God, do not forget who is the cause of this!

CREON Go. It is no use. Spare me the pain of forcing you.

MEDEA I'm spared no pain. I lack no pain to be spared me.

CREON Then you'll be removed by force by one of my men.

MEDEA No, Creon, not that! But do listen, I beg you.

CREON Woman, you seem to want to create a disturbance.

MEDEA I *will* go into exile. *This* is not what I beg for.

CREON Why then this violence and clinging to my hand?

MEDEA Allow me to remain here just for this one day,
So I may consider where to live in my exile,
And look for support for my children, since their father
Chooses to make no kind of provision for them.
Have pity on them! You have children of your own.
It is natural for you to look kindly on them.
For myself I do not mind if I go into exile.
It is the children being in trouble that I mind.

CREON There is nothing tyrannical about my nature,
And by showing mercy I have often been the loser.
Even now I know that I am making a mistake.
All the same you shall have your will. But this I tell you,
That if the light of heaven tomorrow shall see you,
You and your children in the confines of my land,

You die. This word I have spoken is firmly fixed.
But now, if you must stay, stay for this day alone.
For in it you can do none of the things I fear.

Exit Creon with his attendants.

CHORUS Oh, unfortunate one! Oh, cruel!
Where will you turn? Who will help you?
What house or what land to preserve you
From ill can you find?
Medea, a god has thrown suffering
Upon you in waves of despair.

MEDEA Things have gone badly every way. No doubt of that
But not these things this far, and don't imagine so.
There are still trials to come for the new-wedded pair,
And for their relations pain that will mean something.
Do you think that I would ever have fawned on that man
Unless I had some end to gain or profit in it?
I would not even have spoken or touched him with my hands.
But he has got to such a pitch of foolishness
That, though he could have made nothing of all my plans
By exiling me, he has given me this one day
To stay here, and in this I will make dead bodies
Of three of my enemies—father, the girl, and my husband.
I have many ways of death which I might suit to them,
And do not know, friends, which one to take in hand;
Whether to set fire underneath their bridal mansion,
Or sharpen a sword and thrust it to the heart,

Stealing into the palace where the bed is made.
There is just one obstacle to this. If I am caught
Breaking into the house and scheming against it,
I shall die, and give my enemies cause for laughter.
It is best to go by the straight road, the one in which
I am most skilled, and make away with them by poison.
So be it then.
And now suppose them dead. What town will receive
me?
What friend will offer me a refuge in his land,
Or the guaranty of his house and save my own life?
There is none. So I must wait a little time yet,
And if some sure defense should then appear for me,
In craft and silence I will set about this murder.
But if my fate should drive me on without help,
Even though death is certain, I will take the sword
Myself and kill, and steadfastly advance to crime.
It shall not be—I swear it by her, my mistress,
Whom most I honor and have chosen as partner,
Hecate, who dwells in the recesses of my hearth—
That any man shall be glad to have injured me.
Bitter I will make their marriage for them and mournful,
Bitter the alliance and the driving me out of the land.
Ah, come, Medea, in your plotting and scheming
Leave nothing untried of all those things which you
know.
Go forward to the dreadful act. The test has come
For resolution. You see how you are treated. Never
Shall you be mocked by Jason's Corinthian wedding,
Whose father was noble, whose grandfather Helius.
You have the skill. What is more, you were born a
woman,
And women, though most helpless in doing good deeds,
Are of every evil the cleverest of contrivers.

CHORUS Flow backward to your sources, sacred rivers,
And let the world's great order be reversed.
It is the thoughts of *men* that are deceitful,
Their pledges that are loose.
Story shall now turn my condition to a fair one,
Women are paid their due.
No more shall evil-sounding fame be theirs.

Cease now, you muses of the ancient singers,
To tell the tale of my unfaithfulness;
For not on us did Phoebus, lord of music,
Bestow the lyre's divine
Power, for otherwise I should have sung an answer
To the other sex. Long time
Has much to tell of us, and much of them.

You sailed away from your father's home,
With a heart on fire you passed
The double rocks of the sea.
And now in a foreign country
You have lost your rest in a widowed bed,
And are driven forth, a refugee
In dishonor from the land.

Good faith has gone, and no more remains
In great Greece a sense of shame.
It has flown away to the sky.
No father's house for a haven
Is at hand for you now, and another queen
Of your bed has dispossessed you and
Is mistress of your home.

Enter Jason, with attendants.

JASON This is not the first occasion that I have noticed

How hopeless it is to deal with a stubborn temper.
For, with reasonable submission to our ruler's will,
You might have lived in this land and kept your home.
As it is you are going to be exiled for your loose
speaking.
Not that I mind myself. You are free to continue
Telling everyone that Jason is a worthless man.
But as to your talk about the king, consider
Yourself most lucky that exile is your punishment.
I, for my part, have always tried to calm down
The anger of the king, and wished you to remain.
But you will not give up your folly, continually
Speaking ill of him, and so you are going to be banished.
All the same, and in spite of your conduct, I'll not desert
My friends, but have come to make some provision for
you,
So that you and the children may not be penniless
Or in need of anything in exile. Certainly
Exile brings many troubles with it. And even
If you hate me, I cannot think badly of you.

MEDEA O coward in every way—that is what I call you,
With bitterest reproach for your lack of manliness,
You have come, you, my worst enemy, have come to
me!
It is not an example of overconfidence
Or of boldness thus to look your friends in the face,
Friends you have injured—no, it is the worst of all
Human diseases, shamelessness. But you did well
To come, for I can speak ill of you and lighten
My heart, and you will suffer while you are listening.
And first I will begin from what happened first.
I saved your life, and every Greek knows I saved it
Who was a shipmate of yours aboard the Argo,

When you were sent to control the bulls that breathed fire
And yoke them, and when you would sow that deadly field.
Also that snake, who encircled with his many folds
The Golden Fleece and guarded it and never slept,
I killed, and so gave you the safety of the light.
And I myself betrayed my father and my home,
And came with you to Pelias' land of Iolcus.
And then, showing more willingness to help than wisdom,
I killed him, Pelias, with a most dreadful death
At his own daughters' hands, and took away your fear.
This is how I behaved to you, you wretched man,
And you forsook me, took another bride to bed,
Though you had children; for, if that had not been,
You would have had an excuse for another wedding.
Faith in your word has gone. Indeed, I cannot tell
Whether you think the gods whose names you swore by then
Have ceased to rule and that new standards are set up,
Since you must know you have broken your word to me.
O my right hand, and the knees which you often clasped
In supplication, how senselessly I am treated
By this bad man, and how my hopes have missed their mark!
Come, I will share my thoughts as though you were a friend—
You! Can I think that you would ever treat me well?
But I will do it, and these questions will make you
Appear the baser. Where am I to go? To my father's?
Him I betrayed and his land when I came with you.
To Pelias' wretched daughters? What a fine welcome
They would prepare for me who murdered their father!

For this is my position—hated by my friends
At home, I have, in kindness to you, made enemies
Of others whom there was no need to have injured.
And how happy among Greek women you have made
me
On your side for all this! A distinguished husband
I have—for breaking promises. When in misery
I am cast out of the land and go into exile,
Quite without friends and all alone with my children,
That will be a fine shame for the new-wedded groom,
For his children to wander as beggars and she who saved
him.
O God, you have given to mortals a sure method
Of telling the gold that is pure from the counterfeit;
Why is there no mark engraved upon men's bodies,
By which we could know the true ones from the false
ones?

CHORUS It is a strange form of anger, difficult to cure,
When two friends turn upon each other in hatred.

JASON As for me, it seems I must be no bad speaker.
But, like a man who has a good grip of the tiller,
Reef up his sail, and so run away from under
This mouthing tempest, woman, of your bitter tongue.
Since you insist on building up your kindness to me,
My view is that Cypris was alone responsible
Of men and gods for the preserving of my life.
You are clever enough—but really I need not enter
Into the story of how it was love's inescapable
Power that compelled you to keep my person safe.
On this I will not go into too much detail.
In so far as you helped me, you did well enough.
But on this question of saving me, I can prove
You have certainly got from me more than you gave.

Firstly, instead of living among barbarians,
You inhabit a Greek land and understand our ways,
How to live by law instead of the sweet will of force.
And all the Greeks considered you a clever woman.
You were honored for it; while, if you were living at
The ends of the earth, nobody would have heard of you.
For my part, rather than stores of gold in my house
Or power to sing even sweeter songs than Orpheus,
I'd choose the fate that made me a distinguished man.
There is my reply to your story of my labors.
Remember it was you who started the argument.
Next for your attack on my wedding with the princess:
Here I will prove that, first, it was a clever move,
Secondly, a wise one, and, finally, that I made it
In your best interests and the children's. Please keep
calm.
When I arrived here from the land of Iolcus,
Involved, as I was, in every kind of difficulty,
What luckier chance could I have come across than this,
An exile to marry the daughter of the king?
It was not—the point that seems to upset you—that I
Grew tired of your bed and felt the need of a new bride;
Nor with any wish to outdo your number of children.
We have enough already. I am quite content.
But—this was the main reason—that we might live
well,
And not be short of anything. I know that all
A man's friends leave him stone-cold if he becomes
poor.
Also that I might bring my children up worthily
Of my position, and, by producing more of them
To be brothers of yours, we would draw the families
Together and all be happy. You need no children.
And it pays me to do good to those I have now

By having others. Do you think this a bad plan?
You wouldn't if the love question hadn't upset you.
But you women have got into such a state of mind
That, if your life at night is good, you think you have
Everything; but, if in that quarter things go wrong,
You will consider your best and truest interests
Most hateful. It would have been better far for men
To have got their children in some other way, and women
Not to have existed. Then life would have been good.

CHORUS Jason, though you have made this speech of yours look well,
Still I think, even though others do not agree,
You have betrayed your wife and are acting badly.

MEDEA Surely in many ways I hold different views
From others, for I think that the plausible speaker
Who is a villain deserves the greatest punishment.
Confident in his tongue's power to adorn evil,
He stops at nothing. Yet he is not really wise.
As in your case. There is no need to put on the airs
Of a clever speaker, for one word will lay you flat.
If you were not a coward, you would not have married
Behind my back, but discussed it with me first.

JASON And you, no doubt, would have furthered the proposal,
If I had told you of it, you who even now
Are incapable of controlling your bitter temper.

MEDEA It was not that. No, you thought it was not respectable
As you got on in years to have a foreign wife.

JASON Make sure of this: it was not because of a woman
I made the royal alliance in which I now live,
But, as I said before, I wished to preserve you
And breed a royal progeny to be brothers
To the children I have now, a sure defense to us.

MEDEA Let me have no happy fortune that brings pain with it,
Or prosperity which is upsetting to the mind!

JASON Change your ideas of what you want, and show more sense.
Do not consider painful what is good for you,
Nor, when you are lucky, think yourself unfortunate.

MEDEA You can insult me. You have somewhere to turn to.
But I shall go from this land into exile, friendless.

JASON It was what you chose yourself. Don't blame others for it.

MEDEA And how did I choose it? Did I betray my husband?

JASON You called down wicked curses on the king's family.

MEDEA A curse, that is what I am become to your house too.

JASON I do not propose to go into all the rest of it;
But, if you wish for the children or for yourself
In exile to have some of my money to help you,
Say so, for I am prepared to give with open hand,

Or to provide you with introductions to my friends
Who will treat you well. You are a fool if you do not
Accept this. Cease your anger and you will profit.

MEDEA I shall never accept the favors of friends of yours,
Nor take a thing from you, so you need not offer it.
There is no benefit in the gifts of a bad man.

JASON Then, in any case, I call the gods to witness that
I wish to help you and the children in every way,
But you refuse what is good for you. Obstinately
You push away your friends. You are sure to suffer for it.

MEDEA Go! No doubt you hanker for your virginal bride,
And are guilty of lingering too long out of her house.
Enjoy your wedding. But perhaps—with the help of God—
You will make the kind of marriage that you will regret.

Jason goes out with his attendants.

CHORUS When love is in excess
It brings a man no honor
Nor any worthiness.
But if in moderation Cypris comes,
There is no other power at all so gracious.
O goddess, never on me let loose the unerring
Shaft of your bow in the poison of desire.

Let my heart be wise.
It is the gods' best gift.
On me let mighty Cypris
Inflict no wordy wars or restless anger
To urge my passion to a different love.

But with discernment may she guide women's
    weddings,
Honoring most what is peaceful in the bed.

O country and home,
Never, never may I be without you,
Living the hopeless life,
Hard to pass through and painful,
Most pitiable of all.
Let death first lay me low and death
Free me from this daylight.
There is no sorrow above
The loss of a native land.

I have seen it myself,
Do not tell of a secondhand story.
Neither city nor friend
Pitied you when you suffered
The worst of sufferings.
O let him die ungraced whose heart
Will not reward his friends,
Who cannot open an honest mind
No friend will he be of mine.

Enter Aegeus, king of Athens, an old friend of Medea.

AEGEUS Medea, greeting! This is the best introduction
Of which men know for conversation between friends.

MEDEA Greeting to you too, Aegeus, son of King
    Pandion.
Where have you come from to visit this country's soil?

AEGEUS I have just left the ancient oracle of Phoebus.

MEDEA And why did you go to earth's prophetic center?

AEGEUS I went to inquire how children might be born to me.

MEDEA Is it so? Your life still up to this point is childless?

AEGEUS Yes. By the fate of some power we have no children.

MEDEA Have you a wife, or is there none to share your bed?

AEGEUS There is. Yes, I am joined to my wife in marriage.

MEDEA And what did Phoebus say to you about children?

AEGEUS Words too wise for a mere man to guess their meaning.

MEDEA Is it proper for me to be told the god's reply?

AEGEUS It is. For sure what is needed is cleverness.

MEDEA Then what was his message? Tell me, if I may hear.

AEGEUS I am not to loosen the hanging foot of the wine-skin . . .

MEDEA Until you have done something, or reached some country?

AEGEUS Until I return again to my hearth and house.

MEDEA And for what purpose have you journeyed to this land?

AEGEUS There is a man called Pittheus, king of Troezen.

MEDEA A son of Pelops, they say, a most righteous man.

AEGEUS With him I wish to discuss the reply of the god.

MEDEA Yes. He is wise and experienced in such matters.

AEGEUS And to me also the dearest of all my spear-friends.

MEDEA Well, I hope you have good luck, and achieve your will.

AEGEUS But why this downcast eye of yours, and this pale cheek?

MEDEA O Aegeus, my husband has been the worst of all to me.

AEGEUS What do you mean? Say clearly what has caused this grief.

MEDEA Jason wrongs me, though I have never injured him.

AEGEUS What has he done? Tell me about it in clearer words.

MEDEA He has taken a wife to his house, supplanting me.

AEGEUS Surely he would not dare to do a thing like that.

MEDEA Be sure he has. Once dear, I now am slighted by him.

AEGEUS Did he fall in love? Or is he tired of your love?

MEDEA He was greatly in love, this traitor to his friends.

AEGEUS Then let him go, if, as you say, he is so bad.

MEDEA A passionate love—for an alliance with the king.

AEGEUS And who gave him his wife? Tell me the rest of it.

MEDEA It was Creon, he who rules this land of Corinth.

AEGEUS Indeed, Medea, your grief was understandable.

MEDEA I am ruined. And there is more to come: I am banished.

AEGEUS Banished? By whom? Here you tell me of a new wrong.

MEDEA Creon drives me an exile from the land of Corinth.

AEGEUS Does Jason consent? I cannot approve of this.

MEDEA He pretends not to, but he will put up with it.
Ah, Aegeus, I beg and beseech you, by your beard
And by your knees, I am making myself your suppliant,
Have pity on me, have pity on your poor friend,
And do not let me go into exile desolate,
But receive me in your land and at your very hearth.
So may your love, with God's help, lead to the bearing

Of children, and so may you yourself die happy.
You do not know what a chance you have come on here.
I will end your childlessness, and I will make you able
To beget children. The drugs I know can do this.

AEGEUS For many reasons, woman, I am anxious to do
This favor for you. First, for the sake of the gods,
And then for the birth of children which you promise,
For in that respect I am entirely at my wits' end.
But this is my position: if you reach my land,
I, being in my rights, will try to befriend you.
But this much I must warn you of beforehand:
I shall not agree to take you out of this country;
But if you by yourself can reach my house, then you
Shall stay there safely. To none will I give you up
But from this land you must make your escape yourself,
For I do not wish to incur blame from my friends.

MEDEA It shall be so. But, if I might have a pledge from you
For this, then I would have from you all I desire.

AEGEUS Do you not trust me? What is it rankles with you?

MEDEA I trust you, yes. But the house of Pelias hates me,
And so does Creon. If you are bound by this oath,
When they try to drag me from your land, you will not
Abandon me; but if our pact is only words,
With no oath to the gods, you will be lightly armed,
Unable to resist their summons. I am weak,
While they have wealth to help them and a royal house.

AEGEUS You show much foresight for such negotiations.
Well, if you will have it so, I will not refuse.

For, both on my side this will be the safest way
To have some excuse to put forward to your enemies,
And for you it is more certain. You may name the gods.

MEDEA Swear by the plain of Earth, and Helius, father
Of my father, and name together all the gods. . . .

AEGEUS That I will act or not act in what way? Speak.

MEDEA That you yourself will never cast me from your land,
Nor, if any of my enemies should demand me,
Will you, in your life, willingly hand me over.

AEGEUS I swear by the Earth, by the holy light of Helius,
By all the gods, I will abide by this you say.

MEDEA Enough. And, if you fail, what shall happen to you?

AEGEUS What comes to those who have no regard for heaven.

MEDEA Go on your way. Farewell. For I am satisfied.
And I will reach your city as soon as I can,
Having done the deed I have to do and gained my end.

Aegeus goes out.

CHORUS May Hermes, god of travelers,
Escort you, Aegeus, to your home!
And may you have the things you wish
So eagerly; for you
Appear to me to be a generous man.

MEDEA God, and God's daughter, justice, and light of
Helius!
Now, friends, has come the time of my triumph over
My enemies, and now my foot is on the road.
Now I am confident they will pay the penalty.
For this man, Aegeus, has been like a harbor to me
In all my plans just where I was most distressed.
To him I can fasten the cable of my safety
When I have reached the town and fortress of Pallas.
And now I shall tell to you the whole of my plan.
Listen to these words that are not spoken idly.
I shall send one of my servants to find Jason
And request him to come once more into my sight.
And when he comes, the words I'll say will be soft ones.
I'll say that I agree with him, that I approve
The royal wedding he has made, betraying me.
I'll say it was profitable, an excellent idea.
But I shall beg that my children may remain here:
Not that I would leave in a country that hates me
Children of mine to feel their enemies' insults,
But that by a trick I may kill the king's daughter.
For I will send the children with gifts in their hands
To carry to the bride, so as not to be banished—
A finely woven dress and a golden diadem.
And if she takes them and wears them upon her skin
She and all who touch the girl will die in agony;
Such poison will I lay upon the gifts I send.
But there, however, I must leave that account paid.
I weep to think of what a deed I have to do
Next after that; for I shall kill my own children.
My children, there is none who can give them safety.
And when I have ruined the whole of Jason's house,
I shall leave the land and flee from the murder of my
Dear children, and I shall have done a dreadful deed.
For it is not bearable to be mocked by enemies.

So it must happen. What profit have I in life?
I have no land, no home, no refuge from my pain.
My mistake was made the time I left behind me
My father's house, and trusted the words of a Greek,
Who, with heaven's help, will pay me the price for that.
For those children he had from me he will never
See alive again, nor will he on his new bride
Beget another child, for she is to be forced
To die a most terrible death by these my poisons.
Let no one think me a weak one, feeble-spirited,
A stay-at-home, but rather just the opposite,
One who can hurt my enemies and help my friends;
For the lives of such persons are most remembered.

CHORUS Since you have shared the knowledge of your plan with us,
I both wish to help you and support the normal
Ways of mankind, and tell you not to do this thing.

MEDEA I can do no other thing. It is understandable
For you to speak thus. You have not suffered as I have.

CHORUS But can you have the heart to kill your flesh and blood?

MEDEA Yes, for this is the best way to wound my husband.

CHORUS And you, too. Of women you will be most unhappy.

MEDEA So it must be. No compromise is possible.

She turns to the Nurse.

Go, you, at once, and tell Jason to come to me.
You I employ on all affairs of greatest trust.
Say nothing of these decisions which I have made,
If you love your mistress, if you were born a woman.

CHORUS From of old the children of Erechtheus are
Splendid, the sons of blessed gods. They dwell
In Athens' holy and unconquered land,
Where famous Wisdom feeds them and they pass gaily
Always through that most brilliant air where once, they say,
That golden Harmony gave birth to the nine
Pure Muses of Pieria.

And beside the sweet flow of Cephisus' stream,
Where Cypris sailed, they say, to draw the water,
And mild soft breezes breathed along her path,
And on her hair were flung the sweet-smelling garlands
Of flowers of roses by the Lovers, the companions
Of Wisdom, her escort, the helpers of men
In every kind of excellence.

How then can these holy rivers
Or this holy land love you,
Or the city find you a home,
You, who will kill your children,
You, not pure with the rest?
Oh, think of the blow at your children
And think of the blood that you shed.
Oh, over and over I beg you,
By your knees I beg you do not
Be the murderess of your babes!

Oh, where will you find the courage
Or the skill of hand and heart,

When you set yourself to attempt
A deed so dreadful to do?
How, when you look upon them,
Can you tearlessly hold the decision
For murder? You will not be able,
When your children fall down and implore you,
You will not be able to dip
Steadfast your hand in their blood.

Enter Jason with attendants.

JASON I have come at your request. Indeed, although you are
Bitter against me, this you shall have: I will listen
To what new thing you want, woman, to get from me.

MEDEA Jason, I beg you to be forgiving toward me
For what I said. It is natural for you to bear with
My temper, since we have had much love together.
I have talked with myself about this and I have
Reproached myself. "Fool" I said, "why am I so mad?
Why am I set against those who have planned wisely?
Why make myself an enemy of the authorities
And of my husband, who does the best thing for me
By marrying royalty and having children who
Will be as brothers to my own? What is wrong with me?
Let me give up anger, for the gods are kind to me.
Have I not children, and do I not know that we
In exile from our country must be short of friends?"
When I considered this I saw that I had shown
Great lack of sense, and that my anger was foolish.
Now I agree with you. I think that you are wise
In having this other wife as well as me, and I
Was mad. I should have helped you in these plans of yours,

Have joined in the wedding, stood by the marriage bed,
Have taken pleasure in attendance on your bride.
But we women are what we are—perhaps a little
Worthless; and you men must not be like us in this,
Nor be foolish in return when we are foolish.
Now, I give in, and admit that then I was wrong.
I have come to a better understanding now.

She turns toward the house.

Children, come here, my children, come outdoors to us!
Welcome your father with me, and say good-bye to him,
And with your mother, who just now was his enemy,
Join again in making friends with him who loves us.

Enter the children, attended by the Tutor.

We have made peace, and all our anger is over.
Take hold of his right hand—O God, I am thinking
Of something which may happen in the secret future.
O children, will you just so, after a long life,
Hold out your loving arms at the grave? O children,
How ready to cry I am, how full of foreboding!
I am ending at last this quarrel with your father,
And, look my soft eyes have suddenly filled with tears.

CHORUS And the pale tears have started also in my eyes.
Oh, may the trouble not grow worse than now it is!

JASON I approve of what you say. And I cannot blame you
Even for what you said before. It is natural
For a woman to be wild with her husband when he
Goes in for secret love. But now your mind has turned

To better reasoning. In the end you have come to
The right decision, like the clever woman you are.
And of you, children, your father is taking care.
He has made, with God's help, ample provision for you.
For I think that a time will come when you will be
The leading people in Corinth with your brothers.
You must grow up. As to the future, your father
And those of the gods who love him will deal with that.
I want to see you, when you have become young men,
Healthy and strong, better men than my enemies.
Medea, why are your eyes all wet with pale tears?
Why is your cheek so white and turned away from me?
Are not these words of mine pleasing for you to hear?

MEDEA It is nothing. I was thinking about these children.

JASON You must be cheerful. I shall look after them well.

MEDEA I will be. It is not that I distrust your words,
But a woman is a frail thing, prone to crying.

JASON But why then should you grieve so much for these children?

MEDEA I am their mother. When you prayed that they might live
I felt unhappy to think that these things will be.
But come, I have said something of the things I meant
To say to you, and now I will tell you the rest.
Since it is the king's will to banish me from here—
And for me, too, I know that this is the best thing,
Not to be in your way by living here or in
The king's way, since they think me ill-disposed to them—

I then am going into exile from this land;
But do you, so that you may have the care of them,
Beg Creon that the children may not be banished.

JASON I doubt if I'll succeed, but still I'll attempt it.

MEDEA Then you must tell your wife to beg from her father
That the children may be reprieved from banishment.

JASON I will, and with her I shall certainly succeed.

MEDEA If she is like the rest of us women, you will.
And I, too, will take a hand with you in this business,
For I will send her some gifts which are far fairer,
I am sure of it, than those which now are in fashion,
A finely woven dress and a golden diadem,
And the children shall present them. Quick, let one of you
Servants bring here to me that beautiful dress.

One of her attendants goes into the house.

She will be happy not in one way, but in a hundred,
Having so fine a man as you to share her bed,
And with this beautiful dress which Helius of old,
My father's father, bestowed on his descendants.

Enter attendant carrying the poisoned dress and diadem.

There, children, take these wedding presents in your hands.
Take them to the royal princess, the happy bride,
And give them to her. She will not think little of them.

JASON No, don't be foolish, and empty your hands of these.
Do you think the palace is short of dresses to wear?
Do you think there is no gold there? Keep them, don't give them
Away. If my wife considers me of any value,
She will think more of me than money, I am sure of it.

MEDEA No, let me have my way. They say the gods themselves
Are moved by gifts, and gold does more with men than words.
Hers is the luck, her fortune that which God blesses;
She is young and a princess; but for my children's reprieve
I would give my very life, and not gold only.
Go children, go together to that rich palace,
Be suppliants to the new wife of your father,
My lady, beg her not to let you be banished.
And give her the dress—for this is of great importance,
That she should take the gift into her hand from yours.
Go, quick as you can. And bring your mother good news
By your success of those things which she longs to gain.

Jason goes out with his attendants, followed by the Tutor and the children carrying the poisoned gifts.

CHORUS Now there is no hope left for the children's lives.
Now there is none. They are walking already to murder.
The bride, poor bride, will accept the curse of the gold,
Will accept the bright diadem.
Around her yellow hair she will set that dress
Of death with her own hands.

The grace and the perfume and glow of the golden robe
Will charm her to put them upon her and wear the
wreath,
And now her wedding will be with the dead below,
Into such a trap she will fall,
Poor thing, into such a fate of death and never
Escape from under that curse.

You, too, O wretched bridegroom, making your match
with kings,
You do not see that you bring
Destruction on your children and on her,
Your wife, a fearful death.
Poor soul, what a fall is yours!

In your grief, too, I weep, mother of little children,
You who will murder your own,
In vengeance for the loss of married love
Which Jason has betrayed
As he lives with another wife.

Enter the Tutor with the children.

TUTOR Mistress, I tell you that these children are
reprieved,
And the royal bride has been pleased to take in her hands
Your gifts. In that quarter the children are secure.
But come,
Why do you stand confused when you are fortunate?
Why have you turned round with your cheek away
from me?
Are not these words of mine pleasing for you to hear?

MEDEA Oh! I am lost!

TUTOR That word is not in harmony with my tidings.

MEDEA I am lost, I am lost!

TUTOR Am I in ignorance telling you
Of some disaster, and not the good news I thought?

MEDEA You have told what you have told. I do not blame you.

TUTOR Why then this downcast eye, and this weeping of tears?

MEDEA Oh, I am forced to weep, old man. The gods and I,
I in a kind of madness, have contrived all this.

TUTOR Courage! You, too, will be brought home by your children.

MEDEA Ah, before that happens I shall bring others home.

TUTOR Others before you have been parted from their children.
Mortals must bear in resignation their ill luck.

MEDEA That is what I shall do. But go inside the house,
And do for the children your usual daily work.

The Tutor goes into the house. Medea turns to her children.

O children, O my children, you have a city,
You have a home, and you can leave me behind you,
And without your mother you may live there forever.
But I am going in exile to another land
Before I have seen you happy and taken pleasure in you,

Before I have dressed your brides and made your marriage beds
And held up the torch at the ceremony of wedding.
Oh, what a wretch I am in this my self-willed thought!
What was the purpose, children, for which I reared you?
For all my travail and wearing myself away?
They were sterile, those pains I had in the bearing of you.
Oh, surely once the hopes in you I had, poor me,
Were high ones: you would look after me in old age,
And when I died would deck me well with your own hands;
A thing which all would have done. Oh, but now it is gone,
That lovely thought. For, once I am left without you,
Sad will be the life I'll lead and sorrowful for me.
And you will never see your mother again with
Your dear eyes, gone to another mode of living.
Why, children, do you look upon me with your eyes?
Why do you smile so sweetly that last smile of all?
Oh, Oh, what can I do? My spirit has gone from me,
Friends, when I saw that bright look in the children's eyes.
I cannot bear to do it. I renounce my plans
I had before. I'll take my children away from
This land. Why should I hurt their father with the pain
They feel, and suffer twice as much of pain myself?
No, no, I will not do it. I renounce my plans.
Ah, what is wrong with me? Do I want to let go
My enemies unhurt and be laughed at for it?
I must face this thing. Oh, but what a weak woman
Even to admit to my mind these soft arguments.
Children, go into the house. And he whom law forbids
To stand in attendance at my sacrifices,
Let him see to it. I shall not mar my handiwork.
Oh! Oh!

Do not, O my heart, you must not do these things!
Poor heart, let them go, have pity upon the children.
If they live with you in Athens they will cheer you.
No! By Hell's avenging furies it shall not be—
This shall never be, that I should suffer my children
To be the prey of my enemies' insolence.
Every way is it fixed. The bride will not escape.
No, the diadem is now upon her head, and she,
The royal princess, is dying in the dress, I know it.
But—for it is the most dreadful of roads for me
To tread, and them I shall send on a more dreadful still—
I wish to speak to the children.

She calls the children to her.

Come, children, give
Me your hands, give your mother your hands to kiss
them.
Oh, the dear hands, and oh, how dear are these lips to
me,
And the generous eyes and the bearing of my children!
I wish you happiness, but not here in this world.
What is here your father took. Oh, how good to hold
you!
How delicate the skin, how sweet the breath of children!
Go, go! I am no longer able, no longer
To look upon you. I am overcome by sorrow.

The children go into the house.

I know indeed what evil I intend to do,
But stronger than all my afterthoughts is my fury,
Fury that brings upon mortals the greatest evils.

She goes out to the right, toward the royal palace.

CHORUS Often before
I have gone through more subtle reasons,
And have come upon questionings greater
Than a woman should strive to search out.
But we too have a goddess to help us
And accompany us into wisdom.
Not all of us. Still you will find
Among many women a few,
And our sex is not without learning.
This I say, that those who have never
Had children, who know nothing of it,
In happiness have the advantage
Over those who are parents.
The childless, who never discover
Whether children turn out as a good thing
Or as something to cause pain, are spared
Many troubles in lacking this knowledge.
And those who have in their homes
The sweet presence of children, I see that their lives
Are all wasted away by their worries.
First they must think how to bring them up well and
How to leave them something to live on.
And then after this whether all their toil
Is for those who will turn out good or bad,
Is still an unanswered question.
And of one more trouble, the last of all,
That is common to mortals I tell.
For suppose you have found them enough for their living,
Suppose that the children have grown into youth
And have turned out good, still, if God so wills it,
Death will away with your children's bodies,
And carry them off into Hades.
What is our profit, then, that for the sake of
Children the gods should pile upon mortals

After all else
This most terrible grief of all?

Enter Medea, from the spectators' right.

MEDEA Friends, I can tell you that for long I have waited
For the event. I stare toward the place from where
The news will come. And now, see one of Jason's servants
Is on his way here, and that labored breath of his
Shows he has tidings for us, and evil tidings.

Enter, also from the right, the Messenger.

MESSENGER Medea, you who have done such a dreadful thing,
So outrageous, run for your life, take what you can,
A ship to bear you hence or chariot on land.

MEDEA And what is the reason deserves such flight as this?

MESSENGER She is dead, only just now, the royal princess,
And Creon dead, too, her father, by your poisons.

MEDEA The finest words you have spoken. Now and hereafter
I shall count you among my benefactors and friends.

MESSENGER What! Are you right in the mind? Are you not mad,
Woman? The house of the king is outraged by you.
Do you enjoy it? Not afraid of such doings?

MEDEA To what you say I on my side have something too

To say in answer. Do not be in a hurry, friend,
But speak. How did they die? You will delight me twice
As much again if you say they died in agony.

MESSENGER When those two children, born of you, had entered in,
Their father with them, and passed into the bride's house,
We were pleased, we slaves who were distressed by your wrongs.
All through the house we were talking of but one thing,
How you and your husband had made up your quarrel.
Some kissed the children's hands and some their yellow hair,
And I myself was so full of my joy that I
Followed the children into the women's quarters.
Our mistress, whom we honor now instead of you,
Before she noticed that your two children were there,
Was keeping her eye fixed eagerly on Jason.
Afterwards, however, she covered up her eyes,
Her cheek paled, and she turned herself away from him,
So disgusted was she at the children's coming there.
But your husband tried to end the girl's bad temper,
And said "You must not look unkindly on your friends.
Cease to be angry. Turn your head to me again.
Have as your friends the same ones as your husband has.
And take these gifts, and beg your father to reprieve
These children from their exile. Do it for my sake."
She, when she saw the dress, could not restrain herself.
She agreed with all her husband said, and before
He and the children had gone far from the palace,
She took the gorgeous robe and dressed herself in it,
And put the golden crown around her curly locks,
And arranged the set of the hair in a shining mirror,

And smiled at the lifeless image of herself in it.
Then she rose from her chair and walked about the
room,
With her gleaming feet stepping most soft and delicate,
All overjoyed with the present. Often and often
She would stretch her foot out straight and look along it.
But after that it was a fearful thing to see.
The color of her face changed, and she staggered back,
She ran, and her legs trembled, and she only just
Managed to reach a chair without falling flat down.
An aged woman servant who, I take it, thought
This was some seizure of Pan or another god,
Cried out "God bless us," but that was before she saw
The white foam breaking through her lips and her
rolling
The pupils of her eyes and her face all bloodless.
Then she raised a different cry from that "God bless us,"
A huge shriek, and the women ran, one to the king,
One to the newly wedded husband to tell him
What had happened to his bride; and with frequent
sound
The whole of the palace rang as they went running.
One walking quickly round the course of a race-track
Would now have turned the bend and be close to the
goal,
When she, poor girl, opened her shut and speechless eye,
And with a terrible groan she came to herself.
For a twofold pain was moving up against her.
The wreath of gold that was resting around her head
Let forth a fearful stream of all-devouring fire,
And the finely woven dress your children gave to her,
Was fastening on the unhappy girl's fine flesh.
She leapt up from the chair, and all on fire she ran,
Shaking her hair now this way and now that, trying

To hurl the diadem away; but fixedly
The gold preserved its grip, and, when she shook her hair,
Then more and twice as fiercely the fire blazed out.
Till, beaten by her fate, she fell down to the ground,
Hard to be recognized except by a parent.
Neither the setting of her eyes was plain to see,
Nor the shapeliness of her face. From the top of
Her head there oozed out blood and fire mixed together.
Like the drops on pine-bark, so the flesh from her bones
Dropped away, torn by the hidden fang of the poison.
It was a fearful sight; and terror held us all
From touching the corpse. We had learned from what had happened.
But her wretched father, knowing nothing of the event,
Came suddenly to the house, and fell upon the corpse,
And at once cried out and folded his arms about her,
And kissed her and spoke to her, saying, "O my poor child,
What heavenly power has so shamefully destroyed you?
And who has set me here like an ancient sepulcher,
Deprived of you? Oh, let me die with you, my child!"
And when he had made an end of his wailing and crying,
Then the old man wished to raise himself to his feet;
But, as the ivy clings to the twigs of the laurel,
So he stuck to the fine dress, and he struggled fearfully.
For he was trying to lift himself to his knee,
And she was pulling him down, and when he tugged hard
He would be ripping his aged flesh from his bones.
At last his life was quenched, and the unhappy man
Gave up the ghost, no longer could hold up his head.
There they lie close, the daughter and the old father,
Dead bodies, an event he prayed for in his tears.

As for your interests, I will say nothing of them,
For you will find your own escape from punishment.
Our human life I think and have thought a shadow,
And I do not fear to say that those who are held
Wise among men and who search the reasons of things
Are those who bring the most sorrow on themselves.
For of mortals there is no one who is happy.
If wealth flows in upon one, one may be perhaps
Luckier than one's neighbor, but still not happy.

Exit.

CHORUS Heaven, it seems, on this day has fastened many
Evils on Jason, and Jason has deserved them.
Poor girl, the daughter of Creon, how I pity you
And your misfortunes, you who have gone quite away
To the house of Hades because of marrying Jason.

MEDEA Women, my task is fixed: as quickly as I may
To kill my children, and start away from this land,
And not, by wasting time, to suffer my children
To be slain by another hand less kindly to them.
Force every way will have it they must die, and since
This must be so, then I, their mother, shall kill them.
Oh, arm yourself in steel, my heart! Do not hang back
From doing this fearful and necessary wrong.
Oh, come, my hand, poor wretched hand, and take the sword,
Take it, step forward to this bitter starting point,
And do not be a coward, do not think of them,
How sweet they are, and how you are their mother. Just for
This one short day be forgetful of your children,

Afterward weep; for even though you will kill them,
They were very dear—Oh, I am an unhappy woman!

With a cry she rushes into the house.

CHORUS O Earth, and the far shining
Ray of the Sun, look down, look down upon
This poor lost woman, look, before she raises
The hand of murder against her flesh and blood.
Yours was the golden birth from which
She sprang, and now I fear divine
Blood may be shed by men.
O heavenly light, hold back her hand,
Check her, and drive from out the house
The bloody Fury raised by fiends of Hell.

Vain waste, your care of children;
Was it in vain you bore the babes you loved,
After you passed the inhospitable strait
Between the dark blue rocks, Symplegades?
O wretched one, how has it come,
This heavy anger on your heart,
This cruel bloody mind?
For God from mortals asks a stern
Price for the stain of kindred blood
In like disaster falling on their homes.

A cry from one of the children is heard.

Do you hear the cry, do you hear the children's cry?
O you hard heart, O woman fated for evil!

ONE OF THE CHILDREN (*from within*) What can I do and how escape my mother's hands?

ANOTHER CHILD (*from within*) O my dear brother, I cannot tell. We are lost.

CHORUS Shall I enter the house? Oh, surely I should
Defend the children from murder.

A CHILD (*from within*) Oh, help us, in God's name, for now we need your help.
Now, now we are close to it. We are trapped by the sword.

CHORUS Oh, your heart must have been made of rock or steel,
You who can kill
With your own hand the fruit of your own womb.
Of one alone I have heard, one woman alone
Of those of old who laid her hands on her children,
Ino, sent mad by heaven when the wife of Zeus
Drove her out from her home and made her wander;
And because of the wicked shedding of blood
Of her own children she threw
Herself, poor wretch, into the sea and stepped away
Over the sea-cliff to die with her two children.
What horror more can be? O women's love,
So full of trouble,
How many evils have you caused already!

Enter Jason, with attendants.

JASON You women, standing close in front of this dwelling,
Is she, Medea, she who did this dreadful deed,
Still in the house, or has she run away in flight?
For she will have to hide herself beneath the earth,
Or raise herself on wings into the height of air,

If she wishes to escape the royal vengeance.
Does she imagine that, having killed our rulers,
She will herself escape uninjured from this house?
But I am thinking not so much of her as for
The children—her the king's friends will make to suffer
For what she did. So I have come to save the lives
Of my boys, in case the royal house should harm them
While taking vengeance for their mother's wicked deed.

CHORUS O Jason, if you but knew how deeply you are
Involved in sorrow, you would not have spoken so.

JASON What is it? That she is planning to kill me also?

CHORUS Your children are dead, and by their own mother's hand.

JASON What! That is it? O woman, you have destroyed me!

CHORUS You must make up your mind your children are no more.

JASON Where did she kill them? Was it here or in the house?

CHORUS Open the gates and there you will see them murdered.

JASON Quick as you can unlock the doors, men, and undo
The fastenings and let me see this double evil,
My children dead and her—Oh, her I will repay.

His attendants rush to the door. Medea appears above the house in a chariot drawn by dragons. She has the dead bodies of the children with her.

MEDEA Why do you batter these gates and try to unbar them,
Seeking the corpses and for me who did the deed?
You may cease your trouble, and, if you have need of me,
Speak, if you wish. You will never touch me with your hand,
Such a chariot has Helius, my father's father,
Given me to defend me from my enemies.

JASON You hateful thing, you woman most utterly loathed
By the gods and me and by all the race of mankind,
You who have had the heart to raise a sword against
Your children, you, their mother, and left me childless—
You have done this, and do you still look at the sun
And at the earth, after these most fearful doings?
I wish you dead. Now I see it plain, though at that time
I did not, when I took you from your foreign home
And brought you to a Greek house, you, an evil thing,
A traitress to your father and your native land.
The gods hurled the avenging curse of yours on me.
For your own brother you slew at your own hearthside,
And then came aboard that beautiful ship, the Argo.
And that was your beginning. When you were married
To me, your husband, and had borne children to me,
For the sake of pleasure in the bed you killed them.
There is no Greek woman who would have dared such deeds,
Out of all those whom I passed over and chose you
To marry instead, a bitter destructive match,
A monster, not a woman, having a nature
Wilder than that of Scylla in the Tuscan sea.
Ah! no, not if I had ten thousand words of shame
Could I sting you. You are naturally so brazen.
Go, worker in evil, stained with your children's blood.

For me remains to cry aloud upon my fate,
Who will get no pleasure from my newly wedded love,
And the boys whom I begot and brought up, never
Shall I speak to them alive. Oh, my life is over!

MEDEA Long would be the answer which I might have made to
These words of yours, if Zeus the father did not know
How I have treated you and what you did to me.
No, it was not to be that you should scorn my love,
And pleasantly live your life through, laughing at me;
Nor would the princess, nor he who offered the match,
Creon, drive me away without paying for it.
So now you may call me a monster, if you wish,
A Scylla housed in the caves of the Tuscan sea.
I too, as I had to, have taken hold of your heart.

JASON You feel the pain yourself. You share in my sorrow.

MEDEA Yes, and my grief is gain when you cannot mock it.

JASON O children, what a wicked mother she was to you!

MEDEA They died from a disease they caught from their father.

JASON I tell you it was not my hand that destroyed them.

MEDEA But it was your insolence, and your virgin wedding.

JASON And just for the sake of that you chose to kill them.

MEDEA Is love so small a pain, do you think, for a woman?

JASON For a wise one, certainly. But you are wholly evil.

MEDEA The children are dead. I say this to make you suffer.

JASON The children, I think, will bring down curses on you.

MEDEA The gods know who was the author of this sorrow.

JASON Yes, the gods know indeed, they know your loathsome heart.

MEDEA Hate me. But I tire of your barking bitterness.

JASON And I of yours. It is easier to leave you.

MEDEA How then? What shall I do? I long to leave you too.

JASON Give me the bodies to bury and to mourn them.

MEDEA No, that I will not. I will bury them myself,
Bearing them to Hera's temple on the promontory;
So that no enemy may evilly treat them
By tearing up their grave. In this land of Corinth
I shall establish a holy feast and sacrifice
Each year for ever to atone for the blood guilt.
And I myself go to the land of Erechtheus
To dwell in Aegeus' house, the son of Pandion.
While you, as is right, will die without distinction,

Struck on the head by a piece of the Argo's timber,
And you will have seen the bitter end of my love.

JASON May a Fury for the children's sake destroy you,
And justice, Requitor of blood.

MEDEA What heavenly power lends an ear
To a breaker of oaths, a deceiver?

JASON Oh, I hate you, murderess of children.

MEDEA Go to your palace. Bury your bride.

JASON I go, with two children to mourn for.

MEDEA Not yet do you feel it. Wait for the future.

JASON O children I loved!

MEDEA I loved them, you did not.

JASON You loved them, and killed them.

MEDEA To make you feel pain.

JASON Oh, wretch that I am, how I long
To kiss the dear lips of my children!

MEDEA Now you would speak to them, now you would kiss them.
Then you rejected them.

JASON Let me, I beg you,
Touch my boys' delicate flesh.

MEDEA I will not. Your words are all wasted.

JASON O God, do you hear it, this persecution,
These my sufferings from this hateful
Woman, this monster, murderess of children?
Still what I can do that I will do:
I will lament and cry upon heaven,
Calling the gods to bear me witness
How you have killed my boys and prevent me from
Touching their bodies or giving them burial.
I wish I had never begot them to see them
Afterward slaughtered by you.

CHORUS Zeus in Olympus is the overseer
Of many doings. Many things the gods
Achieve beyond our judgment. What we thought
Is not confirmed and what we thought not God
Contrives. And so it happens in this story.

THE BACCHAE

Translated by William Arrowsmith

CHARACTERS

DIONYSUS, *the god, also called Bromius, Evius, and Bacchus*

PENTHEUS, *king of Thebes*

AGAVE, *his mother*

CADMUS, *his grandfather*

TEIRESIAS, *an old blind prophet*

ATTENDANT

FIRST MESSENGER, *a herdsman from Mount Cithaeron*

SECOND MESSENGER

CHORUS OF ASIAN BACCHAE, *followers of Dionysus*

CORYPHAEUS, *chorus leader*

Non-speaking: attendants of Agave; attendants of Cadmus; attendants of Pentheus

For Anne and George

ex voto

XAIPETE

THE BACCHAE

SCENE *Before the royal palace of Thebes. On the left is the way to Cithaeron; on the right, to the city. In the center of the orchestra stands, still smoking, the vine-covered tomb of Semele, mother of Dionysus.*

Enter Dionysus. He is of soft, even effeminate, appearance. His face is beardless; he is dressed in a fawn-skin and carries a thyrsus (i.e., a stalk of fennel tipped with ivy leaves). On his head he wears a wreath of ivy, and his long blond curls ripple down over his shoulders. Throughout the play he wears a smiling mask.

DIONYSUS I am Dionysus, the son of Zeus,
come back to Thebes, this land where I was born.
My mother was Cadmus' daughter, Semele by name,
midwived by fire, delivered by the lightning's
blast.
And here I stand, a god incognito,
disguised as man, beside the stream of Dirce
and the waters of Ismenus. There before the palace
I see my lightning-married mother's grave,
and there upon the ruins of her shattered house
the living fire of Zeus still smolders on
in deathless witness of Hera's violence and rage
against my mother. But Cadmus wins my praise:
he has made this tomb a shrine, sacred to my mother.
It was I who screened her grave with the green
of the clustering vine.
Far behind me lie
those golden-rivered lands, Lydia and Phrygia,

where my journeying began. Overland I went,
across the steppes of Persia where the sun strikes hotly
down, through Bactrian fastness and the grim waste
of Media. Thence to rich Arabia I came;
and so, along all Asia's swarming littoral
of towered cities where Greeks and foreign nations,
mingling, live, my progress made. There
I taught my dances to the feet of living men,
establishing my mysteries and rites
that I might be revealed on earth for what I am:
a god.
        And thence to Thebes.
                                        This city, first
in Hellas, now shrills and echoes to my women's cries,
their ecstasy of joy. Here in Thebes
I bound the fawn-skin to the women's flesh and armed
their hands with shafts of ivy. For I have come
to refute that slander spoken by my mother's sisters—
those who least had right to slander her.
They said that Dionysus was no son of Zeus,
but Semele had slept beside a man in love
and fathered off her shame on Zeus—a fraud, they
   sneered,
contrived by Cadmus to protect his daughter's name.
They said she lied, and Zeus in anger at that lie
blasted her with lightning.
                                        Because of that offense
I have stung them with frenzy, hounded them from
   home
up to the mountains where they wander, crazed of mind,
and compelled to wear my orgies' livery.
Every woman in Thebes—but the women only—
I drove from home, mad. There they sit,
rich and poor alike, even the daughters of Cadmus,
beneath the silver firs on the roofless rocks.
Like it or not, this city must learn its lesson:

it lacks initiation in my mysteries;
that I shall vindicate my mother Semele
and stand revealed to mortal eyes as the god
she bore to Zeus.
Cadmus the king has abdicated,
leaving his throne and power to his grandson Pentheus;
who now revolts against divinity, in *me;*
thrusts *me* from his offerings; forgets *my* name
in his prayers. Therefore I shall *prove* to him
and every man in Thebes that I am God
indeed. And when my worship is established here,
and all is well, then I shall go my way
and be revealed to other men in other lands.
But if the men of Thebes attempt to force
my Bacchae from the mountainside by threat of arms,
I shall marshall my Maenads and take the field.
To these ends I have laid my deity aside
and go disguised as man.

He wheels and calls offstage.

On, my women,
women who worship me, women whom I led
out of Asia where Tmolus heaves its rampart
over Lydia!
On, comrades of my progress here!
Come, and with your native Phrygian drum—
Rhea's drum and mine—pound at the palace doors
of Pentheus! Let the city of Thebes behold you,
while I return among Cithaeron's forest glens
where my Bacchae wait and join their whirling dances.

Exit Dionysus as the Chorus of Asian Bacchae comes dancing in from the right. They are dressed in fawn-skins, crowned with ivy, and carry thyrsi, timbrels, and flutes.

CHORUS Out of the land of Asia,
down from holy Tmolus,
speeding the service of God,
for Bromius we come!
Hard are the labors of God;
hard, but his service is sweet.
Sweet to serve, sweet to cry:
Bacchus! *Evohé!*

—You on the streets!
—You on the roads!
—Make way!
—Let every mouth be hushed. Let no ill-omened words
profane your tongues.
—Make way! Fall back!
—Hush.
—For now I raise the old, old hymn to Dionysus.

—Blessèd, blessèd are those who know the mysteries of
God.
—Blessèd is he who hallows his life in the worship of God,
he whom the spirit of God possesseth, who is one
with those who belong to the holy body of God.
—Blessèd are the dancers and those who are purified,
who dance on the hill in the holy dance of God.
—Blessèd are they who keep the rite of Cybele the
Mother.
—Blessèd are the thyrsus-bearers, those who wield in their
hands the holy wand of God.
—Blessèd are those who wear the crown of the ivy of God.
—Blessèd, blessèd are they: Dionysus is their god!

—On, Bacchae, on, you Bacchae,
bear your god in triumph home!
Bear on the god, son of God,

escort your Dionysus home!
Bear him down from Phrygian hill,
attend him through the streets of Hellas!

—So his mother bore him once
in labor bitter; lightning-struck,
forced by fire that flared from Zeus,
consumed, she died, untimely torn,
in childbed dead by blow of light!
Of light the son was born!

—Zeus it was who saved his son;
with speed outrunning mortal eye,
bore him to a private place,
bound the boy with clasps of gold;
in his thigh as in a womb,
concealed his son from Hera's eyes.

—And when the weaving Fates fulfilled the time,
the bull-horned god was born of Zeus. In joy
he crowned his son, set serpents on his head—
wherefrom, in piety, descends to us
The Maenad's writhing crown, her *chevelure* of snakes.

—O Thebes, nurse of Semele,
crown your hair with ivy!
Grow green with bryony!
Redden with berries! O city,
with boughs of oak and fir,
come dance the dance of God!
Fringe your skins of dappled fawn
with tufts of twisted wool!
Handle with holy care
the violent wand of God!
And let the dance begin!

He is Bromius who runs
to the mountain!
to the mountain!
where the throng of women waits,
driven from shuttle and loom,
possessed by Dionysus!

—And I praise the holies of Crete,
the caves of the dancing Curetes,
there where Zeus was born,
where helmed in triple tier
around the primal drum
the Corybantes danced. They,
they were the first of all
whose whirling feet kept time
to the strict beat of the taut hide
and the squeal of the wailing flute.
Then from them to Rhea's hands
the holy drum was handed down;
but, stolen by the raving Satyrs,
fell at last to me and now
accompanies the dance
which every other year
celebrates your name:
Dionysus!

—He is sweet upon the mountains. He drops to the earth
from the running packs.
He wears the holy fawn-skin. He hunts the wild goat
and kills it.
He delights in the raw flesh.
He runs to the mountains of Phrygia, to the mountains
of Lydia he runs!
He is Bromius who leads us! *Evohé!*

—With milk the earth flows! It flows with wine!
It runs with the nectar of bees!

—Like frankincense in its fragrance
is the blaze of the torch he bears.
Flames float out from his trailing wand
as he runs, as he dances,
kindling the stragglers,
spurring with cries,
and his long curls stream to the wind!

—And he cries, as they cry, *Evohé!* —
On, Bacchae!
On, Bacchae!
Follow, glory of golden Tmolus,
hymning God
with a rumble of drums,
with a cry, *Evohé!* to the Evian god,
with a cry of Phrygian cries,
when the holy flute like honey plays
the sacred song of those who go
to the mountain!
to the mountain!

—Then, in ecstasy, like a colt by its grazing mother,
the Bacchante runs with flying feet, she leaps!

The Chorus remains grouped in two semicircles about the orchestra as Teiresias makes his entrance. He is incongruously dressed in the bacchant's fawn-skin and is crowned with ivy. Old and blind, he uses his thyrsus to tap his way.

TEIRESIAS Ho there, who keeps the gates?
Summon Cadmus—

Cadmus, Agenor's son, the stranger from Sidon
who built the towers of our Thebes.
Go, someone.
Say Teiresias wants him. He will know what errand
brings me, that agreement, age with age, we made
to deck our wands, to dress in skins of fawn
and crown our heads with ivy.

Enter Cadmus from the palace. Dressed in Dionysiac costume and bent almost double with age, he is an incongruous and pathetic figure.

CADMUS My old friend,
I knew it must be you when I heard your summons.
For there's a wisdom in his voice that makes
the man of wisdom known.
But here I am,
dressed in the costume of the god, prepared to go.
Insofar as we are able, Teiresias, we must
do honor to this god, for he was born
my daughter's son, who has been revealed to men,
the god, Dionysus.
Where shall we go, where
shall we tread the dance, tossing our white heads
in the dances of God?
Expound to me, Teiresias.
For in such matters you are wise.
Surely
I could dance night and day, untiringly
beating the earth with my thyrsus! And how sweet it is
to forget my old age.

TEIRESIAS It is the same with me.
I too feel young, young enough to dance.

CADMUS Good. Shall we take our chariots to the mountain?

TEIRESIAS Walking would be better. It shows more honor to the god.

CADMUS So be it. I shall lead, my old age conducting yours.

TEIRESIAS The god will guide us there with no effort on our part.

CADMUS Are we the only men who will dance for Bacchus?

TEIRESIAS They are all blind. Only we can see.

CADMUS But we delay too long. Here, take my arm.

TEIRESIAS Link my hand in yours.

CADMUS I am a man, nothing more. I do not scoff at heaven.

TEIRESIAS We do not trifle with divinity.
No, we are the heirs of customs and traditions
hallowed by age and handed down to us
by our fathers. No quibbling logic can topple *them*,
whatever subtleties this clever age invents.
People may say: "Aren't you ashamed? At your age,
going dancing, wreathing your head with ivy?"
Well, I am *not* ashamed. Did the god declare

that just the young or just the old should dance?
No, he desires his honor from all mankind.
He wants no one excluded from his worship.

CADMUS Because you cannot see, Teiresias, let me be
interpreter for you this once. Here comes
the man to whom I left my throne, Echion's son,
Pentheus, hastening toward the palace. He seems
excited and disturbed. Yes, listen to him.

Enter Pentheus from the right. He is a young man of athletic build, dressed in traditional Greek dress; like Dionysus, he is beardless. He enters excitedly, talking to the attendants who accompany him.

PENTHEUS I happened to be away, out of the city,
but reports reached me of some strange mischief here,
stories of our women leaving home to frisk
in mock ecstasies among the thickets on the mountain,
dancing in honor of the latest divinity,
a certain Dionysus, whoever he may be!
In their midst stand bowls brimming with wine.
And then, one by one, the women wander off
to hidden nooks where they serve the lusts of men.
Priestesses of Bacchus they claim they are,
but it's really Aphrodite they adore.
I have captured some of them; my jailers
have locked them away in the safety of our prison.
Those who run at large shall be hunted down
out of the mountains like the animals they are—
yes, my own mother Agave, and Ino
and Autonoë, the mother of Actaeon.
In no time at all I shall have them trapped
in iron nets and stop this obscene disorder.
I am also told a foreigner has come to Thebes

from Lydia, one of those charlatan magicians,
with long yellow curls smelling of perfumes,
with flushed cheeks and the spells of Aphrodite
in his eyes. His days and nights he spends
with women and girls, dangling before them the joys
of initiation in his mysteries.
But let me bring him underneath that roof
and I'll stop his pounding with his wand and tossing
his head. By God, I'll have his head cut off!
And *this* is the man who claims that Dionysus
is a god and was sewn into the thigh of Zeus,
when, in point of fact, that same blast of lightning
consumed him and his mother both for her lie
that she had lain with Zeus in love. Whoever
this stranger is, aren't such impostures,
such unruliness, worthy of hanging?

For the first time he sees Teiresias and Cadmus in their Dionysiac costumes.

What!
But this is incredible! Teiresias the seer
tricked out in a dappled fawn-skin!
And *you,*
you, my own grandfather, playing at the bacchant
with a wand!
Sir, I shrink to see your old age
so foolish. Shake that ivy off, grandfather!
Now drop that wand. Drop it, I say.

He wheels on Teiresias.

Aha,
I see: this is *your* doing, Teiresias.
Yes, you want still another god revealed to men

so you can pocket the profits from burnt offerings
and bird-watching. By heaven, only your age
restrains me now from sending you to prison
with those Bacchic women for importing here to Thebes
these filthy mysteries. When once you see
the glint of wine shining at the feasts of women,
then you may be sure the festival is rotten.

CORYPHAEUS What blasphemy! Stranger, have you no respect
for heaven? For Cadmus who sowed the dragon teeth?
Will the son of Echion disgrace his house?

TEIRESIAS Give a wise man an honest brief to plead
and his eloquence is no remarkable achievement.
But you are glib; your phrases come rolling out
smoothly on the tongue, as though your words were wise
instead of foolish. The man whose glibness flows
from his conceit of speech declares the thing he is:
a worthless and a stupid citizen.
I tell you,
this god whom you ridicule shall someday have
enormous power and prestige throughout Hellas.
Mankind, young man, possesses two supreme blessings.
First of these is the goddess Demeter, or Earth—
whichever name you choose to call her by.
It was she who gave to man his nourishment of grain.
But after her there came the son of Semele,
who matched her present by inventing liquid wine
as his gift to man. For filled with that good gift,
suffering mankind forgets its grief; from it
comes sleep; with it oblivion of the troubles
of the day. There is no other medicine

for misery. And when we pour libations
to the gods, we pour the god of wine himself
that through his intercession man may win
the favor of heaven.

You sneer, do you, at that story
that Dionysus was sewed into the thigh of Zeus?
Let me teach you what that really means. When Zeus
rescued from the thunderbolt his infant son,
he brought him to Olympus. Hera, however,
plotted at heart to hurl the child from heaven.
Like the god he is, Zeus countered her. Breaking off
a tiny fragment of that ether which surrounds the world,
he molded from it a dummy Dionysus.
This he *showed* to Hera, but with time men garbled
the word and said that Dionysus had been *sewed*
into the thigh of Zeus. This was their story,
whereas, in fact, Zeus *showed* the dummy to Hera
and gave it as a hostage for his son.

Moreover,
this is a god of prophecy. His worshippers,
like madmen, are endowed with mantic powers.
For when the god enters the body of a man
he fills him with the breath of prophecy.

Besides,
he has usurped even the functions of warlike Ares.
Thus, at times, you see an army mustered under arms
stricken with panic before it lifts a spear.
This panic comes from Dionysus.

Someday
you shall even see him bounding with his torches
among the crags at Delphi, leaping the pastures
that stretch between the peaks, whirling and waving
his thyrsus: great throughout Hellas.

Mark my words,
Pentheus. Do not be so certain that power

is what matters in the life of man; do not mistake
for wisdom the fantasies of your sick mind.
Welcome the god to Thebes; crown your head;
pour him libations and join his revels.
  Dionysus does not, I admit, *compel* a woman
to be chaste. Always and in every case
it is her character and nature that keeps
a woman chaste. But even in the rites of Dionysus,
the chaste woman will not be corrupted.
Think:
you are pleased when men stand outside your doors
and the city glorifies the name of Pentheus.
And so the god: he too delights in glory.
But Cadmus and I, whom you ridicule, will crown
our heads with ivy and join the dances of the god—
an ancient foolish pair perhaps, but dance
we must. Nothing you have said would make me
change my mind or flout the will of heaven.
You are mad, grievously mad, beyond the power
of any drugs to cure, for you are drugged
with madness.

CORYPHAEUS Apollo would approve your words.
Wisely you honor Bromius: a great god.

CADMUS My boy,
Teiresias advises well. Your home is here
with us, with our customs and traditions, not
outside, alone. Your mind is distracted now,
and what you think is sheer delirium.
Even if this Dionysus is no god,
as you assert, persuade yourself that he is.
The fiction is a noble one, for Semele will seem
to be the mother of a god, and this confers
no small distinction on our family.

You saw
that dreadful death your cousin Actaeon died
when those man-eating hounds he had raised himself
savaged him and tore his body limb from limb
because he boasted that his prowess in the hunt
surpassed
the skill of Artemis.
Do not let his fate be yours.
Here, let me wreathe your head with leaves of ivy.
Then come with us and glorify the god.

PENTHEUS Take your hands off me! Go worship your
Bacchus,
but do not wipe your madness off on me.
By God, I'll make him pay, the man who taught you
this folly of yours.

He turns to his attendants.

Go, someone, this instant,
to the place where this prophet prophesies.
Pry it up with crowbars, heave it over,
upside down; demolish everything you see.
Throw his fillets out to wind and weather.
That will provoke him more than anything.
As for the rest of you, go and scour the city
for that effeminate stranger, the man who infects our
women
with this strange disease and pollutes our beds.
And when you take him, clap him in chains
and march him here. He shall die as he deserves—
by being stoned to death. He shall come to rue
his merrymaking here in Thebes.

Exeunt attendants.

TEIRESIAS
Reckless fool,
you do not know the consequences of your words.
You talked madness before, but this is raving
lunacy!
Cadmus, let us go and pray
for this raving fool and for this city too,
pray to the god that no awful vengeance strike
from heaven.
Take your staff and follow me.
Support me with your hands, and I shall help you too
lest we stumble and fall, a sight of shame,
two old men together.
But go we must,
acknowledging the service that we owe to God,
Bacchus, the son of Zeus.
And yet take care
lest someday your house repent of Pentheus
in its sufferings. I speak not prophecy
but fact. The words of fools finish in folly.

Exeunt Teiresias and Cadmus. Pentheus retires into the palace.

CHORUS
—Holiness, queen of heaven,
Holiness on golden wing
who hovers over earth,
do you hear what Pentheus says?
Do you hear his blasphemy
against the prince of the blessèd,
the god of garlands and banquets,
Bromius, Semele's son?
These blessings he gave:
laughter to the flute
and the loosing of cares
when the shining wine is spilled

at the feast of the gods,
and the wine-bowl casts its sleep
on feasters crowned with ivy.

—A tongue without reins,
defiance, unwisdom—
their end is disaster.
But the life of quiet good,
the wisdom that accepts—
these abide unshaken,
preserving, sustaining
the houses of men.
Far in the air of heaven,
the sons of heaven live.
But they watch the lives of men.
And what passes for wisdom is not;
unwise are those who aspire,
who outrange the limits of man.
Briefly, we live. Briefly,
then die. Wherefore, I say,
he who hunts a glory, he who tracks
some boundless, superhuman dream,
may lose his harvest here and now
and garner death. Such men are mad,
their counsels evil.

—O let me come to Cyprus,
island of Aphrodite,
homes of the loves that cast
their spells on the hearts of men!
Or Paphos where the hundred-
mouthed barbarian river
brings ripeness without rain!
To Pieria, haunt of the Muses,
and the holy hill of Olympus!

O Bromius, leader, God of joy,
Bromius, take me there!
There the lovely Graces go,
and there Desire, and there
the right is mine to worship
as I please.

—The deity, the son of Zeus,
in feast, in festival, delights.
He loves the goddess Peace,
generous of good,
preserver of the young.
To rich and poor he gives
the simple gift of wine,
the gladness of the grape.
But him who scoffs he hates,
and him who mocks his life,
the happiness of those
for whom the day is blessed
but doubly blessed the night;
whose simple wisdom shuns the thoughts
of proud, uncommon men and all
their god-encroaching dreams.
But what the common people do,
the things that simple men believe,
I too believe and do.

As Pentheus reappears from the palace, enter from the left several attendants leading Dionysus captive.

ATTENDANT Pentheus, here we are; not empty-handed either.
We captured the quarry you sent us out to catch.
But our prey here was tame: refused to run

or hide, held out his hands as willing as you please,
completely unafraid. His ruddy cheeks were flushed
as though with wine, and he stood there smiling,
making no objection when we roped his hands
and marched him here. It made me feel ashamed.
"Listen, stranger," I said, "I am not to blame.
We act under orders from Pentheus. He ordered
your arrest."
As for those women you clapped in chains
and sent to the dungeon, they're gone, clean away,
went skipping off to the fields crying on their god
Bromius. The chains on their legs snapped apart
by themselves. Untouched by any human hand,
the doors swung wide, opening of their own accord.
Sir, this stranger who has come to Thebes is full
of many miracles. I know no more than that.
The rest is your affair.

PENTHEUS Untie his hands.
We have him in our net. He may be quick,
but he cannot escape us now, I think.

While the servants untie Dionysus' hands, Pentheus attentively scrutinizes his prisoner. Then the servants step back, leaving Pentheus and Dionysus face to face.

So,
you *are* attractive, stranger, at least to women—
which explains, I think, your presence here in Thebes.
Your curls are long. You do not wrestle, I take it.
And what fair skin you have—you must take care of
it—
no daylight complexion; no, it comes from the night
when you hunt Aphrodite with your beauty.

Now then,
who are you and from where?

DIONYSUS It is nothing
to boast of and easily told. You have heard, I suppose,
of Mount Tmolus and her flowers?

PENTHEUS I know the place.
It rings the city of Sardis.

DIONYSUS I come from there.
My country is Lydia.

PENTHEUS Who is this god whose worship
you have imported into Hellas?

DIONYSUS Dionysus, the son of Zeus.
He initiated me.

PENTHEUS You have some local Zeus
who spawns new gods?

DIONYSUS He is the same as yours—
the Zeus who married Semele.

PENTHEUS How did you see him?
In a dream or face to face?

DIONYSUS Face to face.
He gave me his rites.

PENTHEUS What form do they take,
these mysteries of yours?

DIONYSUS It is forbidden
to tell the uninitiate.

PENTHEUS Tell me the benefits
that those who know your mysteries enjoy.

DIONYSUS I am forbidden to say. But they are worth knowing.

PENTHEUS Your answers are designed to make me curious.

DIONYSUS No:
our mysteries abhor an unbelieving man.

PENTHEUS You say you saw the god. What form did he assume?

DIONYSUS Whatever form he wished. The choice was his, not mine.

PENTHEUS You evade the question.

DIONYSUS Talk sense to a fool
and he calls you foolish.

PENTHEUS Have you introduced your rites
in other cities too? Or is Thebes the first?

DIONYSUS Foreigners everywhere now dance for Dionysus.

PENTHEUS They are more ignorant than Greeks.

DIONYSUS In this matter
they are not. Customs differ.

PENTHEUS Do you hold your rites
during the day or night?

DIONYSUS Mostly by night.
The darkness is well suited to devotion.

PENTHEUS Better suited to lechery and seducing women.

DIONYSUS You can find debauchery by daylight too.

PENTHEUS You shall regret these clever answers.

DIONYSUS And you,
your stupid blasphemies.

PENTHEUS What a bold bacchant!
You wrestle well—when it comes to words.

DIONYSUS Tell me,
what punishment do you propose?

PENTHEUS First of all,
I shall cut off your girlish curls.

DIONYSUS My hair is holy.
My curls belong to God.

Pentheus shears away the god's curls.

PENTHEUS Second, you will surrender
your wand.

DIONYSUS *You* take it. It belongs to Dionysus.

Pentheus takes the thyrsus.

PENTHEUS Last, I shall place you under guard and confine you
in the palace.

DIONYSUS The god himself will set me free
whenever I wish.

PENTHEUS You will be with your women in prison
when you call on him for help.

DIONYSUS He is here now
and sees what I endure from you.

PENTHEUS Where is he?
I cannot see him.

DIONYSUS With me. Your blasphemies
have made you blind.

PENTHEUS (*to attendants*) Seize him. He is mocking me
and Thebes.

DIONYSUS I give you sober warning, fools:
place no chains on *me*.

PENTHEUS But *I* say: chain him.
And I am the stronger here.

DIONYSUS You do not know
the limits of your strength. You do not know
what you do. You do not know who you are.

PENTHEUS I am Pentheus, the son of Echion and Agave.

DIONYSUS Pentheus: you shall repent that name.

PENTHEUS Off with him.
Chain his hands; lock him in the stables by the palace.
Since he desires the darkness, give him what he wants.
Let him dance down there in the dark.

As the attendants bind Dionysus' hands, the Chorus beats on its drums with increasing agitation as though to emphasize the sacrilege.

As for these women,
your accomplices in making trouble here,
I shall have them sold as slaves or put to work
at my looms. That will silence their drums.

Exit Pentheus.

DIONYSUS I go,
though not to suffer, since that cannot be.
But Dionysus whom you outrage by your acts,
who you deny is God, will call you to account.
When you set chains on me, you manacle the god.

Exeunt attendants with Dionysus captive.

CHORUS
—O Dirce, holy river,
child of Achelöus' water,
yours the springs that welcomed once
divinity, the son of Zeus!
For Zeus the father snatched his son

from deathless flame, crying:
Dithyrambus, come!
Enter my male womb.
I name you Bacchus and to Thebes
proclaim you by that name.
But now, O blessèd Dirce,
you banish me when to your banks I come,
crowned with ivy, bringing revels.
O Dirce, why am I rejected?
By the clustered grapes I swear,
by Dionysus' wine,
someday you shall come to know
   the name of *Bromius!*

—With fury, with fury, he rages,
Pentheus, son of Echion,
born of the breed of Earth,
spawned by the dragon, whelped by Earth!
Inhuman, a rabid beast,
a giant in wildness raging,
storming, defying the children of heaven.
He has threatened me with bonds
though my body is bound to God.
He cages my comrades with chains;
he has cast them in prison darkness.
O lord, son of Zeus, do you see?
O Dionysus, do you see
how in shackles we are held
unbreakably, in the bonds of oppressors?
Descend from Olympus, lord!
Come, whirl your wand of gold
and quell with death this beast of blood
whose violence abuses man and God
   outrageously.

—O lord, where do you wave your wand
among the running companies of God?
There on Nysa, mother of beasts?
There on the ridges of Corycia?
Or there among the forests of Olympus
where Orpheus fingered his lyre
and mustered with music the trees,
mustered the wilderness beasts?
O Pieria, you are blessed!
Evius honors you. He comes to dance,
bringing his Bacchae, fording the race
where Axios runs, bringing his Maenads
whirling over Lydias,
generous father of rivers
and famed for his lovely waters
that fatten a land of good horses.

Thunder and lightning. The earth trembles. The Chorus is crazed with fear.

DIONYSUS (*from within*) Ho!
Hear me! Ho, Bacchae!
Ho, Bacchae! Hear my cry!

CHORUS Who cries?
Who calls me with that cry
of Evius? Where are you, lord?

DIONYSUS Ho! Again I cry—
the son of Zeus and Semele!

CHORUS O lord, lord Bromius!
Bromius, come to us now!

DIONYSUS *Let the earthquake come! Shatter the floor of the world!*

CHORUS
—Look there, how the palace of Pentheus totters.
—Look, the palace is collapsing!
—Dionysus is within. Adore him!
—We adore him!
—Look there!
—Above the pillars, how the great stones gape and crack!
—Listen. Bromius cries his victory!

DIONYSUS *Launch the blazing thunderbolt of God! O lightnings,*
come! Consume with flame the palace of Pentheus!

A burst of lightning flares across the façade of the palace and tongues of flame spurt up from the tomb of Semele. Then a great crash of thunder.

CHORUS Ah,
look how the fire leaps up
on the holy tomb of Semele,
the flame of Zeus of Thunders,
his lightnings, still alive,
blazing where they fell!
Down, Maenads,
fall to the ground in awe! He walks
among the ruins he has made!
He has brought the high house low!
He comes, our god, the son of Zeus!

The Chorus falls to the ground in oriental fashion, bowing their heads in the direction of the palace. A hush; then

Dionysus appears, lightly picking his way among the rubble. Calm and smiling still, he speaks to the Chorus with a solicitude approaching banter.

DIONYSUS What, women of Asia? Were you so overcome with fright
you fell to the ground? I think then you must have seen
how Bacchus jostled the palace of Pentheus. But come, rise.
Do not be afraid.

CORYPHAEUS O greatest light of our holy revels,
how glad I am to see your face! Without you I was lost.

DIONYSUS Did you despair when they led me away to cast me down
in the darkness of Pentheus' prison?

CORYPHAEUS What else could I do?
Where would I turn for help if something happened to you?
But how did you escape that godless man?

DIONYSUS With ease.
No effort was required.

CORYPHAEUS But the manacles on your wrists?

DIONYSUS There I, in turn, humiliated him, outrage for outrage.
He seemed to think that he was chaining me but never once
so much as touched my hands. He fed on his desires.
Inside the stable he intended as my jail, instead of me,
he found a bull and tried to rope its knees and hooves.

He was panting desperately, biting his lips with his teeth,
his whole body drenched with sweat, while I sat nearby,
quietly watching. But at that moment Bacchus came,
shook the palace and touched his mother's grave with tongues
of fire. Imagining the palace was in flames,
Pentheus went rushing here and there, shouting to his slaves
to bring him water. Every hand was put to work: in vain.
Then, afraid I might escape, he suddenly stopped short,
drew his sword and rushed to the palace. There, it seems,
Bromius had made a shape, a phantom which resembled me,
within the court. Bursting in, Pentheus thrust and stabbed
at that thing of gleaming air as though he thought it me.
And then, once again, the god humiliated him.
He razed the palace to the ground where it lies, shattered
in utter ruin—his reward for my imprisonment.
At that bitter sight, Pentheus dropped his sword, exhausted
by the struggle. A man, a man, and nothing more,
yet he presumed to wage a war with God.
For my part,
I left the palace quietly and made my way outside.
For Pentheus I care nothing.
But judging from the sound
of tramping feet inside the court, I think our man
will soon be here. What, I wonder, will he have to say?
But let him bluster. I shall not be touched to rage.
Wise men know constraint: our passions are controlled.

Enter Pentheus, stamping heavily, from the ruined palace.

PENTHEUS But this is mortifying. That stranger, that man
I clapped in irons, has escaped.

He catches sight of Dionysus.

What! *You?*
Well, what do you have to say for yourself?
How did you escape? Answer me.

DIONYSUS Your anger
walks too heavily. Tread lightly here.

PENTHEUS *How did you escape?*

DIONYSUS Don't you remember?
Someone, I said, would set me free.

PENTHEUS Someone?
But who? Who is this mysterious someone?

DIONYSUS [He who makes the grape grow its clusters for mankind.]

PENTHEUS A splendid contribution, that.

DIONYSUS You disparage the gift that is his chiefest glory.

PENTHEUS [If I catch him here, he will not escape my anger.]
I shall order every gate in every tower
to be bolted tight.

DIONYSUS And so? Could not a god
hurdle your city walls?

PENTHEUS You are clever—very—
but not where it counts.

DIONYSUS Where it counts the most,
there I *am* clever.

Enter Messenger, a herdsman from Mount Cithaeron.

But hear this messenger
who brings you news from the mountain of Cithaeron.
We shall remain where we are. Do not fear:
we will not run away.

MESSENGER Pentheus, king of Thebes,
I come from Cithaeron where the gleaming flakes of
snow
fall on and on forever—

PENTHEUS Get to the point.
What is your message, man?

MESSENGER Sir, I have seen
the holy Maenads, the women who ran barefoot
and crazy from the city, and I wanted to report
to you and Thebes what weird fantastic things,
what miracles and more than miracles,
these women do. But may I speak freely
in my own way and words, or make it short?
I fear the harsh impatience of your nature, sire,
too kingly and too quick to anger.

PENTHEUS Speak freely.
You have my promise: I shall not punish you.
Displeasure with a man who speaks the truth is wrong.
However, the more terrible this tale of yours,

that much more terrible will be the punishment
I impose upon that man who taught our womenfolk
this strange new magic.

MESSENGER About that hour
when the sun lets loose its light to warm the earth,
our grazing herds of cows had just begun to climb
the path along the mountain ridge. Suddenly
I saw three companies of dancing women,
one led by Autonoë, the second captained
by your mother Agave, while Ino led the third.
There they lay in the deep sleep of exhaustion,
some resting on boughs of fir, others sleeping
where they fell, here and there among the oak leaves—
but all modestly and soberly, not, as you think,
drunk with wine, nor wandering, led astray
by the music of the flute, to hunt their Aphrodite
through the woods.
But your mother heard the lowing
of our hornèd herds, and springing to her feet,
gave a great cry to waken them from sleep.
And they too, rubbing the bloom of soft sleep
from their eyes, rose up lightly and straight—
a lovely sight to see: all as one,
the old women and the young and the unmarried girls.
First they let their hair fall loose, down
over their shoulders, and those whose straps had slipped
fastened their skins of fawn with writhing snakes
that licked their cheeks. Breasts swollen with milk,
new mothers who had left their babies behind at home
nestled gazelles and young wolves in their arms,
suckling them. Then they crowned their hair with
leaves,
ivy and oak and flowering bryony. One woman
struck her thyrsus against a rock and a fountain
of cool water came bubbling up. Another drove

her fennel in the ground, and where it struck the earth,
at the touch of God, a spring of wine poured out.
Those who wanted milk scratched at the soil
with bare fingers and the white milk came welling up.
Pure honey spurted, streaming, from their wands.
If you had been there and seen these wonders for
  yourself,
you would have gone down on your knees and prayed
to the god you now deny.
                                        We cowherds and shepherds
gathered in small groups, wondering and arguing
among ourselves at these fantastic things,
the awful miracles those women did.
But then a city fellow with the knack of words
rose to his feet and said: "All you who live
upon the pastures of the mountain, what do you say?
Shall we earn a little favor with King Pentheus
by hunting his mother Agave out of the revels?"
Falling in with his suggestion, we withdrew
and set ourselves in ambush, hidden by the leaves
among the undergrowth. Then at a signal
all the Bacchae whirled their wands for the revels
to begin. With one voice they cried aloud:
"O Iacchus! Son of Zeus!" "O Bromius!" they cried
until the beasts and all the mountain seemed
wild with divinity. And when they ran,
everything ran with them.
                                        It happened, however,
that Agave ran near the ambush where I lay
concealed. Leaping up, I tried to seize her,
but she gave a cry: "Hounds who run with me,
men are hunting us down! Follow, follow me!
Use your wands for weapons."
                                        At this we fled
and barely missed being torn to pieces by the women.
Unarmed, they swooped down upon the herds of cattle

grazing there on the green of the meadow. And then
you could have seen a single woman with bare hands
tear a fat calf, still bellowing with fright,
in two, while others clawed the heifers to pieces.
There were ribs and cloven hooves scattered
everywhere,
and scraps smeared with blood hung from the fir trees.
And bulls, their raging fury gathered in their horns,
lowered their heads to charge, then fell, stumbling
to the earth, pulled down by hordes of women
and stripped of flesh and skin more quickly, sire,
than you could blink your royal eyes. Then,
carried up by their own speed, they flew like birds
across the spreading fields along Asopus' stream
where most of all the ground is good for harvesting.
Like invaders they swooped on Hysiae
and on Erythrae in the foothills of Cithaeron.
Everything in sight they pillaged and destroyed.
They snatched the children from their homes. And
when
they piled their plunder on their backs, it stayed in place,
untied. Nothing, neither bronze nor iron,
fell to the dark earth. Flames flickered
in their curls and did not burn them. Then the villagers,
furious at what the women did, took to arms.
And *there,* sire, was something terrible to see.
For the men's spears were pointed and sharp, and yet
drew no blood, whereas the wands the women threw
inflicted wounds. And then the men *ran,*
routed by women! Some god, I say, was with them.
The Bacchae then returned where they had started,
by the springs the god had made, and washed their
hands
while the snakes licked away the drops of blood
that dabbled their cheeks.

Whoever this god may be,
sire, welcome him to Thebes. For he is great
in many other ways as well. It was he,
or so they say, who gave to mortal men
the gift of lovely wine by which our suffering
is stopped. And if there is no god of wine,
there is no love, no Aphrodite either,
nor other pleasure left to men.

Exit Messenger.

CORYPHAEUS I tremble
to speak the words of freedom before the tyrant.
But let the truth be told: there is no god
greater than Dionysus.

PENTHEUS Like a blazing fire
this Bacchic violence spreads. It comes too close.
We are disgraced, humiliated in the eyes
of Hellas. This is no time for hesitation.

He turns to an attendant.

You there. Go down quickly to the Electran gates
and order out all heavy-armored infantry;
call up the fastest troops among our cavalry,
the mobile squadrons and the archers. We march
against the Bacchae! Affairs are out of hand
when we tamely endure such conduct in our women.

Exit attendant.

DIONYSUS Pentheus, you do not hear, or else you disregard
my words of warning. You have done me wrong,

and yet, in spite of that, I warn you once
again: do not take arms against a god.
Stay quiet here. Bromius will not let you
drive his women from their revels on the mountain.

PENTHEUS Don't you lecture me. You escaped from
prison.
Or shall I punish you again?

DIONYSUS If I were you,
I would offer him a sacrifice, not rage
and kick against necessity, a man defying
God.

PENTHEUS I shall give your god the sacrifice
that he deserves. His victims will be his women.
I shall make a great slaughter in the woods of Cithaeron.

DIONYSUS You will all be routed, shamefully defeated,
when their wands of ivy turn back your shields
of bronze.

PENTHEUS It is hopeless to wrestle with this man.
Nothing on earth will make him hold his tongue.

DIONYSUS Friend,
you can still save the situation.

PENTHEUS How?
By accepting orders from my own slaves?

DIONYSUS No.
I undertake to lead the women back to Thebes.
Without bloodshed.

PENTHEUS This is some trap.

DIONYSUS A trap?
How so, if I save you by my own devices?

PENTHEUS . I know.
You and they have conspired to establish your rites forever.

DIONYSUS True, I *have* conspired—with God.

PENTHEUS Bring my armor, someone. And *you* stop talking.

Pentheus strides toward the left, but when he is almost offstage, Dionysus calls imperiously to him.

DIONYSUS *Wait!*
Would you like to *see* their revels on the mountain?

PENTHEUS I would pay a great sum to see that sight.

DIONYSUS Why are you so passionately curious?

PENTHEUS Of course
I'd be sorry to see them drunk—

DIONYSUS But for all your sorrow,
you'd like very much to see them?

PENTHEUS Yes, very much.
I could crouch beneath the fir trees, out of sight.

DIONYSUS But if you try to hide, they may track you down.

PENTHEUS Your point is well taken. I will go openly.

DIONYSUS Shall I lead you there now? Are you ready to go?

PENTHEUS The sooner the better. The loss of even a moment
would be disappointing now.

DIONYSUS First, however,
you must dress yourself in women's clothes.

PENTHEUS *What?*
You want *me,* a man, to wear a woman's dress. But why?

DIONYSUS If they knew you were a man, they would kill you instantly.

PENTHEUS True. You are an old hand at cunning, I see.

DIONYSUS Dionysus taught me everything I know.

PENTHEUS Your advice is to the point. What I fail to see
is what we do.

DIONYSUS I shall go inside with you
and help you dress.

PENTHEUS Dress? In a *woman's* dress,
you mean? I would die of shame.

DIONYSUS Very well.
Then you no longer hanker to see the Maenads?

PENTHEUS What is this costume I must wear?

DIONYSUS On your head
I shall set a wig with long curls.

PENTHEUS And then?

DIONYSUS Next, robes to your feet and a net for your hair.

PENTHEUS Yes? Go on.

DIONYSUS Then a thyrsus for your hand
and a skin of dappled fawn.

PENTHEUS I could not bear it.
I *cannot* bring myself to dress in women's clothes.

DIONYSUS Then you must fight the Bacchae. That means bloodshed.

PENTHEUS Right. First we must go and reconnoiter.

DIONYSUS Surely a wiser course than that of hunting bad with worse.

PENTHEUS But how can we pass through the city
without being seen?

DIONYSUS We shall take deserted streets.
I will lead the way.

PENTHEUS Any way you like,
provided those women of Bacchus don't jeer at me.
First, however, I shall ponder your advice,
whether to go or not.

DIONYSUS Do as you please.
I am ready, whatever you decide.

PENTHEUS Yes.
Either I shall march with my army to the mountain
or act on your advice.

Exit Pentheus into the palace.

DIONYSUS Women, our prey now thrashes
in the net we threw. He shall see the Bacchae
and pay the price with death.
O Dionysus,
now action rests with you. And you are near.
Punish this man. But first distract his wits;
bewilder him with madness. For sane of mind
this man would never wear a woman's dress;
but obsess his soul and he will not refuse.
After those threats with which he was so fierce,
I want him made the laughingstock of Thebes,
paraded through the streets, a woman.
Now
I shall go and costume Pentheus in the clothes
which he must wear to Hades when he dies, butchered
by the hands of his mother. He shall come to know
Dionysus, son of Zeus, consummate God,
most terrible, and yet most gentle, to mankind.

Exit Dionysus into the palace.

CHORUS
—When shall I dance once more
with bare feet the all-night dances,
tossing my head for joy
in the damp air, in the dew,

as a running fawn might frisk
for the green joy of the wide fields,
free from fear of the hunt,
free from the circling beaters
and the nets of woven mesh
and the hunters hallooing on
their yelping packs? And then, hard pressed,
she sprints with the quickness of wind,
bounding over the marsh, leaping
to frisk, leaping for joy,
gay with the green of the leaves,
to dance for joy in the forest,
to dance where the darkness is deepest,
where no man is.

—What is wisdom? What gift of the gods
is held in honor like this:
to hold your hand victorious
over the heads of those you hate?
Honor is precious forever.

—Slow but unmistakable
the might of the gods moves on.
It punishes that man,
infatuate of soul
and hardened in his pride,
who disregards the gods.
The gods are crafty:
they lie in ambush
a long step of time
to hunt the unholy.
Beyond the old beliefs,
no thought, no act shall go.
Small, small is the cost
to believe in this:

whatever is God is strong;
whatever long time has sanctioned,
that is a law forever;
the law tradition makes
is the law of nature.

—What is wisdom? What gift of the gods
is held in honor like this:
to hold your hand victorious
over the heads of those you hate?
Honor is precious forever.

—Blessèd is he who escapes a storm at sea,
who comes home to his harbor.
—Blessèd is he who emerges from under affliction.
—In various ways one man outraces another in the
race for wealth and power.
—Ten thousand men possess ten thousand hopes.
—A few bear fruit in happiness; the others go awry.
—But he who garners day by day the good of life,
he is happiest. Blessèd is he.

Re-enter Dionysus from the palace. At the threshold he turns and calls back to Pentheus.

DIONYSUS Pentheus if you are still so curious to see
forbidden sights, so bent on evil still,
come out. Let us see you in your woman's dress,
disguised in Maenad clothes so you may go and spy
upon your mother and her company.

Enter Pentheus from the palace. He wears a long linen dress which partially conceals his fawn-skin. He carries a thyrsus in his hand; on his head he wears a wig with long blond curls bound by a snood. He is dazed and completely in the power of the god who has now possessed him.

Why,
you look exactly like one of the daughters of Cadmus.

PENTHEUS I seem to see two suns blazing in the heavens.
And now two Thebes, two cities, and each
with seven gates. And you—you are a bull
who walks before me there. Horns have sprouted
from your head. Have you always been a beast?
But now I see a bull.

DIONYSUS It is the god you see.
Though hostile formerly, he now declares a truce
and goes with us. You see what you could not
when you were blind.

PENTHEUS (*coyly primping*) Do I look like anyone?
Like Ino or my mother Agave?

DIONYSUS So much alike
I almost might be seeing one of them. But look:
one of your curls has come loose from under the snood
where I tucked it.

PENTHEUS It must have worked loose
when I was dancing for joy and shaking my head.

DIONYSUS Then let me be your maid and tuck it back.
Hold still.

PENTHEUS Arrange it. I am in your hands
completely.

Dionysus tucks the curl back under the snood.

DIONYSUS And now your strap has slipped. Yes,
and your robe hangs askew at the ankles.

PENTHEUS (*bending backward to look*) I think so.
At least on my right leg. But on the left the hem
lies straight.

DIONYSUS You will think me the best of friends
when you see to your surprise how chaste the Bacchae
are.

PENTHEUS But to be a real Bacchante, should I hold
the wand in my right hand? Or this way?

DIONYSUS No.
In your right hand. And raise it as you raise
your right foot. I commend your change of heart.

PENTHEUS Could I lift Cithaeron up, do you think?
Shoulder the cliffs, Bacchae and all?

DIONYSUS If you wanted.
Your mind was once unsound, but now you think
as sane men do.

PENTHEUS Should we take crowbars with us?
Or should I put my shoulders to the cliffs
and heave them up?

DIONYSUS What? And destroy the haunts
of the nymphs, the holy groves where Pan plays
his woodland pipe?

PENTHEUS You are right. In any case,
women should not be mastered by brute strength.
I will hide myself beneath the firs instead.

DIONYSUS You will find all the ambush you deserve,
creeping up to spy on the Maenads.

PENTHEUS Think.
I can see them already, there among the bushes,
mating like birds, caught in the toils of love.

DIONYSUS Exactly. This is your mission: you go to watch.
You may surprise them—or they may surprise you.

PENTHEUS Then lead me through the very heart of Thebes,
since I, alone of all this city, dare to go.

DIONYSUS You and you alone will suffer for your city.
A great ordeal awaits you. But you are worthy
of your fate. I shall lead you safely there;
someone else shall bring you back.

PENTHEUS Yes, my mother.

DIONYSUS An example to all men.

PENTHEUS It is for that I go.

DIONYSUS You will be carried home—

PENTHEUS O luxury!

DIONYSUS Cradled in your mother's arms.

PENTHEUS You will spoil me.

DIONYSUS I *mean* to spoil you.

PENTHEUS I go to my reward.

DIONYSUS You are an extraordinary young man, and you go

to an extraordinary experience. You shall win
a glory towering to heaven and usurping
God's.

Exit Pentheus.

Agave and you daughters of Cadmus,
reach out your hands! I bring this young man
to a great ordeal. The victor? Bromius.
Bromius—and I. The rest the event shall show.

Exit Dionysus.

CHORUS
—Run to the mountain, fleet hounds of madness!
Run, run to the revels of Cadmus' daughters!
Sting them against the man in women's clothes,
the madman who spies on the Maenads, who peers
from behind the rocks, who spies from a vantage!
His mother shall see him first. She will cry
to the Maenads: "Who is this spy who has come
to the mountains to peer at the mountain-revels
of the women of Thebes? What bore him, Bacchae?
This man was born of no woman. Some lioness
gave him birth, some one of the Libyan gorgons!"

—O Justice, principle of order, spirit of custom,
come! Be manifest; reveal yourself with a sword!
Stab through the throat that godless man,
the mocker who goes, flouting custom and outraging
God!
O Justice, stab the evil earth-born spawn of Echion!

—Uncontrollable, the unbeliever goes,
in spitting rage, rebellious and amok,

madly assaulting the mysteries of God,
profaning the rites of the mother of God.
Against the unassailable he runs, with rage
obsessed. Headlong he runs to death.
For death the gods exact, curbing by that bit
the mouths of men. They humble us with death
that we remember what we are who are not God,
but men. We run to death. Wherefore, I say,
accept, accept:
humility is wise; humility is blest.
But what the world calls wise I do not want.
Elsewhere the chase. I hunt another game,
those great, those manifest, those certain goals,
achieving which, our mortal lives are blest.
Let these things be the quarry of my chase:
purity; humility; an unrebellious soul,
accepting all. Let me go the customary way,
the timeless, honored, beaten path of those who walk
with reverence and awe beneath the sons of heaven.

—O Justice, principle of order, spirit of custom,
come! Be manifest; reveal yourself with a sword!
Stab through the throat that godless man,
the mocker who goes, flouting custom and outraging
God!
O Justice, destroy the evil earth-born spawn of Echion!

—O Dionysus, reveal yourself a bull! Be manifest,
a snake with darting heads, a lion breathing fire!
O Bacchus, come! Come with your smile!
Cast your noose about this man who hunts
your Bacchae! Bring him down, trampled
underfoot by the murderous herd of your Maenads!

Enter Second Messenger from Cithaeron.

SECOND MESSENGER How prosperous in Hellas these halls once were,
this house founded by Cadmus, the stranger from Sidon
who sowed the dragon seed in the land of the snake!
I am a slave and nothing more, yet even so
I mourn the fortunes of this fallen house.

CORYPHAEUS What is it?
Is there news of the Bacchae?

SECOND MESSENGER This is my news:
Pentheus, the son of Echion, is dead.

CORYPHAEUS All hail to Bromius! Our god is a great god!

SECOND MESSENGER What is this you say, women? You dare to rejoice
at these disasters which destroy this house?

CORYPHAEUS I am no Greek. I hail my god
in my own way. No longer need I
shrink with fear of prison.

SECOND MESSENGER If you suppose this city is so short of men—

CORYPHAEUS Dionysus, Dionysus, not Thebes,
has power over me.

SECOND MESSENGER Your feelings might be forgiven, then. But this,
this exultation in disaster—it is not right.

CORYPHAEUS Tell us how the mocker died.
How was he killed?

SECOND MESSENGER There were three of us in all:
Pentheus and I,
attending my master, and that stranger who volunteered
his services as guide. Leaving behind us
the last outlying farms of Thebes, we forded
the Asopus and struck into the barren scrubland
of Cithaeron.
There in a grassy glen we halted,
unmoving, silent, without a word,
so we might see but not be seen. From that vantage,
in a hollow cut from the sheer rock of the cliffs,
a place where water ran and the pines grew dense
with shade, we saw the Maenads sitting, their hands
busily moving at their happy tasks. Some
wound the stalks of their tattered wands with tendrils
of fresh ivy; others, frisking like fillies
newly freed from the painted bridles, chanted
in Bacchic songs, responsively.
But Pentheus—
unhappy man—could not quite see the companies
of women. "Stranger," he said, "from where I stand,
I cannot see these counterfeited Maenads.
But if I climbed that towering fir that overhangs
the banks, then I could see their shameless orgies
better."
And now the stranger worked a miracle.
Reaching for the highest branch of a great fir,
he bent it down, down, down to the dark earth,
till it was curved the way a taut bow bends
or like a rim of wood when forced about the circle
of a wheel. Like that he forced that mountain fir
down to the ground. No mortal could have done it.
Then he seated Pentheus at the highest tip
and with his hands let the trunk rise straightly up,
slowly and gently, lest it throw its rider.

And the tree rose, towering to heaven, with my master
huddled at the top. And now the Maenads saw him
more clearly than he saw them. But barely had they
seen,
when the stranger vanished and there came a great voice
out of heaven—Dionysus', it must have been—
crying: "Women, I bring you the man who has mocked
at you and me and at our holy mysteries.
Take vengeance upon him." And as he spoke
a flash of awful fire bound earth and heaven.
The high air hushed, and along the forest glen
the leaves hung still; you could hear no cry of beasts.
The Bacchae heard that voice but missed its words,
and leaping up, they stared, peering everywhere.
Again that voice. And now they knew his cry,
the clear command of God. And breaking loose
like startled doves, through grove and torrent,
over jagged rocks, they flew, their feet maddened
by the breath of God. And when they saw my master
perching in his tree, they climbed a great stone
that towered opposite his perch and showered him
with stones and javelins of fir, while the others
hurled their wands. And yet they missed their target,
poor Pentheus in his perch, barely out of reach
of their eager hands, treed, unable to escape.
Finally they splintered branches from the oaks
and with those bars of wood tried to lever up the tree
by prying at the roots. But every effort failed.
Then Agave cried out: "Maenads, make a circle
about the trunk and grip it with your hands.
Unless we take this climbing beast, he will reveal
the secrets of the god." With that, thousands of hands
tore the fir tree from the earth, and down, down
from his high perch fell Pentheus, tumbling

to the ground, sobbing and screaming as he fell,
for he knew his end was near. His own mother,
like a priestess with her victim, fell upon him
first. But snatching off his wig and snood
so she would recognize his face, he touched her cheeks,
screaming, *"No, no, Mother! I am Pentheus,
your own son, the child you bore to Echion!
Pity me, spare me, Mother! I have done a wrong,
but do not kill your own son for my offense."*
But she was foaming at the mouth, and her crazed eyes
rolling with frenzy. She was mad, stark mad,
possessed by Bacchus. Ignoring his cries of pity,
she seized his left arm at the wrist; then, planting
her foot upon his chest, she pulled, wrenching away
the arm at the shoulder—not by her own strength,
for the god had put inhuman power in her hands.
Ino, meanwhile, on the other side, was scratching off
his flesh. Then Autonoë and the whole horde
of Bacchae swarmed upon him. Shouts everywhere,
he screaming with what little breath was left,
they shrieking in triumph. One tore off an arm,
another a foot still warm in its shoe. His ribs
were clawed clean of flesh and every hand
was smeared with blood as they played ball with scraps
of Pentheus' body.
The pitiful remains lie scattered,
one piece among the sharp rocks, others
lying lost among the leaves in the depths
of the forest. His mother, picking up his head,
impaled it on her wand. She seems to think it is
some mountain lion's head which she carries in triumph
through the thick of Cithaeron. Leaving her sisters
at the Maenad dances, she is coming here, gloating
over her grisly prize. She calls upon Bacchus:

he is her "fellow-huntsman," "comrade of the chase,
crowned with victory." But all the victory
she carries home is her own grief.
Now,
before Agave returns, let me leave
this scene of sorrow. Humility,
a sense of reverence before the sons of heaven—
of all the prizes that a mortal man might win,
these, I say, are wisest; these are best.

Exit Second Messenger.

CHORUS
—We dance to the glory of Bacchus!
We dance to the death of Pentheus,
the death of the spawn of the dragon!
He dressed in woman's dress;
he took the lovely thyrsus;
it waved him down to death,
led by a bull to Hades.
Hail, Bacchae! Hail, women of Thebes!
Your victory is fair, fair the prize,
this famous prize of grief!
Glorious the game! To fold your child
in your arms, streaming with his blood!

CORYPHAEUS But look: there comes Pentheus' mother, Agave,
running wild-eyed toward the palace.
—Welcome,
welcome to the reveling band of the god of joy!

Enter Agave with other Bacchantes. She is covered with blood and carries the head of Pentheus impaled upon her thyrsus.

AGAVE Bacchae of Asia—

CHORUS Speak, speak.

AGAVE We bring this branch to the palace,
this fresh-cut spray from the mountains.
Happy was the hunting.

CHORUS I see.
I welcome our fellow-reveler of God.

AGAVE The whelp of a wild mountain lion,
and snared by me without a noose.
Look, look at the prize I bring.

CHORUS Where was he caught?

AGAVE On Cithaeron—

CHORUS On Cithaeron?

AGAVE Our prize was killed.

CHORUS Who killed him?

AGAVE I struck him first.
The Maenads call me "Agave the blest."

CHORUS And then?

AGAVE Cadmus'—

CHORUS Cadmus'?

AGAVE Daughters.
After me, they reached the prey.
After me. Happy was the hunting.

CHORUS Happy indeed.

AGAVE Then share my glory,
share the feast.

CHORUS Share, unhappy woman?

AGAVE See, the whelp is young and tender.
Beneath the soft mane of its hair,
the down is blooming on the cheeks.

CHORUS With that mane he *looks* a beast.

AGAVE Our god is wise. Cunningly, cleverly,
Bacchus the hunter lashed the Maenads
against his prey.

CHORUS Our king is a hunter.

AGAVE You praise me now?

CHORUS I praise you.

AGAVE The men of Thebes—

CHORUS And Pentheus, your son?

AGAVE Will praise his mother. She caught
a great quarry, this lion's cub.

CHORUS Extraordinary catch.

AGAVE Extraordinary skill.

CHORUS You are proud?

AGAVE Proud and happy.
I have won the trophy of the chase,
a great prize, manifest to all.

CORYPHAEUS Then, poor woman, show the citizens of Thebes
this great prize, this trophy you have won
in the hunt.

Agave proudly exhibits her thyrsus with the head of Pentheus impaled upon the point.

AGAVE You citizens of this towered city,
men of Thebes, behold the trophy of your women's
hunting! *This* is the quarry of our chase, taken
not with nets nor spears of bronze but by the white
and delicate hands of women. What are they worth,
your boastings now and all that uselessness
your armor is, since we, with our bare hands,
captured this quarry and tore its bleeding body
limb from limb?
—But where is my father Cadmus?
He should come. And my son. Where is Pentheus?
Fetch him. I will have him set his ladder up
against the wall and, there upon the beam,
nail the head of this wild lion I have killed
as a trophy of my hunt.

Enter Cadmus, followed by attendants who bear upon a bier the dismembered body of Pentheus.

CADMUS Follow me, attendants.
Bear your dreadful burden in and set it down,
there before the palace.

The attendants set down the bier.

This was Pentheus
whose body, after long and weary searchings
I painfully assembled from Cithaeron's glens
where it lay, scattered in shreads, dismembered
throughout the forest, no two pieces
in a single place.
Old Teiresias and I
had returned to Thebes from the orgies on the mountain
before I learned of this atrocious crime
my daughters did. And so I hurried back
to the mountain to recover the body of this boy
murdered by the Maenads. There among the oaks
I found Aristaeus' wife, the mother of Actaeon,
Autonoë, and with her Ino, both
still stung with madness. But Agave, they said,
was on her way to Thebes, still possessed.
And what they said was true, for there she is,
and not a happy sight.

AGAVE Now, Father,
yours can be the proudest boast of living men.
For you are now the father of the bravest daughters
in the world. All of your daughters are brave,
but I above the rest. I have left my shuttle
at the loom; I raised my sight to higher things—
to hunting animals with my bare hands.
You see?
Here in my hands I hold the quarry of my chase,

a trophy for our house. Take it, Father, take it.
Glory in my kill and invite your friends to share
the feast of triumph. For you are blest, Father,
by this great deed I have done.

CADMUS This is a grief
so great it knows no size. I cannot look.
This is the awful murder your hands have done.
This, this is the noble victim you have slaughtered
to the gods. And to share a feast like this
you now invite all Thebes and me?
O gods,
how terribly I pity you and then myself.
Justly—too, too justly—has lord Bromius,
this god of our own blood, destroyed us all,
every one.

AGAVE How scowling and crabbed is old age
in men. I hope my son takes after his mother
and wins, as she has done, the laurels of the chase
when he goes hunting with the younger men of Thebes.
But all my son can do is quarrel with God.
He should be scolded, Father, and you are the one
who should scold him. Yes, someone call him out
so he can see his mother's triumph.

CADMUS Enough. No more.
When you realize the horror you have done,
you shall suffer terribly. But if with luck
your present madness lasts until you die,
you will seem to have, not having, happiness.

AGAVE Why do you reproach me? Is there something wrong?

CADMUS First raise your eyes to the heavens.

AGAVE There.
But why?

CADMUS Does it look the same as it did before?
Or has it changed?

AGAVE It seems—somehow—clearer,
brighter than it was before.

CADMUS Do you still feel
the same flurry inside you?

AGAVE The same—flurry?
No, I feel—somehow—calmer. I feel as though—
my mind were somehow—changing.

CADMUS Can you still hear me?
Can you answer clearly?

AGAVE No. I have forgotten
what we were saying, Father.

CADMUS Who was your husband?

AGAVE Echion—a man, they said, born of the dragon seed.

CADMUS What was the name of the child you bore your husband?

AGAVE Pentheus.

CADMUS And whose head do you hold in your hands?

AGAVE (*averting her eyes*) A lion's head—or so the hunters told me.

CADMUS Look directly at it. Just a quick glance.

AGAVE What is it? What am I holding in my hands?

CADMUS Look more closely still. Study it carefully.

AGAVE *No!* O gods, I see the greatest grief there is.

CADMUS Does it look like a lion now?

AGAVE No, no. It is—
Pentheus' head—I hold—

CADMUS And mourned by me
before you ever knew.

AGAVE But *who* killed him?
Why am *I* holding him?

CADMUS O savage truth,
what a time to come!

AGAVE For God's sake, speak.
My heart is beating with terror.

CADMUS *You* killed him.
You and your sisters.

AGAVE But where was he killed?
Here at home? Where?

CADMUS He was killed on Cithaeron,
there where the hounds tore Actaeon to pieces.

AGAVE But why? Why had Pentheus gone to Cithaeron?

CADMUS He went to your revels to mock the god.

AGAVE But *we*—
what were we doing on the mountain?

CADMUS You were mad.
The whole city was possessed.

AGAVE Now, now I see:
Dionysus has destroyed us all.

CADMUS You outraged him.
You denied that he was truly God.

AGAVE Father,
where is my poor boy's body now?

CADMUS There it is.
I gathered the pieces with great difficulty.

AGAVE Is his body entire? Has he been laid out well?

CADMUS [All but the head. The rest is mutilated
horribly.]

AGAVE But why should Pentheus suffer for my crime?

CADMUS He, like you, blasphemed the god. And so
the god has brought us all to ruin at one blow,

you, your sisters, and this boy. All our house
the god has utterly destroyed and, with it,
me. For I have no sons left, no male heir;
and I have lived only to see this boy,
this branch of your own body, most horribly
and foully killed.

He turns and addresses the corpse.

—To you my house looked up.
Child, you were the stay of my house; you were
my daughter's son. Of you this city stood in awe.
No one who once had seen your face dared outrage
the old man, or if he did, you punished him.
Now I must go, a banished and dishonored man—
I, Cadmus the great, who sowed the soldiery
of Thebes and harvested a great harvest. My son,
dearest to me of all men—for even dead,
I count you still the man I love the most—
never again will your hand touch my chin;
no more, child, will you hug me and call me
"Grandfather" and say, "Who is wronging you?
Does anyone trouble you or vex your heart, old man?
Tell me, Grandfather, and I will punish him."
No, now there is grief for me; the mourning
for you; pity for your mother; and for her sisters,
sorrow.
If there is still any mortal man
who despises or defies the gods, let him look
on this boy's death and believe in the gods.

CORYPHAEUS Cadmus, I pity you. Your daughter's son
has died as he deserved, and yet his death
bears hard on you.

[*At this point there is a break in the manuscript of nearly fifty lines. The following speeches of Agave and Coryphaeus and the first part of Dionysus' speech have been conjecturally reconstructed from fragments and later material which made use of the Bacchae. Lines which can plausibly be assigned to the lacuna are otherwise not indicated. My own inventions are designed, not to complete the speeches, but to effect a transition between the fragments, and are bracketed. —Translator*]

AGAVE O Father, now you can see
how everything has changed. I am in anguish now,
tormented, who walked in triumph minutes past,
exulting in my kill. And that prize I carried home
with such pride was my own curse. Upon these hands
I bear the curse of my son's blood. How then
with these accursed hands may I touch his body?
How can I, accursed with such a curse, hold him
to my breast? O gods, what dirge can I sing
[that there might be] a dirge [for every]
broken limb?

. . . .

Where is a shroud to cover up his corpse?
O my child, what hands will give you proper care
unless with my own hands I lift my curse?

She lifts up one of Pentheus' limbs and asks the help of Cadmus in piecing the body together. She mourns each piece separately before replacing it on the bier.

Come, Father. We must restore his head
to this unhappy boy. As best we can, we shall make
him whole again.
—O dearest, dearest face!
Pretty boyish mouth! Now with this veil

I shroud your head, gathering with loving care
these mangled bloody limbs, this flesh I brought
to birth

. . . .

CORYPHAEUS Let this scene teach those [who see these
things:
Dionysus is the son] of Zeus.

Above the palace Dionysus appears in epiphany.

DIONYSUS [I am Dionysus,
the son of Zeus, returned to Thebes, revealed,
a god to men.] But the men [of Thebes] blasphemed me.
They slandered me; they said I came of mortal man,
and not content with speaking blasphemies,
[they dared to threaten my person with violence.]
These crimes this people whom I cherished well
did from malice to their benefactor. Therefore,
I now disclose the sufferings in store for them.
Like [enemies], they shall be driven from this city
to other lands; there, submitting to the yoke
of slavery, they shall wear out wretched lives,
captives of war, enduring much indignity.

He turns to the corpse of Pentheus.

This man has found the death which he deserved,
torn to pieces among the jagged rocks.
You are my witnesses: he came with outrage;
he attempted to chain my hands, abusing me
[and doing what he should least of all have done.]
And therefore he has rightly perished by the hands
of those who should the least of all have murdered him.
What he suffers, he suffers justly.

Upon you,
Agave, and on your sisters I pronounce this doom:
you shall leave this city in expiation
of the murder you have done. You are unclean,
and it would be a sacrilege that murderers
should remain at peace beside the graves [of those
whom they have killed].

He turns to Cadmus.

. . . .

Next I shall disclose the trials
which await this man. You, Cadmus, shall be changed
to a serpent, and your wife, the child of Ares,
immortal Harmonia, shall undergo your doom,
a serpent too. With her, it is your fate
to go a journey in a car drawn on by oxen,
leading behind you a great barbarian host.
For thus decrees the oracle of Zeus.
With a host so huge its numbers cannot be counted,
you shall ravage many cities; but when your army
plunders the shrine of Apollo, its homecoming
shall be perilous and hard. Yet in the end
the god Ares shall save Harmonia and you
and bring you both to live among the blest.
So say I, born of no mortal father,
Dionysus, true son of Zeus. If then,
when you would not, you had muzzled your madness,
you should have an ally now in the son of Zeus.

CADMUS We implore you, Dionysus. We have done wrong.

DIONYSUS Too late. When there was time, you did not know me.

CADMUS We have learned. But your sentence is too harsh.

DIONYSUS I am a god. I was blasphemed by you.

CADMUS Gods should be exempt from human passions.

DIONYSUS Long ago my father Zeus ordained these things.

AGAVE It is fated, Father. We must go.

DIONYSUS Why then delay?
For you must go.

CADMUS Child, to what a dreadful end
have we all come, you and your wretched sisters
and my unhappy self. An old man, I must go
to live a stranger among barbarian peoples, doomed
to lead against Hellas a motley foreign army.
Transformed to serpents, I and my wife,
Harmonia, the child of Ares, we must captain
spearsmen against the tombs and shrines of Hellas.
Never shall my sufferings end; not even
over Acheron shall I have peace.

AGAVE (*embracing Cadmus*) O Father,
to be banished, to live without you!

CADMUS Poor child,
like a white swan warding its weak old father,
why do you clasp those white arms about my neck?

AGAVE But banished! Where shall I go?

CADMUS I do not know,
my child. Your father can no longer help you.

AGAVE Farewell, my home! City, farewell.
O bridal bed, banished I go,
in misery, I leave you now.

CADMUS Go, poor child, seek shelter in Aristaeus' house.

AGAVE I pity you, Father.

CADMUS And I pity you, my child,
and I grieve for your poor sisters. I pity them.

AGAVE Terribly has Dionysus brought
disaster down upon this house.

DIONYSUS I was terribly blasphemed,
my name dishonored in Thebes.

AGAVE Farewell, Father.

CADMUS Farewell to you, unhappy child.
Fare well. But you shall find your faring hard.

Exit Cadmus.

AGAVE Lead me, guides, where my sisters wait,
poor sisters of my exile. Let me go
where I shall never see Cithaeron more,
where that accursed hill may not see me,

where I shall find no trace of thyrsus!
That I leave to other Bacchae.

Exit Agave with attendants.

CHORUS The gods have many shapes.
The gods bring many things
to their accomplishment.
And what was most expected
has not been accomplished.
But God has found his way
for what no man expected.
So ends the play.